GW01238315

LE QUESNOY
NEW ZEALAND'S LAST BATTLE
1918

CHRISTOPHER PUGSLEY

Oratia

'I owe it to him to care about what happened'
— Euan Kennedy

To the men and women of the New Zealand Expeditionary Force who served on the Western Front and to their families who live with that memory. Remembering.

10586 **Gunner Frank Warren Gardner**
2/2853 **Gunner Donald Stewart Kennedy**
57685 **Driver Andrew Mather**

Killed in action with No. 2 Battery New Zealand Field Artillery, 7 November 1918

Published by Oratia Books, Oratia Media Ltd, 783 West Coast Road, Oratia, Auckland 0604, New Zealand (www.oratia.co.nz).

Copyright © 2018 Christopher Pugsley
Copyright © 2018 Oratia Books — published work

The copyright holders assert their moral rights in the work.
This book is copyright. Except for the purposes of fair reviewing, no part of this publication may be reproduced or transmitted in any form or by any means, whether electronic, digital or mechanical, including photocopying, recording, any digital or computerised format, or any information storage and retrieval system, including by any means via the Internet, without permission in writing from the publisher. Infringers of copyright render themselves liable to prosecution.

ISBN 978-0-947506-49-0

The author acknowledges the support of the Literary Trust of the National Army Museum for this publication.

Jacket imagery and previous page: Soldiers of Major Harold Barrowclough's 4 Rifles of 3rd Rifle Brigade in the front line facing Le Quesnoy on 4 November 1918. Note the reverse triangle, which is the insignia of 4 Rifles, on the arm of the nearest soldier on the right of picture. The corporal (with two stripes), standing on the left, has served overseas for two years, indicated by the reverse stripes on his lower jacket sleeve. NZ RSA Collection, Photographer: Captain H.A. Sanders, NZEF Official H Series H1247, Ref. MNZ-1996-1/2-F, Alexander Turnbull Library, Wellington, New Zealand

Endpapers: Detail, France: Sheet 12, Valenciennes, May 1915, Geographical Section, General Staff, War Office, 1:100,000. Author's collection

Editorial: Carolyn Lagahetau, Frances Chan
Design: Susan Harris

First published 2018
Printed in New Zealand

CONTENTS

TOWN PLAN OF LE QUESNOY
SCALE 1/5000.

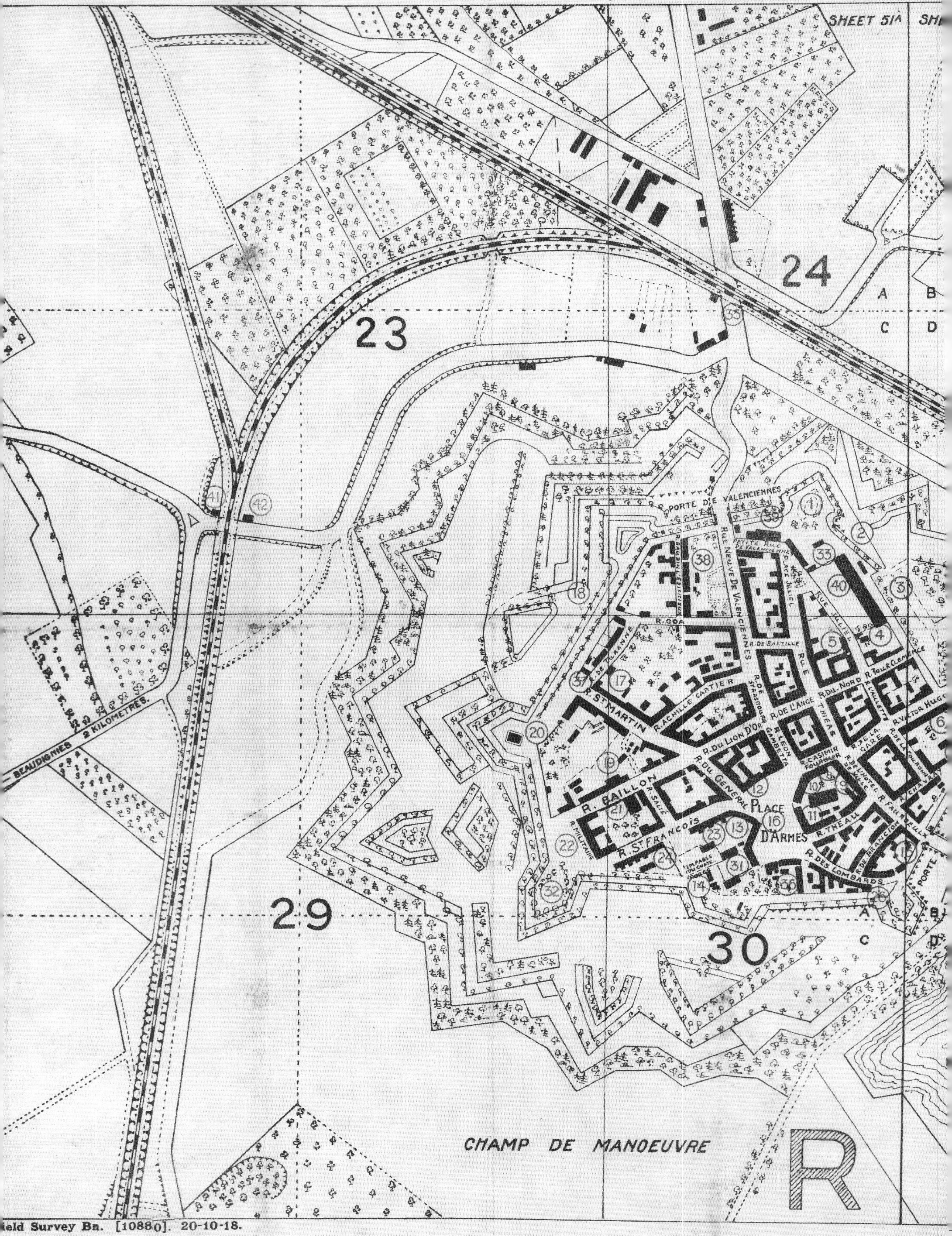

SHEET 51ᴬ

PORTE DE VALENCIENNES

RUE NEUVE DE VALENCIENNES

R. GOA

R. ST MARTIN

R. ACHILLE CARTIER

R. DE LA SAPINE

R. DU LION D'OR

R. DU GENERAL

R. BAILLON

R. MILITAIRE

R. ST FRANCOIS

PLACE D'ARMES

R. THEA

R. DES LOMBARDS

R. CASIMIR FOURNIER

R. VICTOR HUGO

BEAUDIGNIES 2 KILOMETRES.

CHAMP DE MANOEUVRE

Field Survey Bn. [10880]. 20-10-18.

YARDS 100   0   500   1000 YARDS.

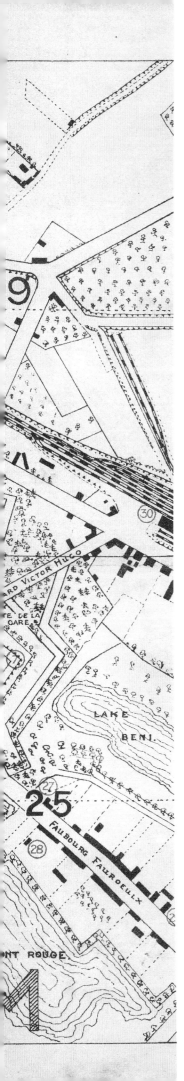

Introduction

THE STORMING OF LE QUESNOY — 'NEW ZEALANDERS DID IT'

Dear Eleanor,

I got this paper in Les [sic] Quesnoy, a little town surrounded by high walls and a double moat. Ask your mother to tell you a story about a knight who had to rescue a lady he loved from a big castle many years ago and your mother will tell you what Le Quesnoy is like. This town was surrounded and captured by soldiers from New Zealand so when you grow older and bigger you will learn more about it.[1]

This is an extract of a letter from 24-year-old Rifleman William Jack, a warehouseman of Dunedin serving with 3 Rifles in France, written on 17 November 1918 to his seven-year-old goddaughter Eleanor Hunt, living with her family in Haitaitai, Wellington. It captures a hint of the romanticism and mythology attached to this last battle fought by New Zealanders on the Western Front.

On 7 November 1918 *The New York Times* reported the taking of Le Quesnoy (pronounced Le Ken-wah) by the New Zealand Division under the headline 'Great Exploits by Haig's Men: Their Winning of Le Quesnoy was a Triumph of Valor and Tactics. New Zealanders Did It'.[2]

The New Zealanders had been mentioned regularly in the paper's columns throughout September and October 1918 but this was the first headline where they featured. New Yorkers were not alone in reading of the New Zealanders' exploits. It appeared in newspapers around the world. Philip Gibb's despatches, and those of Malcolm Ross, the New Zealand official war correspondent, were avidly read in New Zealand. The news of Le Quesnoy provided echoes of war as it once may have been: a throwback to the storming of citadels more reminiscent of the sieges of the Middle Ages. The *Grey River Argus* reported the battle under the heading 'New Zealanders' Great Exploits':

> Yesterday's victory was a most sweeping one. The German defeat could not be more complete … The capture of Le Quesnoy will be remembered as one of the most thrilling episodes in this campaign.

Town plan of Le Quesnoy, Field Survey Battalion, 20 October 1918.
Ref. 17917-1918, Auckland War Memorial Museum Tamaki Paenga Hira

A tale of knights rescuing fair ladies from castles of long ago. A letter on paper taken in Le Quesnoy written by Rifleman William Jack, 3 Rifles, to his seven-year-old goddaughter on 17 November 1918.
Ref. MS-Papers-7483-01, Alexander Turnbull Library, Wellington, New Zealand

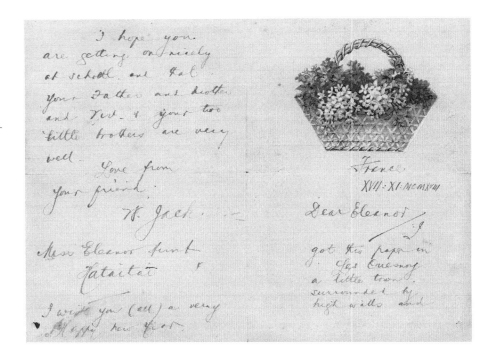

> It is believed to be the first time [in this war] that a besieged town has been formally summoned to submit by British troops.[3]

The besieging of a walled fortress, the scaling of its walls and the surrender of the garrison suggests that our soldiers were something special — something above the ordinary — necessary words for an exhausted New Zealand public in November 1918. It meant that our war ended with a bang and not simply peters out. It is New Zealand's Waterloo moment: a great victory at a decisive moment, and one that, unlike Waterloo, which the Duke of Wellington shares with the Prussians under Field Marshal Blücher, we do not have to share with anyone — it is New Zealand's alone. That is not strictly true, the battle involved three British, one American and one French army, but this taking of a small fortress town in northern France with its obsolete complex of outer ramparts, moats and inner walls and bastions captured public attention, and while on the scale of things it is but one incident in a large and complex battle — it is New Zealand's moment.

'The storming of Le Quesnoy' became the grand finale for New Zealand in their military campaigning with reports of New Zealanders being greeted rapturously by Le Quesnoy's citizens. It was liberation from a harsh regime. Major James Evans, MC and Bar, of 2 Auckland reports on visiting the town on 9 November that people are "half-starved & in very weak state of health & one is not surprised after what they have been through".[4] Thirty-six-year-old Evans was a veteran of the 1916 Sinai Campaign with the Auckland Mounted Rifles, transferred to the Auckland Infantry Regiment and received the Military Cross and Bar (a second award of the Military Cross) for his leadership and

The New York Times,
7 November 1918, p. 7

GREAT EXPLOITS
BY HAIG'S MEN

Their Winning of Le Quesnoy Was a Triumph of Valor and Tactics.

NEW ZEALANDERS DID IT

bravery in 1917–18. To him and his fellow New Zealanders, the relief of these French citizens from the yoke of German imperialism is why this war is being fought, and the manner of the town's surrender without civilian casualties gives it a romanticism missing from earlier battles such as the Somme, Messines and Passchendaele, where the villages and towns had been cleared of their civilian populations.

'The storming of Le Quesnoy' was included in the Minister of Defence Colonel Sir James Allen's Armistice message to the troops overseas.

> From the landing at Anzac on the 25th April 1915, to the surrender of Turkey and to the storming of Le Quesnoy on 4th November 1918, you have fought and conquered in battles whose names shall be familiar in our mouths as household words. You have won for New Zealand a fame imperishable. God bless you and bring you safely home to us.[5]

The report in *The Times* placed it in the wider context of the three British armies engaged in the Battle of the Sambre on 4 November 1918:

> The outstanding incidents of the attack were the crossing of the Canal and the capture of Catillon by the 1st Division, the surrounding and final reduction of Le Quesnoy by New Zealanders and the rapid advance on Landrecies and its capture by 25th Division.
>
> Undoubtedly, however, the most dramatic episode was the capture of Le Quesnoy. It is an old fortified town, with huge earth ramparts, which have stood many sieges. It was held in great strength and the New Zealanders were compelled to draw back from the first attempt to storm it frontally, though they succeeded in carrying the outer circuit of the ramparts. They then proceeded to encircle the town, and worked round both north and south in the face of determined resistance, until the two parties met on the opposite side. Leaving Le Quesnoy thus beleaguered, the main body of New Zealanders went on and got among the German guns, and this division alone took about 100, with the wagons and personnel of all the batteries practically complete.
>
> Going on, the New Zealanders carried all before them, having stubborn opposition to overcome at many points, notably at Jolimetz and Herbignies. All this time Le Quesnoy within its ancient fortifications was still German. We dropped invitations to surrender from aeroplanes, but with no response, and demands for surrender under the white flag were also refused. In the afternoon, therefore, the attack was resumed, and the New Zealanders fought their way into the streets, when the German officer commanding made formal surrender of himself and the garrison of 1,000 men. It was like a passage from some old war suddenly interpolated into a modern battle.[6]

Lieutenant-General Sir George Montague Harper, commander of IV Corps, in his farewell letter to New Zealand Division Commander Major-General Sir Andrew Russell, praised the New Zealand achievement since joining his corps in the critical days of the German March 1918 offensive. He succinctly spelt out the details of the division's performance from its involvement in the Allied offensive on 23 August to November 1918. "Finally on the 4th November the Division by an attack which did much to decide the finish of the war forced the surrender of the fortress of Le Quesnoy and drove

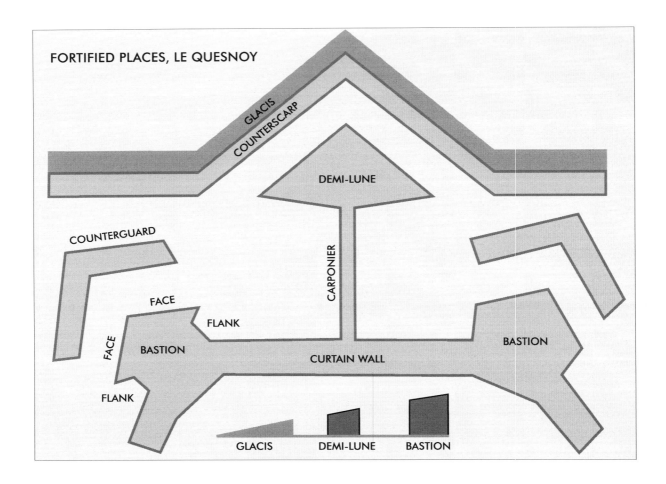

FORTIFIED PLACES, LE QUESNOY

GLACIS

COUNTERSCARP

DEMI-LUNE

CARPONIER

COUNTERGUARD

FACE

FLANK

FACE

BASTION

BASTION

CURTAIN WALL

FLANK

GLACIS DEMI-LUNE BASTION

'Fortified Places, Le Quesnoy,' http://fortified-places.com/quesnoy.html

Basic outline of a Vauban Fortress, all of which can be seen in the plan of Le Quesnoy. Note the progressively increasing height from outer glacis to the demi-lune to the bastions built to cover the inner walls. Each fortification was faced with stone or brick but backed by metres of earth to absorb the impact of the siege cannon. The geometric design was to ensure that all angles were covered by fire and as the attackers made their way over the glacis they were channelled into killing grounds for the defenders' muskets and cannon. The outer network of defences were open to the rear so that the defenders on the inner defences could fire into them if they were captured.

Glacis — a sloped bank in earth or stone that exposes the attacker to fire.

Counterscarp — a scarp and a counterscarp are the inner and outer sides of a ditch or moat that breaks up the attackers' formation and exposes them to fire from the demi-lune and counterguard.

Demi-Lune (or Ravelin) — an outer fortification that both protects the inner fortification and breaks up the attackers formations. It also prevents the besiegers' artillery firing directly onto the inner fortress walls.

Counterguard — a fortification with a low rampart that mounted cannon or musketeers positioned in front or within the fortress moat to protect the inner walls and bastions. The inner walls and bastions were able to sweep the counterguard with cannon and musket fire if captured.

Carponier — a covered access way to the outer fortifications that also served to divide the attacking force and provide musket fire into the open areas and moats on either side.

Bastion — a projecting part of a fortification built at an angle to the line of a wall, so as to allow defensive fire in several directions, particularly along the line of the curtain walls that formed the inner ramparts.

Hornwork — a freestanding fortification with angular points or horns serving to enclose an area immediately adjacent to a fort and add an extra layer of defence.

the enemy back through the Forest of Mormal." Harper concludes, "The continuous successes enumerated above constitute a record of which the Division may well be proud. It is a record which I may safely say has been unsurpassed in the final series of attacks which led to the enemy's sueing [sic] for peace."[7] Praise at the end of a victorious campaign is to be expected, but Harper had the reputation of being a demanding and tactically innovative divisional commander who saw the importance of training and thorough preparation for operations and was not quick to praise. He clearly saw much of himself in his New Zealand subordinate and recognised the excellence of the division he commanded.

Le Quesnoy earns it place in the *History of the Great War* by official historian Brigadier-General Sir James Edmonds. After describing New Zealand's part in the battle in some detail, he states: "The 4th November, 1918, was for the New Zealand Division one of the most outstanding days of the War."[8] In part 4 of *History of the Great War: Order of Battle* series under the entries for Third Army and IV Corps it lists the 37th and New Zealand

Aerial photo of Le Quesnoy with signatures (left to right) of Brigadier-General Herbert Hart, commanding 3rd Rifle Brigade; Field-Marshal Sir Douglas Haig, Commander-in-Chief, British Expeditionary Force; Lieutenant-General Sir George Harper, commanding IV Corps; Major-General Sir Andrew Russell, commanding New Zealand Division; Brigadier-General George Napier Johnston, commanding Royal Artillery New Zealand Division. Ref. PH-RESOS-136, PH-CNEG-CN757, Auckland War Memorial Museum Tamaki Paenga Hira

Divisions as taking part in the Battle of the Sambre on 4 November and then as a separate entry for the same day 'Capture of Le Quesnoy' is reserved for the New Zealand Division alone.[9]

This praise continues up to the present. Canadian historian Jeffery Williams in his biography of General Byng who commands the Third Army in this battle, writes: "In Le Quesnoy and during the advance beyond it the New Zealand Division captured over 2450 prisoners and more than 100 guns. It was a remarkable achievement, even for this outstanding division."[10] A former Sandhurst colleague, Dr J.P. Harris in his study of the British Expeditionary Force in the 100 Days campaign leading to the Armistice on 11 November states: "The most remarkable feature of the fighting on the front of Harper's IV Corps — which attacked at 05.30 with the New Zealand Division and the 37th Division, supported by 12 field and five heavy artillery brigades — was the capture of Le Quesnoy."[11]

Jonathan Boff in his study of the British Third Army and the defeat of Germany in 1918, agrees:

> The New Zealand Division scored a notable success, surrounding and capturing Le Quesnoy. The technology they used was medieval. Burning oil was projected onto the ramparts before infantry climbed scaling ladders to capture the walls and overwhelm the defenders. The New Zealanders rounded up 2,450 prisoners. Total POW's captured by Third Army were 6,000.[12]

This highlights the New Zealanders having the lion's share of prisoners, given that eight infantry divisions of the Third Army took part. The authors of *The British Army and the First World War* do not mention the New Zealand Division by name, but recognise its achievement. "Le Quesnoy was taken in an impressive operation making elaborate use of Livens Projectors to throw cylinders of flaming oil at the ramparts and a carefully planned infantry envelopment covered by artillery."[13]

It obviously features in New Zealand histories both past and present. Of the original studies Stewart's *The New Zealand Division 1916–1919* and Austin's *The Official History of the New Zealand Rifle Brigade* provide the most detail, but all of the regimental histories mention it, if only to put their part of the battle in context.[14] Mythology plays its part. Ferguson in *The History of the Canterbury Regiment* writes: "At Le Quesnoy the garrison numbering about a thousand, had held out until about 4.30 p.m., when the 3rd (Rifle) Brigade stormed the ramparts and entered the town after strenuous and picturesque fighting."[15] Ormond Burton's *The Auckland Regiment* has the least to say and in featuring one of the regiment's outstanding soldiers, Peter Prendergast, MM and Bar, a soldier of "desperate, reckless daring" intent on winning the Victoria Cross, Burton has him mortally wounded on 4 November 1918, when he was already a month dead, having died of wounds on 2 October 1918.[16]

More recently Ian McGibbon in *New Zealand's Western Front Campaign* gives a lucid, balanced account, as does John Gray in *From the Uttermost Ends of the Earth*, a history and travel guide to the New Zealand Division on the Western Front.[17] The voices of those that fought there speak to us in Glyn Harper's *Johnny ENZED* and Jane Tolerton's *An Awfully Big Adventure: New Zealand World War One veterans tell their stories*.[18] Certainly the most vivid individual account is the published diary of Private Monty Ingram, but forgotten stories of the signallers, the Army Service Corps' supply columns of wagon

The former mayor's residence in Le Quesnoy which is part of the former gendarmerie barracks that includes a number of maisonettes. This has been purchased by the War Memorial Museum Trust made up of a group of New Zealanders, with plans to establish a museum, conference facility and accommodation as a centre for touring the area, research and fostering links between New Zealand and France.
Le Quesnoy War Memorial Museum

and horses and the gunners have also been told.[19] Finally Le Quesnoy is the centrepiece of Nathalie Philippe's *The Great Adventure Ends: New Zealand and France on the Western Front*. Its chapters are the fruit of a successful conference held in Le Quesnoy in 2008 and, as its introduction states, is written, "by a diverse group of French, German and New Zealand writers and researchers".[20]

The 2018 anniversary prompts this examination. This is spurred by the initiative taken by a trust established in 2011 by New Zealand Military Society president, Herb Farrant, together with Major (Retired) Greg Moyle ED, JP, for Le Quesnoy to become home for New Zealand's first war memorial museum in Europe. This private initiative, chaired by former Commonwealth secretary-general Sir Don McKinnon, has purchased the former gendarmerie headquarters on a one-hectare site within the walls of the town. It includes a grand 19th century previous mayor's residence and nine maisonettes that were used to accommodate the families of the gendarmerie. This is planned to become a museum and conference centre with the houses providing "self-catering accommodation for staff, visitors, school parties and tour groups, and there is the potential for academic and cultural residencies, and exchanges with New Zealand".[21] There are also plans for a purpose-built museum and potentially a 40-room hotel within the grounds. It is a bold undertaking of a scale similar to that which saw the New Zealand government in the 1920s commit itself to erecting battlefield monuments to commemorate New Zealand's war effort at Messines and Gravenstafel in Belgium and at Longueval on the Somme, and at Le Quesnoy in France. In the same vein, New Zealand chose not to have its missing commemorated at the Menin Gate at Ypres, the Thiepval Monument on the Somme or at the Helles Memorial on the Gallipoli Peninsula in Turkey. Instead it decided on its own memorials to the New Zealand missing on the battlefields of the Western Front and on the Gallipoli Peninsula.

But what of Le Quesnoy itself? The old fortress town has a habit of sneaking up on you before you know it is there. I first came with the family in a hired campervan in 1988, after I left the New Zealand Army earlier that year. It was a trip to Belgium and France to visit the New Zealand battlefields with a promise to the family of days in Paris, the Loire, Normandy and Brittany as reward.

Driving from the village of Beaudignies on the route taken by the New Zealand Division in 1918, the town and the imposing brick ramparts are hidden by the trees that cover the outer earthworks, despite the road's approach through open fields. All one sees are trees on the skyline with a glimpse of rooftops. Suddenly one is at the roundabout that straddles what was once the railway line and you are there and driving through the walls into the town, without warning or any sense of scale.

Walking to the monument was also confusing — it is far easier and better signposted today with Google and a smartphone with the Ngā Tapuwae Western Front app as a guide, but in 1988 we parked in the square, and looked for signage. By as much luck as judgement, we walked through the old arched castle gate down Avenue des Néo Zélandais, a footpath that edges its way round inside the ramparts, until we passed through the archway surmounted by the New Zealand crest, and then we were on the outside looking back across the moat up at the ramparts. In front of us was the marble bas-relief carving of the Diggers, or 'Dinks', of the 3rd New Zealand Rifle Brigade clambering up the ladder and into the town as a winged Victorious Peace looks on.

I was back again in November 2000. I postponed my arrival as a senior lecturer in War Studies at the Royal Military Academy Sandhurst to accompany the All Blacks who were playing a Remembrance Day test against France in Paris on 11 November. Together with fellow historian Ian McGibbon we spent a glorious week in France. This was at the invitation of Andrew Martin, the team manager and a former army colleague. We were with them for the week leading up to the test with a visit to the captain of the original All Blacks, Dave Gallaher's grave at Nine Elms Cemetery at Poperinge and a trip to Le Quesnoy. We also watched the New Zealand 'A' Team game at Lens before the All Blacks in Paris. I went back to my diary to capture the day of our visit.

Arrive in a suspiciously quiet Le Quesnoy to find that the town has gathered with bands, and flags and great enthusiasm in the square. Andrew's plan for a quick getaway around the back does not work. We line up behind the band and are swamped by happy townsfolk and kids seeking autographs. We parade through the streets towards the gate leading to the New Zealand Memorial. All Blacks are interspersed among the crowd, and they have to be called forward, although many hide back with their friends in the NZ "A" side. The narrow tree lined path is crammed with people and the small space facing the monument is full of the team, the media, officials of the town, the New Zealand ambassador and those who can also cram in, while hundreds close up behind or overlook the gathering from the walls above. It's a fun mood, wreaths are laid, anthems played, and Andrew asks me to stand up on a stone bench in the throng and tell them why we are here. I do and it's bizarre, but I speak of the last battle and why they scaled the walls and there are appreciative murmurs and translations in the crowd. Bushy gives me a thumb's up and despite the happy chaos it seems to have worked … Move to the water gate and talk quickly about how they got over the wall, and then the whole thing dissolves into chaos as people move back into town for the reception in the town hall. We straggle back … At the town hall it is total confusion, the townsfolk have got inside but the team is left outside because there is no room!!! We stand and chat and the All

Fortunino Mantania's imaginative illustration of the storming of Le Quesnoy that reflected public perceptions of the New Zealand action in their last battle of the Great War. *The Sphere*, 18 January 1919, p. 69, Mary Evans Picture Library, London

Blacks are surrounded by interested youngsters … After a while as it gets cold, we head for home … It has been an amazing day.[22]

My 12 years at Sandhurst allowed me to go back many times. In 2008 I took part in a conference that was a true exchange between French and New Zealand perceptions of this battle and the impact of the First World War on French and New Zealand society. Too often conferences overseas can be New Zealanders talking to and about themselves in exotic locations. This was different. It was an eclectic group of French, German and New Zealand scholars and writers. Superbly organised and administered with immediate headphone translation, we talked to each other about respective national perspectives, from rugby and living in occupied France to the battle and the soldiers' return home. Thanks to Le Quesnoy historian and novelist Franck Bruyère who weaved a tale of enchantment about the ladder of Le Quesnoy, I came back fascinated by the story of the ladders, who provided them and the role they played. I was also grateful to Peter Lee from Cambridge, a Waipa

District councillor and a professional fireman, who made us all appreciate how impossible it was to have all those fully laden soldiers climbing the ladder, as depicted on the memorial sculpture, and in the beautiful glass window of St Andrew's Anglican Church in Cambridge. Any more than one fully laden soldier would have seen the ladder extension ropes break, and the Dinks come tumbling down, Humpty-Dumpty fashion. It was one at a time or nothing, exactly as George Butler painted it in *The Scaling of the Walls of Le Quesnoy*, 1920: Second Lieutenant Leslie Averill at the top with drawn revolver, Second Lieutenant Harry Kerr, similarly armed, beginning to clamber up the ladder behind him. Historically correct but boring, with no sense of tension or excitement. No wonder New Zealand architect Samuel Hurst Seager chose Fortunino Mantania's much more vivid sketch from *The Sphere* as the model for the memorial, but I suspect Seager was not aware of Butler's version.

The mythology that grows out of this incident momentarily captures the attention of the world. It is an exit from four years of war where, for a moment, New Zealand is in the headlines. In Western Front terms casualties were few, but no less heart-wrenching for families who live forever with the memories of a loved one's death delivered by telegram or letter as peace is being announced. Their names, occupations, ages and where they came from and where they now lie, are listed here. In the same way I have written this story in the present tense because to those fighting it was not over until it was over, and then these exhausted men had to deal with the swathe cut by Spanish Flu, which reappears in its most virulent and deadly form.

What stands out most to me about the fighting for Le Quesnoy and the villages around it, is more than the gritty, stoic professionalism of this division, but, that for the first time New Zealanders are meeting local civilians in large numbers who have been living under German occupation for four years, and who ecstatically welcome our arrival, even if they have no idea where we have come from. Their tearful joy reminded our soldiers why this war is being fought — to stop the aggression of Imperial Germany, who determined, regardless of diplomacy, to invade Belgium and France. Knowing what we know of the 20th century may make that argument derisible today, but the reasons why 21st-century wars are being fought should temper our criticism of 1914–18: the ignorant and often wilful blindness of politicians who see war as a solution continues. Le Quesnoy is the meeting of strangers, French and New Zealanders, for the best of reasons.

A century on we still have a bridgehead of memory in Europe, in the small towns of Messines and Zonnebeke in Belgium, in Longueval on the Somme. Until the centenary anniversaries the memories of New Zealanders who fought there have been kept alive more by local initiatives than New Zealand's efforts. What New Zealanders did lives on because these small towns and villages choose to remember and honour the presence of our dead. One could say this for Le Quesnoy as well, but here veterans such as Leslie Averill and Lawrence 'Curly' Blyth sustained the links for as long as they lived. Now the initiative has been taken up by a bold team of New Zealand visionaries with plans to establish a New Zealand War Memorial Museum centre. Not just looking back to a memory of a century-old war but also eyeing the future to build on what happened and take it into the next century. An opportunity to change perspectives — our view of France, the French view of New Zealand and on a scale we can manage. Such a centre would be lost in Paris, but means a great deal in Le Quesnoy. It is an opportunity to enlarge a New Zealand bridgehead, maintained by the Cambridge/Le Quesnoy Friendship Association, in a small town in France first taken in 1918 and give it a dimension that may surprise both our countries. Let us hope so.

I am grateful to Nathalie Philippe and Richard Stowers — this was to be their book but circumstances frustrated their efforts, and I am thankful to step into the breach. My thanks also to Peter Dowling at Oratia Media who allowed this to happen at short notice and has taken this gamble. I am grateful to Peter's team, editor Carolyn Lagahetau and copy editor Frances Chan, for again tackling my drafts with marvellous care and attention. Herb Farrant, perhaps the one who knows Le Quesnoy best, has provided a great deal of valuable information, as has Bob Cameron who has generously shared his research into the First World War manuscripts in the Alexander Turnbull Library. I am also grateful to Euan Kennedy for telling me his uncle's story that provides a fitting coda. The manuscripts collection at the Alexander Turnbull Library has been mined for memoirs and diaries and I thank the library staff for their friendly support. Jane Tolerton and Nicholas Boyack have allowed me to quote from their invaluable World War 1 Oral History Archive in the Alexander Turnbull Library. The growing online websites provided by the National Library of New Zealand have been very important to my research and in particular Paper's Past has been an essential tool. The Library's online photographic archive has been invaluable and I thank Natalie Marshall and her team for prompt answers to my many queries. Archives New Zealand has again been a rich source of official material. At Kippenberger Military Research Library, National Army Museum, Waiouru, Dolores Ho provided a rich vein of material on Le Quesnoy, and I am grateful to her, the curator, Windsor Jones, and the library and museum staff for their always friendly reception and willingness to assist. I gratefully acknowledge the ongoing support of the Literary Trust of the National Army Museum whose financial assistance underpins military history research in New Zealand. Auckland War Memorial Museum has generously provided unique illustrations and maps of the battle and their Cenotaph website has once again been an invaluable research tool. Sean Brosnahan at Toitū Otago Settlers Museum provided the portrait of the young Harold Barrowclough. Mrs Cynthia Brown generously made available the memoirs of her father, Brigadier H. Selwyn Kenrick. There are many others who I have talked Le Quesnoy with over the years, all have a part of this work and have my thanks.

Ray Grover, Herb Farrant, Aaron Fox, Bob Anderson and Paul Koorey have generously read parts of the manuscript at short notice and in haste. My daughter Susan Harris took time out from celebrating her successful completion of a Master of Arts at the Royal College of Art in London to provide the stellar design including the cover and the maps. Any sins or omissions are mine, and I would be grateful for any additions or corrections to the list of New Zealanders who died in this last battle of the First World War.

My family, Deanna, Joanna, Susan and Ian Harris, David and Camilla and Dylan our grandson looked on with concern at my willingness to embark on this project so soon after *The Camera in the Crowd*, but the writing habit is a crazy compulsive thing, even if the garden suffers. In compensation, I offer them all my love.

Christopher Pugsley
Waikanae Beach, 2018

H1115

Chapter 1

PREPARING FOR ARMAGEDDON

Yesterday I went forward to the front line for liaison duty with the New Zealand Division, which has relieved the tattered remnants of our own infantry. What a grand crowd they are! Sunburnt, powerful steady men — they look as if they had just yesterday come from their cattle or sheep ranches to put things to right here; and they are completely confident that they can wipe the floor with the Boches, though they talk quietly and without boasting.[1]

This is the view of the New Zealand Division by a British soldier in early 1918. A young British artillery officer of a heavy artillery brigade reflecting on how the war has progressed in 1918 writes in a similar vein.

Optimism did not come till August, anticipation of final victory, even later — and when it did come, almost with a rush. But from April onwards, at any rate in our sector of the front, one was conscious of a prevailing spirit of profound thankfulness, almost of satisfaction, that the Germans were securely held. Of the two factors which contributed to this happy feeling, the first was the daily evidence around us that now it was ourselves and not the Germans who were living and fighting in a green and wooded countryside hardly touched by the spoiling hand of war. The second and greater factor was our rapidly growing friendship with the New Zealand Division, with whom we were now working as closely as if we had been their own Divisional field artillery brigade.

We admired them more than any Division we had previously met, and not only because we knew them better. They accepted us too, and in a matter of days they looked upon us as their private heavy artillery.

A platoon of Major Harold Barrowclough's 4 Rifles, 3rd Rifle Brigade, eating a meal in Solesmes on 28 October 1918 on the edge of the village among the vegetable fields. They wear their battalion identification, a black reverse triangle on their left sleeve. Each soldier's years of service are indicated by the stripes on the lower right sleeve. At this time 4 Rifles, and the other battalions in the 3rd Rifle Brigade, are at half-strength. The Allied advance has halted west of Le Quesnoy and supplies and ammunition are being brought forward for the next stage of the offensive that will start on 4 November. NZ RSA Collection, Photographer: Captain H.A. Sanders, NZEF Official H Series H1115, Ref. 1/2-013672-G, Alexander Turnbull Library, Wellington, New Zealand

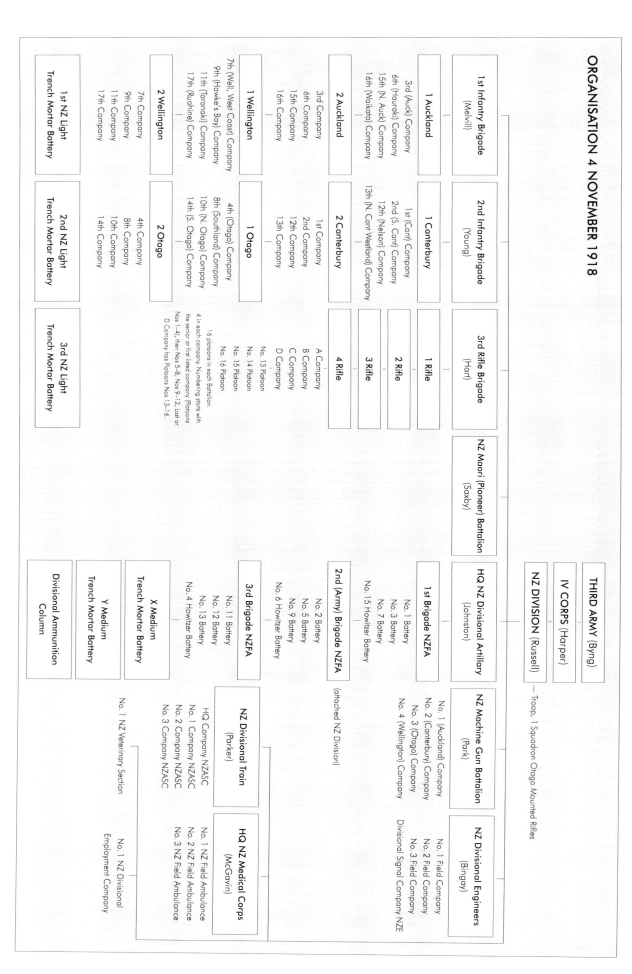

ORGANISATION 4 NOVEMBER 1918

THIRD ARMY (Byng)

IV CORPS (Harper)

NZ DIVISION (Russell) — Troop, 1 Squadron Otago Mounted Rifles

1st Infantry Brigade (Melvill)

1 Auckland
- 3rd (Auck) Company
- 6th (Hauraki) Company
- 15th (N. Auck) Company
- 16th (Waikato) Company

1 Canterbury
- 1st (Cant) Company
- 2nd (S. Cant) Company
- 12th (Nelson) Company
- 13th (N. Cant Westland) Company

2nd Infantry Brigade (Young)

2 Auckland
- 3rd Company
- 6th Company
- 15th Company
- 16th Company

2 Canterbury
- 1st Company
- 2nd Company
- 12th Company
- 13th Company

1 Wellington
- 7th (Well, West Coast) Company
- 9th (Hawke's Bay) Company
- 11th (Taranaki) Company
- 17th (Ruahine) Company

1 Otago
- 4th (Otago) Company
- 8th (Southland) Company
- 10th (N. Otago) Company
- 14th (S. Otago) Company

2 Wellington
- 7th Company
- 9th Company
- 11th Company
- 17th Company

2 Otago
- 4th Company
- 8th Company
- 10th Company
- 14th Company

3rd Rifle Brigade (Hart)

1 Rifle

2 Rifle

3 Rifle

4 Rifle
- A Company
- B Company
- C Company
- D Company
  - No. 13 Platoon
  - No. 14 Platoon
  - No. 15 Platoon
  - No. 16 Platoon

16 platoons in each Battalion. 4 in each company. Numbering starts with the senior or first listed company (Platoons Nos 1–4), then Nos 5–8, Nos 9–12, Last or D Company has Platoons Nos 13–16.

NZ Maori (Pioneer) Battalion (Saxby)

HQ NZ Divisional Artillary (Johnston)

1st Brigade NZFA
- No. 1 Battery
- No. 3 Battery
- No. 7 Battery
- No. 15 Howitzer Battery

2nd (Army) Brigade NZFA (attached NZ Division)
- No. 2 Battery
- No. 5 Battery
- No. 9 Battery
- No. 6 Howitzer Battery

3rd Brigade NZFA
- No. 11 Battery
- No. 12 Battery
- No. 13 Battery
- No. 4 Howitzer Battery

X Medium Trench Mortar Battery

Y Medium Trench Mortar Battery

1st NZ Light Trench Mortar Battery

2nd NZ Light Trench Mortar Battery

3rd NZ Light Trench Mortar Battery

Divisional Ammunition Column

NZ Machine Gun Battalion (Park)
- No. 1 (Auckland) Company
- No. 2 (Canterbury) Company
- No. 3 (Otago) Company
- No. 4 (Wellington) Company

NZ Divisional Engineers (Bingay)
- No. 1 Field Company
- No. 2 Field Company
- No. 3 Field Company
- Divisional Signal Company NZE

NZ Divisional Train (Parker)
- HQ Company NZASC
- No. 1 Company NZASC
- No. 2 Company NZASC
- No. 3 Company NZASC

HQ NZ Medical Corps (McGavin)
- No. 1 NZ Field Ambulance
- No. 2 NZ Field Ambulance
- No. 3 NZ Field Ambulance
- No. 1 NZ Veterinary Section
- No. 1 NZ Divisional Employment Company

Except when they were out of the line we were in daily contact with them till the end of the war — and with battalions and even companies as well as with their Divisional and Brigade headquarters. I cannot recall a single occasion when either side let the other down. For us, bearing in mind that Heavy Artillery Brigades were Corps troops, it was a novel and stimulating experience, and I have no doubt we shot all the better for it. For no words of mine can convey to the layman the feeling of heaven when an artilleryman knows when the Division he is supporting is a good one, and of all the good and very good Divisions of the British Army I would rate the New Zealand Division high among the highest.[2]

ORGANISATION OF THE NEW ZEALAND DIVISION

The year 1918 is a year of battle and shifting fortunes. The German March offensive threatens to separate the British and French armies but is held. Both sides lose heavily, but the German armies fail to take the critical communication centres such as Amiens. The destruction of German elite Stormtrooper formations means that the remaining divisions are weak in strength and have been robbed of their best soldiers. They hold an extended frontline against the French, British and the ever-expanding American armies who have both the material advantage and, increasingly, the operational and tactical skills to exploit German weaknesses.

The New Zealand Division is rested and trained for mobile warfare when it is thrown in to fill the gap between Colincamps and Hébuterne on 26 March 1918. It held the position and defeated German attempts to break through. It is committed to battle on 23 August as part of the Allied advance that sees the German armies forced into a series of withdrawals. The New Zealand Division is constantly engaged in fighting as it takes a leading role in the encirclement of Bapaume and the advance to the high ground beyond. After a short rest the division is again committed on 29 September in the advance to the Hindenburg Line and subsequent breakthrough. In October it is involved again in heavy fighting as the Allied armies advance with the final attacks bringing the Allied front to face the so-called Herman I Position with the New Zealand Division positioned opposite Le Quesnoy on 26 October 1918.

In November 1918 the New Zealand Division is larger than the standard British Division. Its approximate effective strength on 31 October 1918 is 853 officers and 16,581 all ranks, a total of 17,434 personnel. To this must be added the strength of 2nd (Army) Brigade, New Zealand Field Artillery, and its ammunition column: 31 officers and 730 other ranks in the brigade and four officers and 137 other ranks in the ammunition column, a total of 902 personnel, bringing the strength of the New Zealand Division to 18,336.[3] Although 2nd Brigade is not strictly part of the division, it is attached to the New Zealand Division for this last battle and is one of the last New Zealand formations in action before the Armistice on 11 November 1918.

The New Zealand Division benefits from a regular supply of trained manpower guaranteed by conscription in New Zealand. Two thousand reinforcements arrive from New Zealand every month. James Allen, the Minister of Defence, assesses that he can sustain the division until late 1920. The German March offensive saw the New Zealand government accelerate the dispatch of reinforcements from New Zealand to ensure that the numbers are there to meet the crisis.[4] By 31 October 1918 the accumulated reinforcements in New Zealand training camps in the United

Kingdom number 313 officers and 8765 other ranks, plus 547 undergoing commissioning training in British Officer Cadet battalions. In addition, there are 72 officers and 780 other ranks in the infantry and General Base Depot at Étaples in France, making an available reinforcement pool of 930 officers and 9545 other ranks, not counting those in transit from New Zealand. No other division in the British armies has the luxury of such a reinforcement pool, indeed, the lack of manpower sees British divisions reduced in strength to between 10,000 and 12,000 men.[5]

Reinforcements must be trained to be effective or else they are nothing more than cannon fodder. New Zealand prides itself on its training regime and each Reinforcement sailing is carefully assessed on arrival and their standard is reported back to New Zealand, so adjustments may be made to the training programme. In November 1918 the 3rd Rifle Brigade makes the following assessment:

> the men are strong and well set up and the proportion of young men about 22 years of age is very high … they were moderately well trained but lack finish in drill. At bayonet fighting they were fair. The discipline was only fair, and they were very poor at saluting, and in addressing their officers. Their knowledge of tactical work was of course nil. These men are very keen and have turned out very well indeed in the recent fighting when they displayed great dash.[6]

It is government policy to ensure that when the war ends, a New Zealand Division is still on operations as part of the British Expeditionary Force (BEF); only in this way does the New Zealand government believe that it can demand a say in the post-war settlements. In 1917 it bows to British War Office pressure to produce more manpower for the front in the form of an additional brigade — 4th Brigade. This makes the New Zealand Division the odd one out among the infantry divisions of the BEF and its commander Major-General Sir Andrew Russell believes that having an additional brigade means it is liable to be taken away from him and misused. The 4th Brigade is disbanded in 1918 when the strengths of the British infantry divisions are reduced. Russell is unhappy that its members are formed into an Entrenching Group for labouring tasks with pick and shovel, until they are called forward as fighting reinforcements. He believes this will diminish their level of training and preparedness. These experienced men are invaluable additions during the fighting in 1918. However, he does not want the War Office to cast covetous eyes at the build-up of New Zealand reinforcements.

The New Zealand Division retains the 12 infantry battalion structure, each approximately 1000-strong in January 1918 instead of the nine battalions that British divisions are reduced to, due to critical manpower shortages. It also retains four platoons per company in the four companies in the battalion, while British infantry companies are reduced to three. The three infantry brigades of the New Zealand Division are: the 3rd (Rifle) Brigade with its four rifle battalions: 1, 2, 3 and 4 Rifles. The 1st and 2nd Brigades are organised respectively into the North and South Island Brigades: 1 and 2 Wellington battalions and 1 and 2 Auckland battalions in 1st Brigade; and 1 and 2 Canterbury and 1 and 2 Otago in 2nd Brigade.[7]

An examination of the strength returns of 2nd Brigade for the month of October 1918 shows that the New Zealanders are operating on a long-term personnel management cycle and not committing the maximum manpower resources to each battle. This is evident when comparing the trench or fighting strengths of the four battalions with the actual posted or effective strength of each battalion. 1 Canterbury: trench strength 15 officers, 434 other ranks, effective strength 39 officers, 781 other ranks; 2 Canterbury: trench strength 20:554, effective strength 41:947; 1 Otago: trench strength 17:546, effective strength 39:906; 2 Otago: trench strength 17:557, effective strength: 40:899.[8]

The effective strengths show that each battalion is close to full strength, yet the fighting strength is greatly reduced, often by some 300 men, in each case. Examination of the detail in each battalion shows some 50 men on leave in the UK or Paris, 150 men in Left out of Battle parties, which allows the battalion to be rebuilt in the event of heavy casualties, or detached to other duties, 10–20 men on courses and an average of 20 sick and remaining with unit, which is remarkably low.

It shows that the battalions are geared for the long term, accepting workable fighting strengths that can be sustained while veterans are deliberately left out of battle, sent on courses or on leave, and if it is your turn in the cycle, you go, regardless of whether the next battle is due. It caters for the fact that the fighting is a constant, but the men need to be rested and refreshed so that they can do their job when it is their turn. It anticipates by 90 years the rotation cycle of the All Blacks or the contemporary Super Rugby teams. The effective strength of the New Zealand Division allows this approach and it is one of the factors that accounts for its discipline, high morale and professionalism in 1918.

Both 1st and 2nd Brigades benefit from having additional reinforcements available from the Entrenching Group formed from the disbanded 4th Brigade. This allows the two brigades to be topped up throughout September and October 1918 with designated Auckland, Wellington, Canterbury and Otago men, most of whom have battle experience — a reinforcement luxury that the Rifles do not have. It is because of this that Russell determines that 3rd Rifle Brigade does not have the staying power to advance through Forêt de Mormal and designates it as the force to encircle Le Quesnoy — a difficult task but one that Russell anticipates will be within its capabilities and he has great faith in Brigadier-General Herbert Hart, its commander. He also allocates one battalion from 1st Brigade to assist in the encirclement.

Russell knows his infantry brigades with their four battalions and greater strength per battalion has far more punch that those in the British divisions on either flank. Experience makes him assume that British divisions attacking on his flanks may not succeed. Writing in his diary on 1 October: "It's useless to depend on British divisions — they may succeed or they may not."[9] His planning always takes this into consideration. He anticipates and plans for the need for flank protection so that his division can push on and achieve their objectives regardless of what is happening on either flank.

Preparation and planning are Russell's hallmarks. He, like other British divisional commanders, has been warned of the coming German offensive in early 1918 and Russell anticipates the change to open and more mobile warfare in his training in early March. He also vets his commanders at every level, demanding that those who are no longer up to it, because of the strains of war, be sent home, and those he assesses as not being good enough, are also replaced.

By this stage experienced officers of the New Zealand Staff Corps (NZSC) fill most brigade-level staff appointments, however, the principal divisional operational staff appointment, that of the GSO1 Operations is filled by a seconded British officer, Lieutenant-Colonel Henry Wilson, DSO, Rifle Brigade, later Field Marshal Sir Henry 'Jumbo' Wilson. Russell wants the best available man in this position and does not believe he has a New Zealander of the necessary experience and quality. National pride plays no part in selection — for Russell, it is always the best man for the job. He sees trained staff as the key to his division's success and insists they all have combat experience before being tested as understudies and then attend appropriate staff courses in readiness for the post.[10]

He is equally careful in vetting his commanders at every level. Brigadier-General George Napier Johnston is the commander of the New Zealand Divisional Artillery and deputises for Russell as acting divisional commander in his absence. Canadian-born, he is a British regular officer with long experience with New Zealand Military Forces before the war. A highly skilled and demanding officer, he has a correct rather than warm relationship with Russell, but provides superbly trained artillery formations: 1st, 2nd (Army) and 3rd New Zealand Field Artillery Brigades, the Divisional Ammunition Column and 2nd (Army) Brigade Ammunition Column, which ensures the supply of gun ammunition. Each brigade has four batteries, each of six guns. Three are 18-pounder batteries and one a 4.5-inch howitzer battery. Johnston also has X and Y medium trench mortar batteries armed with 6-inch Newton mortars which complement the three light trench mortar batteries, armed with 3-inch Stokes mortar, that are attached to each infantry brigade.

Integral to the divisional fire plan are the four machine gun companies of the New Zealand Machine Gun Battalion: No. 1 (Auckland) Company, No. 2 (Wellington) Company, No. 3 (Canterbury) Company and No. 4 (Otago) Company, each with 16 Vickers medium machine guns.

Forty-one-year-old Brigadier-General Charles Melvill commands 1st Brigade. Melvill was a British regular officer, who was one year old in 1879 when his father was killed at Buffalo River in Zululand attempting

A New Zealand battery of 18-pounders move into position near Beaudignies for the attack on Le Quesnoy. Artillery limbers unload of their ammunition while the gunners dig in, 28 October 1918. NZ RSA Collection, Photographer: Captain H.A. Sanders, NZEF Official H Series H1136, Ref: G13691-1/2, Alexander Turnbull Library, Wellington, New Zealand

A New Zealand artillery fitter of one of the two New Zealand medium trench mortar batteries checks the fittings on the baseplate of one of the 6-inch Newton trench mortars at Beauvois on 21 October 1918. There are six mortars in each battery. The specially designed carriage for the baseplate and mortar tube can be seen behind the two gunners. This was a New Zealand-designed modification to enable the mortars to keep up with the advance that started in August 1918. They were dismounted and fired from the ground as seen with the mortar on the right. NZ RSA Collection, Photographer: Captain H.A. Sanders, NZEF Official H Series H1126, Ref: 1/2-013682-G, Alexander Turnbull Library, Wellington, New Zealand

to save the 'Colours' of the 24th Regiment of Foot. After years of agitation, Lieutenants Melvill and Nevill Coghill were posthumously awarded the Victoria Cross in 1907, some 27 years later. Melvill was attached to the New Zealand Military Forces in 1911–12. He was wounded in France in 1914 serving with the South Lancashire Regiment. He was appointed a captain in the Wellington Battalion on joining the NZEF in November 1915, and through talent rises rapidly to command 1st Brigade in June 1917.[11] It is interesting to note that Russell bemoans the fact that although Melvill is a skilled commander, he considers that in hindsight he would be of better value to the division as a staff officer; Russell being always conscious of his lack of depth in staff officers compared to potential infantry commanders in his division.

2nd Brigade is commanded by 41-year-old Brigadier-General Robert 'Bobby' Young, a dentist from Marton. He was active in the territorials in August 1914 and was appointed a company commander in the Wellington Infantry Battalion. He becomes commanding officer of the Auckland Infantry Battalion and serves as a battalion commander in France, being promoted to brigadier-general in 1917. He was sniped and badly wounded immediately after assuming command.

Thirty-six-year-old Brigadier-General Herbert Hart, a Carterton lawyer from farming stock, commands 3rd Rifle Brigade. A Boer War veteran and active in the territorials, in August 1914 he was appointed second-in-command of the Wellington Infantry Battalion. Badly wounded on Gallipoli, he is an outstanding officer and was the first territorial officer promoted to command an infantry brigade in the division in 1917.[12] Both Hart and Young serve under Lieutenant-Colonel William Malone of Chunuk Bair fame, the first commanding officer of the Wellington Infantry Battalion. The promotion of both reflects the high professional standards that Malone inculcates in the officers of his original battalion.[13]

By 1918 the subalterns of 1914–15 are the commanding officers in the battalions; all are battle hardened and strict disciplinarians in matters relating to fighting efficiency. The series of battles in 1918 have winnowed the officer ranks and in this battle many of the company commanders are comparatively junior officers, but despite their rank, have a great deal of fighting experience for by now almost all newly commissioned officers are drawn from the ranks.[14]

Russell grooms New Zealand officers to command the combat support and supply services. In this advance the engineers have a critical role that is carried out by the three field engineer companies supported by the 1000-strong New Zealand Maori Pioneer Battalion.[15] The engineers also provide the Divisional Signal Company that is largely drawn from New Zealand Post and Telegraph staff.[16] In the same way the three field ambulances of the New Zealand Medical Corps are carefully harnessed from the graduates of Otago Medical School and rotate staff experienced in battlefield surgery and war medicine through the division, the stationary hospital in France and the three general hospitals in the United Kingdom. The logistic glue that keeps this together are the horse-drawn general service wagons of the Divisional Train of the Army Service Corps with its three companies serving the brigades. It is still a horse-drawn division with over 5000 horses when one includes the third artillery brigade and its ammunition column.[17]

BATTLE OF THE SAMBRE — 'THE ARMAGEDDON OF THE WAR'

In early November 1918 Field Marshal Douglas Haig's armies, after being forced to gather breath and gain logistic relief in late October, regroup and are striking toward the key communication centres vital to the supply and movement of the German armies in northern France. It is a year of constant battle and in every army, including General Sir Julian Byng's Third Army, the divisions, with the exception of the New Zealand Division, are reduced in strength to an average of 10,000 personnel. By comparison their German opponents are reduced in some cases to a divisional fighting strength of 2000 and there are few, if any, reinforcements. Both sides face logistic problems: for the Germans this involves a dwindling supply of horses that cannot be replaced, despite the fact that they are falling back on to their supply dumps. For the Allies, they are now operating some 40–50 kilometres from their railheads, which places enormous strain on their Army Service Corps' motor and horse transport.

The offensive that began in August 1918 is now operating in a very different country from where it started. It is thickly populated in rolling country with densely planted hedgerows and orchards with steep banked streams and rivers. There are five and a half hours less daylight than in August and the winter rains are beginning. It is an offensive made possible by the transport drivers and the field engineers, supported by the pioneers, who disarm the mines, fill in the cratered roads and build temporary bridges to replace those that the retreating Germans have destroyed.

The Canadian Corps seize Valenciennes on 3 November and the next day, the British First, Third and Fourth Armies are to attack on a frontage of some 48 kilometres from the Sambre north of Oisy to Valenciennes.[18] Byng's Third Army includes Lieutenant-General Harper's IV Corps and the New Zealand Division is one of Harper's four divisions: 5th, 37th, 42nd and New Zealand Divisions. The corps is tasked with advancing on the rail centre of Maubeuge. This means negotiating the obstacles presented in turn by the walled fortress town of Le Quesnoy, Forêt de Mormal and the steep-banked Sambre River. Byng gives his corps commanders the intermediate objective of the road running south from Bavay, which forms the eastern

boundary of Forêt de Mormal, and in the IV Corps sector he orders that Le Quesnoy be enveloped and bypassed, but not attacked in order to prevent civilian casualties. The New Zealand Division in conjunction with the 37th Division to the south on the right flank and the 62nd (2nd West Riding) Division in the neighbouring VI Corps to the north, are to attack and establish themselves on the line Franc a Louer–Herbignies–Tous Vents, "and to exploit success eastward through the Forêt de Mormal towards the River Sambre".[19]

The situation of the German forces demands the least possible delay. As the official despatch details, that military cliché "the maintenance of momentum" is all important.

> The capitulation of Turkey and Bulgaria and the imminent collapse of Austria — consequently upon Allied successes which the desperate position of her own armies on the western front had rendered her powerless to prevent — had made Germany's military position ultimately impossible. If her armies were allowed to withdraw undisturbed to shorter lines, the struggle might still be protracted over the winter. The British Armies, however, were now in a position to prevent this by a direct attack upon a vital centre, which should anticipate the enemy's withdrawal and force an immediate conclusion.[20]

The New Zealanders have no doubts and this is the message that is given at the planning and orders groups in early November. Brigadier-General Herbert Hart in 3rd Rifle Brigade outlines its detail to his four battalion commanders on 1 November. "The attack is to be on a huge scale, the Armageddon of the War. Three British Armies, 1st, 3rd & 4th attacking the centre of the German line, & French & American Armies pushing up from the South on both banks of the Meuse."[21]

Rifleman of Lieutenant-Colonel Jardine's 2 Rifles of 3rd Rifle Brigade, identified by square black unit insignia on the left sleeve, digging in the support trench facing Le Quesnoy in early November in preparation for the 4 November 1918 attack. One sign that the supply chain is stretched is the fact that there is only one man smoking a cigarette. NZ RSA Collection, Photographer: Captain H.A. Sanders, NZEF Official H Series H1310, Ref: 1/2-013800-G, Alexander Turnbull Library, Wellington, New Zealand

The New Zealanders carried out intensive patrolling to gain information on the German defences and identification of German units. Here, two German prisoners are interrogated by divisional intelligence officer Lieutenant Silston Cory-Wright, MC, a 30-year-old civil engineer from Auckland who is fluent in German, and an accomplished intelligence staff officer. George Edmond Butler, 'Interrogating the prisoners, Masnieres,' Pastel, 456 x 354 mm, Ref: AAAC 898 NCWA 502, Archives New Zealand

THE PLAN

Lieutenant-General Harper, commanding IV Corps, gives the New Zealand Division the task of encircling Le Quesnoy and advancing east through Forêt de Mormal. It is a difficult task but it is the measure of Harper's faith in the quality of its commander and his division, which has been proven in the months of battle since August. IV Corps has advanced 97 kilometres and fought in eight battles with the New Zealanders playing a critical role in each.[22] Major-General Sir Andrew Russell, commanding the New Zealand Division, is the longest-serving divisional commander in the 16 attacking divisions in the three British armies mounting the attack. He has commanded his New Zealanders since he raised the division in February 1916. He commanded its predecessor, the New Zealand & Australian Division, since November 1915 until it dissolved and reformed as the New Zealand Division.

Russell's problem is to pass the bulk of his division either side of the fortress town, which is the cork in the bottle straddling the routes into the forest that leads to the crossings over the Sambre River. It is a complex operation.

Le Quesnoy has been a fortress since at least the mid-12th century. Its defences were developed when the town was part of the Spanish Netherlands and were redesigned and improved by the great French military architect and engineer, Sébastien Le Prestre, Marquis de Vauban (1633–1707). The fortifications were further improved in the early 18th century by the addition of the huge protruding hornwork, so named because its two bastions on each of the outer corners gave it the impression of a pair of horns. This form of defensive work was unique in the world at that time, surrounded by lakes, leading to the Fauroeulx Gate. The fortifications have been fought over many times, and if we bring it forward to the next war, most recently in 1940 when a small French garrison held out for four days against the German 5th Panzer Division.[23]

In 1918 Le Quesnoy has a civilian population of some 1600 that have not been evacuated. Because of this the centre of the town is not to be subjected to intense artillery fire. This directive is passed down from General Byng at Third Army to Lieutenant-General Harper at Headquarters IV Corps then on to Russell. It fits in with Russell's view of the villages and towns they have encountered in the advance to date. Russell sees them as obstacles to be avoided.

Bypassing towns and villages is the New Zealand Division's modus operandi during the 1918 advance. In the previous attacks such as before Bapaume to the west, Russell is intent on ringing the city rather than attacking it head-on. He is critical of the tendency to see major centres as objectives, and insists to his brigade commanders that "villages are only obstacles — not ends in themselves".[24] He appreciates the skilled German tactics: their withdrawing in good order, based on clever siting and use of machine guns to allow the withdrawal of his infantry and artillery. Where the ground allows Russell directs his brigades to prise them out by a series of flanking movements, with the emphasis on achieving success with "as few casualties as possible".[25] The bypassing of Le Quesnoy is simply a continuation of this well-practised tactical doctrine.

THE BATTLE OF THE COLOURED LINES

To the uninitiated, this is very much a battle for the coloured lines. In what is now a war of movement, the objectives are marked out in different colours and provide commanders and staff with a means of assessing progress across a wide front involving potentially hundreds of thousands of men. In this battle the initial objective is the Blue Line, which is marked just beyond the main German defensive position. Then there is the Blue Dotted Line. A dotted line generally represents an intermediate position or one that, if it is possible to exploit to and take, then it should be done without stopping and reorganising for a separate attack. The next line in this battle is the Green Line. When the New Zealanders reach this line, Le Quesnoy has been bypassed with an encircling movement on either side. It is now necessary to pause, organise the next lot of battalions to be ready to attack, and also have the artillery fire that has been moving forward keeping just ahead of the infantry halt but keep on firing, so as to cover this reorganisation. At a given time, it all starts again and the New Zealanders, as well as the British divisions on each flank, push on to the Red Line. This is the objective that General Byng, the Third Army commander, has laid down as his goal for this battle. In this case the Red Line is the road in front of a very formidable obstacle, Forêt de Mormal. This forest runs across the front of the advancing British forces and is ideal for defence, so the Red Line is the point where the British stop and consolidate and pass through fresh troops to move through the forest. However, all this depends of the level of German resistance, and if it proves to be less than expected, then Byng and his corps commander have given his divisions the latitude to exploit success and advance into the forest to the Red Dotted Line, which as you will see as the story unfolds, they do. All of this is carefully thought through in the planning process by commanders and staff who have been adapting to the techniques of a war of movement since the Battle of Amiens on 8 August 1918.

Effective communications was very difficult to achieve during the First World War. By 1918 cable was rapidly laid between headquarters and battalions and to the artillery brigades and the batteries. Wireless, signal lamps, runners and despatch riders by motorcycle and horse were also used. Here a signaller at a howitzer battery of the New Zealand Field Artillery receives the target and range instructions in 1917. NZ RSA Collection, Photographer: Captain H.A. Sanders, NZEF Official H Series H199, Ref: 1/2-012898-G, Alexander Turnbull Library, Wellington, New Zealand

At zero hour, 5.30 a.m., the barrage will start and 3rd Rifle Brigade with three battalions in line are to advance and capture the railway and "draw an arc round the western side of Le Quesnoy from south to north" on the Blue Line. Once achieved, 3 Rifles, the reserve battalion, will pass south of the town and advance to the Blue-Dotted Line. The 1st Infantry Brigade is to pass one battalion, 1 Auckland, through 2 Rifles battalion north of the town, and advance to a similar position on the Blue Dotted Line.

A further two battalions of Brigadier-General Melvill's 1st Brigade, 1 and 2 Wellingtons, will pass through and form up along the Green Line linking up with 3 Rifles from 3rd Rifle Brigade who will move forward and secure the Green Line on the right flank. At this point the advance to the Red Line becomes the responsibility of 1st Brigade, who with 1 Wellington on the right and 2 Wellington on the left will secure the road running along the western edge of Forêt de Mormal. Then, if the opportunity offers, the battalions will exploit through the forest to the Red Dotted Line, otherwise Young's 2nd Brigade will move forward and take over the advance.

By 1918 Russell's division is a professional citizen force, very different from the raw division that landed in France in April–May 1916. On 16 September 1918 Russell gives an assessment of his division and of the operational situation to Colonel James Allen, the New Zealand Minister of Defence. It is worth reading in detail.

The actual operations have been very much more interesting than the offensives in which we took part in 1916 and 1917. Then we no longer exceeded on the first day or two the same set pieces in which by dint of careful rehearsing and limited objectives, we succeeded in winning a meagre two or three thousand yards, but it would be wrong to suppose the tactical successes are due to altered or improved methods so much as to the fact that we had not got in front of us the same thoroughly organised defence with which were face to face last year, nor had we troops of the same fighting quality to overcome. When the Germans had reached the extreme length of their tether during their offensives, they found themselves with their impetus lost, their organisation severely strained, their ranks very considerably depleted, and, I imagine, with the unpleasant conviction that they had failed to achieve a measure commensurate with their effort and likely to bring about the hoped for peace by victory ... They preferred to risk a war of movement in which they imagined themselves vastly our superiors. They were wrong. There is not much to choose between the two Armies; both being I take it pretty bad. It could not well be otherwise when you think of the combings out on both sides which have been stuffed into the ranks of the opposing Armies to fill them out and give them at any rate a semblance of military strength.

I make no rash surmises as to future developments of active operations this Autumn, but I am convinced that the Bosche [sic] is a beaten man and that he knows it, and that, providing the men are available, we should go on attacking and attacking and so confirm that encouraging habit that he has formed of surrendering at the first opportunity. Such a policy, if the means exist, would lead us to the banks of the Rhine before Christmas, or at any rate to the Meuse.[26]

This is a picture of an enemy declining in strength and morale, pitted against in some cases equally tired but generally stronger British forces, but Russell is confident in the calibre of his commanders and in the training and morale of his men to defeat the Germans in mobile warfare. He also knows that his division has advantages in organisation and manpower not available to other British divisions.

PREPARING FOR BATTLE

The battalions of 3rd Brigade hold the front line with Le Quesnoy visible as a series of treed mounds beyond the railway line on the skyline. Melvill's 1st Brigade is billeted in Solesmes, 15 kilometres to the southwest, and spends the first days of November training for operations. This is very much part of the New Zealand Division's operating procedures as Russell insists that his

New Zealand engineers replacing bridges destroyed by the Germans during their retreat. This is likely to be one of the bridges at Pont à Pierres between Solesmes and Beaudignies that remained under German artillery fire until 4 November 1918.
NZ RSA Collection, Photographer: Captain H.A. Sanders, NZEF Official H Series H1150, Ref: 1/2-013703-G, Alexander Turnbull Library, Wellington, New Zealand

brigadiers and commanding officers leave nothing to chance. In 1 Wellington tactical training by platoons is carried out, as well as range firing for Lewis guns, rifles and rifle grenades. The warning order is received for the operations against Le Quesnoy and the commanding officer and company commanders reconnoitre the routes forward to the brigade assembly area.[27] The attack is practised the following morning "in drizzly rain and men all worked well". The battalion band gives a concert in the afternoon and the men rest. The company commanders and the commanding officer discuss the impending operations in a planning session in the afternoon.[28]

Similar procedures occur in all battalions. Private Neil 'Monty' Ingram is a scout attached to the Intelligence Section in Battalion Headquarters, 2 Wellington. "In company with the other scouts and the Battalion Intelligence Officer rode up to the front to reconnoitre. It was indeed a pleasure to push an old bike along again after nearly two years footslogging and our job was completed in half the usual time."[29]

The following day orders for the operation are issued at 9 a.m. The day is spent preparing for the move forward and the attack and "completing deficiencies in arms, equipment, etc. At 4.25 p.m. 2 Wellington march through Town headed by the Band and watched by the local population. The march is a slow and tiring one."[30] In his diary 'Monty' Ingram writes:

Marched to position near Beaudignies this evening in drizzling rain and over broken muddy roads. Heavy going and tiring. We sleep in the open here tonight and at 5.30 a.m. tomorrow morning we "go over the top" … It started to rain at 5.30 and continued intermittently throughout the night … There was little sleep for us on the night of the 3rd, lying on the ground under a

steady drenching rain for most of the dark hours. Before daybreak we were aroused, and after a hasty breakfast, mustered ready for zero hour to arrive.[31]

In 1 Auckland, companies are "engaged in Lewis Gun and Musketry practice, also undergoing instruction in the throwing of the German stick bombs".[32] On 3 November the battalion holds a church parade in Solesmes and marches out of the town at 4.30 p.m. to the brigade assembly area passing through the villages of Romeries and Beaudignies before reaching the area immediately west of the Beaudignies–Ruesnes road, where it bivouacs for the night.[33]

The field engineers and pioneers are fully engaged in building temporary bridges and clearing routes forward into the gun lines and assembly areas. Three artillery bridges and 14 infantry foot bridges are built over the Ecaillon River, all constructed from timber growing along its banks. Engineer effort is also needed at the dual temporary bridges at Pont à Pierres on the road to the west of Beaudignies, which is subject to ongoing German artillery fire. In addition, barns and orchards are scoured for extending ladders with which to surmount the ramparts if needed, and cork lifejackets are also brought up in case it is necessary to cross the moat.[34]

The road traffic forward is busy with men, guns, ammunition and supplies moving forward. Scotsman George Soutar is a 28-year-old wagon driver in the Maori Pioneer Battalion. He was transferred into the battalion from the Otago Mounted Rifles in March 1916, and remained on as a driver after it became the Maori Pioneer Battalion on 1 September 1917. In November 1918 Soutar is "on limber" delivering rations forward to the Pioneer companies working on the roads and bridges. On 3 November the wagon lines are preparing to move forward. "Brighter and warmer. On limber

A New Zealand supply convoy of horse-drawn wagons GS (General Service, the nearest wagon) and carts move toward the bridge at Pont à Pierres, marked by the chimney on the skyline, with Beaudignies and Le Quesnoy beyond, while Army Service Corps motor transport return from unloading ammunition and supplies, 30 October 1918. NZ RSA Collection, Photographer: Captain H.A. Sanders, NZEF Official H Series H1141, Ref: 1/2-013696-G, Alexander Turnbull Library, Wellington, New Zealand

Diggers of the New Zealand Machine Gun Battalion loading ammunition belts with a machine gun belt loader in preparation for battle, May 1918. Feeding the guns demanded preparation of hundreds of belts. NZ RSA Collection, Photographer: Captain H.A. Sanders, NZEF Official H Series H583, Ref.1/2-013194-G, Alexander Turnbull Library, Wellington, New Zealand

Watering artillery horses at Louvencourt. Horses were the critical element in providing mobility to the New Zealand Division by towing guns, bringing up supplies and ammunition. In 1918 the New Zealand Division had over 5000 horses that had to be watered and fed. NZ RSA Collection, Photographer: Captain H.A. Sanders, NZEF Official H Series H1186, Ref. 1/2-013735-G, Alexander Turnbull Library, Wellington, New Zealand

at 8.30 carting refuse from Q.M. [quartermaster] and coys to incinerator, and getting ready to shift later … Plenty of 'toot sweeters' during the night but he's missed us again, though we are directly in his line of fire evidently."[35] According to Soutar, the "'toot sweeters' are longer long rangers [German artillery] of very high velocity about 4.5" or so".[36]

The signallers of the Divisional Signal's Company are also at full stretch. On 2 November "Orders having been received for the resumption of the offensive on the 4th November general preparations were made today. Cable Wagons were got ready for work and detachments told off."[37] The cable wagon teams are busy connecting the two artillery groups and their headquarters to the exchange. On the following day cable parties move forward to Beaudignies to set up communications for Russell's advanced divisional headquarters that will take over the headquarters building currently occupied by 3rd Rifle Brigade, once they move forward.

A pair of lines are laid to the Advanced Headquarters of 62nd Division in VI Corps on the left flank and two pairs are laid to the site of Headquarters 1st Brigade, one pair for the brigade and one pair for its accompanying artillery group whose headquarters are located alongside each other. All pairs of cables were laid and tested to see that line communications were established. In the forward areas this is done by man-powered wheelbarrow and limber cart as it is too close to the front line and under observation from Le Quesnoy to be carried out by the cable wagons.

Signal personnel are sent forward to Beaudignies and the Advanced Divisional Signal Office is opened there at 9 p.m., which is when Major-General Russell's Advanced Divisional Headquarters also opens. The war diary reports on a busy day. "Owing to indiscriminate shellfire and the large amount of traffic on roads and across fields, a considerable amount of difficulty was experienced through the night in the maintenance of the forward lines to the Brigades and Groups. This difficulty was, however, successfully overcome and no disconnections for any time occurred."[38]

A visual signal scheme is set up from the Advanced Divisional Headquarters forward to the brigades. Power buzzers and amplifiers are supplied to 1st Brigade and 3rd Rifle Brigade for ground induction signalling. A Wilson wireless set is set up at Advanced Divisional Headquarters to work forward to a trench set at each of the two brigade headquarters. Despatch riders on motorcycles and mounted men from the Otago Mounted Rifles are based at the Advanced Divisional Headquarters, "should the roads have become impassable".[39]

In the New Zealand Division all preparations are complete with the troops forward in their assembly areas. Armageddon awaits tomorrow.

New Zealand infantrymen in the front line facing Le Quesnoy, November 1918. This forward platoon are in hastily dug fighting trenches. The near pair is one of the platoon Lewis gun teams, with the No. 1 on the gun and his No. 2 on the right observing for targets with his binoculars. The platoon medic has his stretcher behind his trench. NZ RSA Collection, Photographer: Captain H.A. Sanders, NZEF Official H Series H1243, Ref. 1/2-013790, Alexander Turnbull Library, Wellington, New Zealand

Chapter 2

THE 'DINKS' ENCIRCLE LE QUESNOY

> The attack was launched half-an hour before dawn on a beautiful autumn morning. My Hdqrs [Headquarters] was established during the night at Ferme du Fort Martin. The 1st Battn was on my right, the 4th in the centre & the 2nd on the left. The 3rd Battn had to leapfrog the 1st Battn on the blue line, two hours after zero & advance 2000 yards completing the investment of the town.[1]

This is Brigadier-General Herbert Hart's diary entry for 4 November 1918. The riflemen of his 3rd Rifle Brigade or 'Dinks'* as they call themselves, are tasked with investing the fortress town, allowing the remaining brigades to bypass Le Quesnoy and push on through Forêt de Mormal and, if the opportunity allows, seize crossings over the Sambre River. Hart adjusts the organisation of his four battalions to cater for the fact that his brigade is 976 men below strength by reducing the number of platoons in his rifle companies from four to three platoons, each of at least 28 men in three sections.[2] He organises his attack frontage so that each of his three attacking battalions cover a frontage of one thousand yards [914 metres]. "The enemy was holding strong positions in front of the town, mainly on the railway line which crossed our whole frontage. We had first to storm & capture these positions before we reached the town."[3]

The first phase is to capture the Blue Line marked by the general line of the railway line immediately west of the town, extending north from Le Quesnoy to the village of Orsinval, which, as the map shows, is over the Army Corps boundary in the area held by 62nd Division, which is part of

*The term 'fair dinkum' was originally a term of derision coined by the Main Body to explain why the men of the Rifle Brigade took so long to enlist. It was shortened to 'Dinks' and became the proud nickname of the men of the 3rd Rifle Brigade.

A 3-inch Stokes mortar crew, supporting 1 Rifles, 3rd Rifle Brigade, fire at German positions on the railway that is the main German defensive line west of Le Quesnoy. The mortar is with the reserve company of the battalion in the sunken road near 'Le Tilleul' or Linden, named after a local farmhouse noted for the Linden or lime trees in its garden. The sunken road runs north from the junction on the Beaudignies–Le Quesnoy road. NZ RSA Collection, Photographer: Captain H.A. Sanders, NZEF Official H Series H 1308, Ref: 1/2-013798-G, Alexander Turnbull Library, Wellington, New Zealand

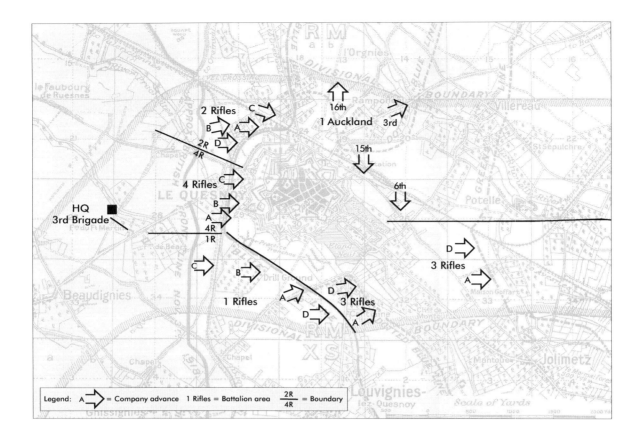

Progress of Attack,
3rd Rifle Brigade,
4 November 1918.

the neighbouring VI Corps. To the south the Blue Line swings to the east of the railway line and runs across a large hedged apple orchard and then the open area marked as the Drill Ground to intercept the road from Louvignies to Le Quesnoy, at which point it turns south, running to the east of the road where it crosses the interdivisional boundary with the 37th Division, the other leading division in IV Corps.

All is quiet on a fine but misty morning. It is evident from the German posts along the line of the railway that they do not expect the attack this morning, but are in position to defend against it when it comes. Hart's battalions have sent out patrols during the night to confirm that the Germans have not withdrawn. Lieutenant-Colonel Leonard Jardine's 2 Rifles on the left or northern flank sends out two patrols. Both report that he is still there. As on previous nights, there is intermittent German shelling. Fortunately for Jardine's 2 Rifles, this falls in the area immediately west of where the battalion is assembled, landing along a general line running north–south where the divisional boundary intersects Préchettes River to the chapel at the crossroads on the Ruesnes–Le Quesnoy road, which is the headquarters of Major Harold Barrowclough's 4 Rifles.

ZERO HOUR 5.30: THE ROAR OF THE GUNS

Along came 5.30, zero time, and just on tick, a big gun fired on the right and left flank. I believe that was signal that all was ready, then before a man could say Jack Robinson, every gun on the sector opened out at once, even the machine gunners. The vic[k]ers gun and I was told that there were only 66 of them covering [our] division I must say that I think it was one of the priettest [sic] sights I have ever see, because all along the front line was liquid fire enough to put the wind up anybody.[4]

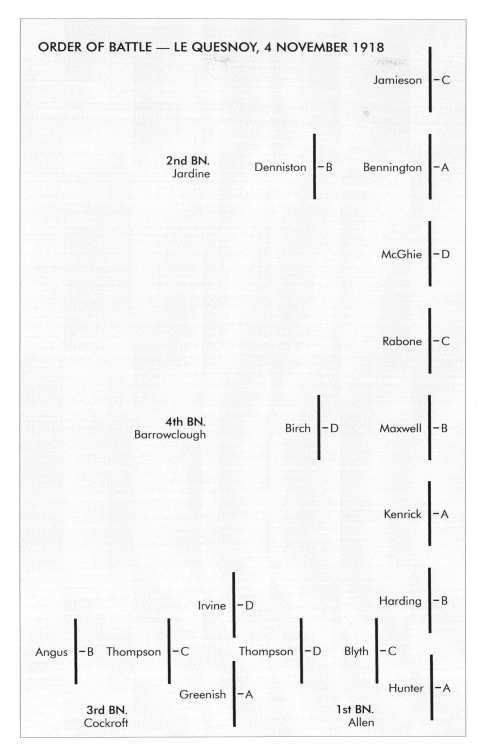

ORDER OF BATTLE — LE QUESNOY, 4 NOVEMBER 1918

Jamieson – C

2nd BN.
Jardine

Denniston – B   Bennington – A

McGhie – D

Rabone – C

4th BN.
Barrowclough

Birch – D   Maxwell – B

Kenrick – A

Irvine – D   Harding – B

Angus – B   Thompson – C   Thompson – D   Blyth – C

Greenish – A   Hunter – A

3rd BN.
Cockroft

1st BN.
Allen

Order of Battle, 3 (Rifle) Brigade, 4 November 1918, with company commanders and battalion commanders named. Austin, *Official History of the New Zealand Rifle Brigade*, p. 446

This is the view of Corporal Norman Coop, a 26-year-old section commander in D Company, 3 Rifles. Throughout the night the riflemen in the front line report that the German posts fire double red flares at intervals and at 5.20 a.m. two orange flares are fired, perhaps to indicate all clear. Ten minutes later the silence is shattered by the roar of the British barrage. Hart writes: "The advance of our men in the early morning was covered by the usual field artillery barrage, one gun to 30 yards upon which was superimposed the fire from 12/6" Medium & 16 Light Trench Mortars, & in addition smoke & burning oil were projected on to the ramparts."[5] Hart's matter-of-fact statement highlights the degree with which the battle of materiel has swung in the Allies' favour in 1918. British artillery is the dominant force on the battlefield at this stage of the war.

Zero hour is at 5.30 a.m. on 4 November 1918. There is no preliminary bombardment. Major Lindsay Inglis of the New Zealand Machine Gun Corps later records: "At 5.30 a.m. on 4th November our last day's fighting was ushered in by the usual stupendous crash of guns, mortars and machine guns opening the barrage at the exact second of zero."[6] Massed machine gun fire is essential to the fire plan and integrated in with the artillery and mortar barrage. The Auckland and Otago Machine Gun Companies of the division's machine gun battalion fire in support of the 3rd Rifle Brigade operation. In addition, two sections (eight guns) of the Canterbury Machine Gun Company fire over the ramparts and into the streets of the town and the main square to keep the garrison under cover.

The division is supported by seven artillery brigades, including 1st, 2nd and 3rd New Zealand Field Artillery Brigades, each consisting of four 6-gun/ howitzer batteries: 24 per brigade, 168 guns in all, as well as three batteries of 6-inch howitzers of 90th (Heavy) Brigade Royal Garrison Artillery. These are divided into two artillery groups.[7] The Right Group is commanded by Lieutenant-Colonel Frank 'Batt' Symon, a 39-year-old regular officer of the Royal New Zealand Artillery who was commissioned as a lieutenant in the New Zealand Militia in 1900. Symon commanded No. 1 Battery on Gallipoli and was promoted to lieutenant-colonel commanding 1st Brigade New Zealand Field Artillery in August 1915. He was awarded the CMG (Companion of the Order of St Michael and St George) for his work on Gallipoli and the Distinguished Service Order in 1917. His group consists of 1st and 2nd Brigades, New Zealand Field Artillery, and 211th Brigade, Royal Field Artillery.

The Left Group is commanded by 31-year-old Lieutenant-Colonel Robert McQuarrie. McQuarrie was a pre-war territorial and one of the first to volunteer for the Advance Party to Samoa in August 1914. He sailed for Egypt with the 5th Reinforcements and was wounded on Gallipoli in 1915. He was awarded the Military Cross for his command of No. 9 Battery on the Somme in 1916. He was promoted to lieutenant-colonel in command of 3rd Brigade, New Zealand Field Artillery, on 30 May 1918. His leadership in this coming battle sees McQuarrie receive the Distinguished Service Order.[8] He is one of a number of comparatively young but very experienced New Zealand artillery officers, both regular and territorial, who perfect their trade under the stern eye and very high standards demanded by Brigadier-General George Napier Johnston, Commander Royal Artillery New Zealand Division, or 'Blinky' as his gunners called him.

McQuarrie's artillery group consists of 3rd Brigade, New Zealand Field Artillery, 210th and 72nd Brigades, Royal Field Artillery, and 14th (Army) Brigade, Royal Horse Artillery. Three batteries of six 6-inch howitzers of 90th (Heavy) Brigade, Royal Garrison Artillery, also support the attack.

In addition, X and Y trench mortar batteries of the New Zealand Division are placed in support of the Rifle Brigade. As the New Zealand artillery history states, the barrage is to be carried out to a depth of 6000 yards [5486 metres]. To achieve this it is necessary to advance four of the six brigades while the barrage is being fired to ensure enough guns have sufficient range to carry out their tasks. This involves brigades moving forward, one battery at a time; the remaining batteries distributing their fire across the front of the

barrage and increasing their rate of fire to ensure that the intensity of the fire on each barrage line does not lessen.

It is a complex fire plan and reflects the highly developed techniques and skills of British artillery at this stage of the war. A moving barrage advances ahead of the three battalions of the 3rd Rifle Brigade, the rate of the artillery barrage on the left or north of the town is based on the speed of that of 62nd Division, while the barrage to the south of the town is based on that required by 37th Division. What this means is that the two artillery groups supporting the New Zealanders are firing on different programmes. For example, the rate for 62nd Division north of the town is for three lifts of fire from zero hour, of 100 yards every three minutes and then at a rate of 100 yard lifts every four minutes — all based on a calculation of how long it is going to take the advancing infantry to move forward. In the south, 37th Division wants the first lift at zero plus four minutes, followed by seven lifts of 100 yards every four minutes, then at a rate of 100 yards every six minutes. Each programme is determined by the difficulty of the ground that the infantry has to cross and the estimated strength of the German opposition.[9]

Five artillery brigades will continue to fire up to the Green Line with two brigades firing the barrage with them up to the Blue Line and then shifting their fire in order to fire smoke and shrapnel onto the ramparts of the town. The infantry advance is supported by a barrage consisting of 50% high explosive shells and 50% shrapnel, which continues for 5000 yards to the Green Line and sees the guns fire continuously for 290 minutes. The standard rate of fire is four rounds per minute and so the effort needed by each gun team to maintain this rate of fire speaks for itself.

In addition, the division's trench mortars and Vickers machine guns of the Machine Gun Battalion fire in support of the artillery fire plan with

A New Zealand gun team sponging out a Newton 6-inch mortar after firing in the line facing Le Quesnoy on 28 October 1918. There are six of these mortars in each of X and Y New Zealand trench mortar batteries. NZ RSA Collection, Photographer: Captain H.A. Sanders, NZ Official H Series H1155, Ref: 1/2-013732-G, Alexander Turnbull Library, Wellington, New Zealand

Thirty-six-year-old Private Arthur John Lloyd (1882–1948), New Zealand Machine Gun Battalion, was a cream tester for the Waikato Dairy Company at Mercer. An accomplished artist who delighted in painting New Zealand shipping scenes, Lloyd painted a series of works showing a machine gunner's experience on the Western Front 1916–18. These are now part of the Auckland War Memorial Collection. Here we see the No. 1 on the Vickers medium machine gun firing on fixed lines over the ramparts of Le Quesnoy so that the bullets land along the Place d'Armes and the streets leading into it. We see the No. 2 on the gun collect boxes of belted ammunition while in the trench the rest of the gun team link the belts together. New Zealand gunners tended to fire in bursts of 40–50 rounds and each gun would fire thousands of rounds. Wounded make their way back in the distance. Arthur Lloyd, 'One of the guns of the 2nd NZ M.G. Coy firing barrage into the main street of Le Quesnoy, 4 Nov 1918,' watercolour and ink., Ref. ID PD 1929-3-2, Auckland War Memorial Museum Tamaki Paenga Hira

specific mortars and machine guns then detached and supporting the advancing infantry, with others suppressing any fire from the ramparts. Overhead No. 59 Squadron RAF provide a contact aircraft to report progress by wireless and also fly a counterattack aircraft to direct fire onto any developing German counterattack and to also indicate obvious artillery targets for counterbattery fire.[10]

Artillery fire on the walled town of Le Quesnoy itself is limited to shrapnel fire and smoke on the ramparts of the town but not onto the buildings within the walls. At zero hour 'Q' Special Company Royal Engineers fire 500 drums of burning oil onto the western ramparts blinding any garrison manning the walls while No. 5 Special Company Royal Engineers thicken this with a timed programme of smoke projectiles onto the ramparts, which will stop and start depending on when units are moving past the town. This programme is fired from banks of Livens Projectors assembled in rows. At zero hour these are electrically detonated and lob canisters of petroleum onto the walls where they burst into flame with thick clouds of black smoke that mingle with the mist and make it impossible for friend or foe to see more than ten or so metres distant.

There is one exception to excluding artillery fire on the town and that is the prominent tower of the Hotel de Ville. Inglis records:

> The 6-inch Howitzers made practise on the tower of the Le Quesnoy Maire, which, overlooking nearly the whole of the brigade area, was a too convenient observation post for the German artillery. After we entered the town we found that, although the tower had been completely demolished and the town hall gutted, only two "overs" had missed to explode in other buildings.[11]

AT THE GUN LINE

At zero hour the guns begin and the barrage lifts forward to cover the infantry advance. The *Chronicles of the N.Z.E.F.* catches the reality of life at the gun line:

> Behind the guns the gunners themselves toil on. The ground is sodden through recent rains, and the gun wheels in some instances sink almost to the axle. The trails dig in deeper and deeper as the shock and concussion of each shell send it down a little further … By this time the enemy has joined in the turmoil. His fire of retaliation comes down, but it is a feeble effort compared to our own tremendous concentration.[12]

Some 400 rounds have been stockpiled by each gun in preparation for the barrage. Gunner William Jamieson, a 24-year-old carpenter from Carterton, is in No. 3 Battery, 1st Brigade, New Zealand Field Artillery. In old age he remembers the massed lines of guns ready to fire the barrage:

> The ammunition was taken up in the limbers and you would either go back to the dump and pick up ammunition and take it up and make a pile at the gun pit or where it was. At that time the guns were out in the paddock … And there would be a row of the guns there, a couple of hundred yards behind them there would be a sixty pounder battery, that was a bigger gun, English guns, and back behind them would be the eight inch, the big heavy guns. They would be lined up in battle formation …[13]

Some of the 18-pounders are of the latest type fitted with an air recuperator buffer that had a range of 9600 yards compared to guns with the older spring recuperator whose range is 6600 yards. These new guns remain firing the barrage as long as possible while one by one the batteries limber up to their horse teams and together with ammunition limbers move forward to battery positions east of the town to keep the barrage going for the advancing infantry.

Guns fired for 141 minutes at a rate of four shells a minute between the Start Line for the attack up to the Blue Line. By the time guns are firing on the Red Line immediately west of the forest they had been firing for 386 minutes. The coordination needed to keep this barrage of fire going is exceptional and the impact on the crews feeding the guns also has to be realised. Jamieson recalls his time at the guns.

> With the firing of the guns, you see you get the concussion every time you have a stunt. We used to bung our ears up with a bit of cotton wool, if you

H1116

An 18-pounder field gun of one of the New Zealand batteries firing on German positions forward of Le Quesnoy on 29 October 1918. There were nine New Zealand 18-pounder batteries, each armed with six 18-pounder field guns, totalling 54 guns. NZ RSA Collection, Photographer: Captain H.A. Sanders, NZEF Official H Series H1116, Ref: 1/2-013673-G, Alexander Turnbull Library, Wellington, New Zealand

had time. And by the time you been through one stunt there, you got rid of a lot of ammunition and you would be deaf for a day or two, or pretty deaf anyway …[14]

Adapting to mobile warfare with artillery is learnt on the job. The New Zealand Divisional Artillery has little time to train in mobile operations as they have to stay in position supporting the front line, when the infantry are rotated in turn to go out for training. However, in April–May 1918 while holding the defensive line east of Amiens, Major-General Russell directs that his infantry battalions train in offensive operations with support by artillery batteries who rotate in turn out of the line to fire live rounds for each infantry practice attack, leapfrogging the horse-drawn guns forward by sections at the gallop, so that the infantry has continuous fire support.

It becomes standard practice to attach a section or battery to move forward with the leading battalions. On 4 November 1918 a section of 4.5-inch howitzers from 1st Brigade and a section of 18-pounders from each of the 2nd and 3rd Brigades are detailed to move forward with the advancing infantry who bypass the town. These are tasked to engage enemy tanks (usually captured British tanks) and to firing on any massed body of men or strong point. In addition, every battery designates one gun to be prepared to move forward and engage enemy tanks in the direct fire role.[15] All this is proven by trial and error in the battles or 'stunts', as the Diggers call them, leading up to 4 November. Each stunt is carefully analysed for tactical lessons that can be applied in future fighting. "The utility of having a section of 18-pounders was proved again and again. They were especially useful in putting isolated machine guns out of action."[16]

Under Brigadier-General Johnston, New Zealand artillery is adept at providing quick 'shell storms' of fire on suspected strongpoints, and if necessary quickly drawing up artillery barrages for the infantry to advance behind.

New Zealand 4.5-inch howitzers of No. 15 Battery, 1st Brigade, New Zealand Field Artillery, in an orchard firing on German positions around Le Quesnoy, 29 October 1918. There were three New Zealand howitzer batteries, each of six howitzers. There is some dispute over individual identifications in this photo. The loader (with one sleeve rolled up) has been identified as A.C. Hall by one researcher, and as 21-year-old Gunner Hamish Howard from Blackball on the West Coast by a second researcher. The second researcher has also identified the layer (man smoking a pipe) as Gunner Geoffrey Challies, a 22-year-old carpenter from Richmond. NZ RSA Collection, Photographer: Captain H.A. Sanders, NZEF Official H Series, H1128, Ref: 1/2-013684-G, Alexander Turnbull Library, Wellington, New Zealand

A great saving of casualties can be made by using artillery freely to deal with machine guns. Machine guns disposed in depth can hold up any attack unsupported by Artillery. When the attack is held up it is far better to wait artillery support than to go forward with the certainty of getting heavy casualties and probably not gaining the objective.[17]

In the series of battles leading to Le Quesnoy, the coordination between infantry and artillery is refined, so that simple concentrations could be made immediately or if needed and time was available a barrage could be coordinated. "The simpler the Barrage the better; but 'Halts' on a more or less even line in order to dwell on strong points is not hard to arrange, and provided they did not complicate matters for the Infantry would, I think, prove very effective."[18]

THE GERMAN GUNS RETALIATE

The 15th Battery had a gun position in an orchard and the Hun caused us a few casualties, one of which was Jack Hogg, one of our original gunners who came right through all the fighting, his death was a sad loss especially as the armistice came within a few days.[19]

Major Lindsay Inglis is forward with the Vickers machine guns of his 4th Otago Machine Gun Company of the New Zealand Machine Gun Battalion. He is witness to the barrage. The German artillery and mortars (*minenwerfer*) respond immediately and Inglis moves forward to assess the damage to his guns.

The gun positions and the infantry near them were heavily shelled for some time at the outset; but thanks to our good digging in, we suffered only three casualties, two killed and one wounded, during this period. The casualties were three new reinforcements who had dug wide and shallow instead of narrow and deep and had been cleaned up by a shell which

Deaths New Zealand Field Artillery
EDWARDS, Harry Grosvenor Brundell 50506 Gunner
HARDING, Francis Smith 9/1567 Gunner
HARDY, Colin Conrad 2/2837 Gunner
HOGG, John Alexander 2/2437 Bombardier
JOHNSON, Ernest George 12794 Gunner
McKENZIE, Kenneth 10645 Gunner[20]

would not have harmed them if they had constructed the same type of slit as the old hands.

The other two casualties were Corporal George Gunn and Private Tweedie [Tweedy] of the company signallers, who were hit within a few feet of my H.Q., when a shell burst alongside of them while they were mending our wire to brigade.

Gunn, a fine, fearless chap, who had been with the Company from its formation, was very badly hit — one arm nearly severed and a great hole in a lung, he died the next day. Tweedie, who had a few chips hardly more than skin deep in a shoulder blade and the back of one knee, asked me while I was dressing him if he was very badly hit. I told him he could not have wished himself a cushier Blighty than he had. We heard a few days later that he died of shock; but his name is not in the list of Killed published in the official history of the NZ MG Corps, and I hope the rumour was false.[21]

Sadly it is true, Sapper Glenholme Francis Tweedy is evacuated to 3rd Field Ambulance where he dies the following day, 5 November 1918. He is buried in Caudry British Cemetery.[22] Some riflemen received artillery fire in their assembly areas. Inglis recalled the scene:

A good many of the Riflemen who had assembled just in front of us in shallow pits dug during the night were killed and wounded. Roy Ayling[23] and I with a party of spare [machine gun] numbers rendered some first aid to the wounded and roped in a party of German prisoners to carry them down to the Aid Post. One corporal was sitting quietly on the edge of a hole. He looked such a good colour that I did not think he was seriously hurt and asked, "Can you manage to walk down, Corporal?"

"Afraid not, sir," he replied, nodding towards his legs which were dangling inside the rifle pit, "My leg is a bit damaged."

A bit damaged — it was held together only by the blood drenched puttee, through which splintered bone protruded in several places.[24]

The wounded are evacuated by stretcher bearers and coopted German prisoners according to the divisional medical plan, which establishes a stretcher bearer post near Hart's headquarters at Ferme du Fort Martin on the sunken road from Beaudignies to Orsinval. Here motor ambulances collect the stretcher cases and evacuate them back to the Advanced Dressing Station (ADS) at Beaudignies and from there to the Main Dressing Station (MDS) at Solesmes. It is planned that the ADS will move forward to the east of Le Quesnoy after midday.[25]

The increasingly cold weather saw particular measures taken to treat the wounded in this battle. The Rifles regimental history records:

Elaborate precautions were taken to counteract the deadly shock produced by the action of cold upon wounded men. Teams of three were trained just as precisely as a gun-team, each man being allotted a particular task which he alone was permitted to perform. The senior soldier was the surgeon's immediate assistant. The second placed waterproofs and towels in the desired positions, and stood by to hold the bowls of lotion or the tins of dressings. The third cut off the soiled clothing and first field dressing, held the limbs in position as directed by the surgeon, and, where necessary, also held the electric torch. The teams were under the control of a Senior N.C.O., who directed the rendering of further assistance when required, called for the evacuating stretcher-staff waiting in readiness at the door to remove the cases dealt with, and gave the word for the bringing in of the next cases for treatment. In addition there was a separate staff detailed to attend to the special heating arrangements and to the feeding of the patients. Each case, whilst being treated, was placed over a blanketed frame heated by oil stoves.[27]

Deaths New Zealand Machine Gun Corps
DUNCAN, David 42062 Private
FITZGERALD, John Lawrence 55845 Private
GRAHAM, Hugh Murray 68576 Private
GREENWOOD, Eric Percy 54684 Private
GUNN, William George 23/440 Corporal
HOOPER, Charles Leonard 62000 Sergeant
KING, Charles Frederick 10458 Private
MANSON, William 26/1044 Corporal
MYLES, Sidney Austin Wilson 59696 Private
SHELTON, Frederick 14494 Private
STOCKMAN, Leslie Campbell 17870 Sergeant[26]

Company Quartermaster Sergeant (CQMS) Harold Green is a 30-year-old cabinetmaker from Petone, Wellington. As CQMS he is up early in the morning at 1 a.m. to supervise a hot breakfast to his company, C Company, 3 Rifles, in the assembly area of which, as he notes that even before the attack begins, "only 83 were left". Green is wounded by artillery shrapnel in the right forearm, which fortunately misses the bone. "Got the wound fixed with a field dressing and walked back to the dressing station where I got aboard a horse ambulance."[28] Green is shuttled down the line, being moved on from the near casualty clearing stations that are full of more serious cases. He is eventually evacuated back to 'Blighty' arriving at New End Military Hospital, Hampstead, on Thursday 7 November 1918. The reaction sets in as he passes down the evacuation chain. "The amount of gas I swallowed during the past week began to have its affect [sic] on me and I was coughing and my eyes were running and smarting continually. Generally I felt played out."[29]

New Zealand stretcher bearers bringing in a wounded New Zealander at Le Quesnoy. NZ RSA Collection, Photographer: Captain H.A. Sanders, NZEF Official H Series H1148, Ref.1/2-013701-G, Alexander Turnbull Library, Wellington, New Zealand

H1148

THE RIFLES SECURE THE BLUE LINE

Behind the artillery barrage the infantry advance. The three leading battalions
of the 3rd Rifle Brigade move forward in extended order with gaps of some
six paces between each man in what is known as artillery formation: 1 Rifles
on the right or southern flank, 4 Rifles in the centre whose three companies
encompassed the entire frontage of the fortress, and 2 Rifles on the left. This
is to the north of Le Quesnoy to take the strongly defended area of ground
known as the 'railway triangle' and the area of the town outside the walls and
north of the railway line as far as the road to Orsinval. The fourth battalion,
in this case 3 Rifles, follows on behind 1 Rifles on the right, ready to push on
through in the next phase of the attack to encircle the fortress by securing the
Blue Dotted Line. 1 Auckland of 1st Brigade similarly is tasked to seize the
Blue Dotted Line from the north in the next phase of the attack.

The initial objective is the railway line, which is the general line of
today's D934 motorway. It is the principal German defensive line with a
series of dug-in machine gun posts. Each of these has been identified and
studied in detail by the attackers. Lack of manpower and the dwindling
number of horse teams available to move artillery guns sees a change in
German defensive tactics. Instead of defence in depth, the emphasis is
now on holding the main defensive line in strength and at all costs to give
time for artillery to withdraw. At Le Quesnoy the railway line is designated
the main line of resistance. This is part of the so-called Herman Position I,
which despite its title, is little more than a line of scratch trenches, except
of course where it can be backed up with the ramparts of Le Quesnoy.[30]
Manning the line are *landser* (soldiers) of the 22nd Division. This division
is not classed very highly in Allied intelligence assessments but shows that
"On the defensive the Division appears to have done better than many
divisions of a higher rating."[31] The 22nd Division consists of four regiments:
Infantry Regiments 82, 83 and 167 with Reserve Infantry Regiment 83.
These are supported by Field Artillery Regiment 11. However, all four
regiments are badly understrength. Infantry Regiment 167 holds the railway
line immediately west of Le Quesnoy with Regiment 83 to its south. There
are three designated defensive lines. The main position is on the railway. A
second line protects the bulk of the German artillery in position to the east
of Le Quesnoy and to the south of the village of Frasnoy and a third line runs
along the western edge of Forêt de Mormal. As we shall see, these last two
lines exist in name only. Every available German soldier is holding the main
line of defence.

The three battalions of Reserve Infantry Regiment 83 are attached to
bolster the strength of the two regiments holding the main defensive line.
The soldiers of III Battalion, Reserve Infantry Regiment 83, are deployed
within Le Quesnoy itself, with its No. 10 and 11 Companies manning the
western ramparts supported by five light machine guns of No. 1 Machine
Gun Company. The remaining infantry company, No. 9 Company, occupies
the ramparts to the south. They are supported by two light machine guns. In
addition, one light mortar (*minenwerfer*) and three 77-mm field guns of Field
Artillery Regiment 11 are deployed within the walls as fire support. These
are infantry companies in name only as their combined strengths amount
to 53 men — making each company about 17 strong — far less than the
average strength of 28 riflemen in any one of the three platoons that make
up the rifle companies of the attacking battalions. The total strength of the

garrison within the town including machine gunners and artillerymen is in the vicinity of 120–130 soldiers, not counting the hospital staff and patients in the military hospital in the town.[32] The majority of the defenders are in the two regiments holding the railway line defences. When the garrison in Le Quesnoy surrenders later that afternoon, 711 prisoners are taken, most of whom must have retired into the fortress when driven back from their defensive line on the railway.

Immediately after zero hour the German defenders respond with machine gun, mortar and artillery fire. The attacking rifle companies reacted with well-honed tactical drills that they have trained for and practised. Each battalion of Hart's brigade has a different story to tell.

2 RIFLES AND THE 'RAILWAY TRIANGLE'

In the north on the left flank of the New Zealand attack, the 2 Rifles' war diary notes that, "All [our] guns opened up together, creating an awful din. The enemy fired double red and golden rain flares."[33] This is no doubt an SOS signal from the German infantry in the front line to the German artillery to bring down artillery fire on the western approaches to the town. Lieutenant-Colonel Jardine's battalion objective is the railway triangle, which is known to be heavily defended. Jardine, a 28-year-old surveyor, is one of the outstanding commanding officers in the New Zealand Division. A platoon commander with the Wellington Battalion on Gallipoli, he was awarded the Military Cross for his leadership as a company commander on the Somme in 1916, and will be awarded a Distinguished Service Order and Bar for his command of the battalion in 1918.[34] He attacks with three companies forward: 23-year-old former student Lieutenant John McGhie's D Company on the right, 29-year-old government clerk Lieutenant Francis Bennington's A Company in the centre and 34-year-old regular soldier Captain George Jamieson's C Company on the left. B Company, commanded by 32-year-old judge's associate Lieutenant Leslie Denniston, is in reserve, centrally positioned following behind A Company. The soldiers advance, moving as close as possible to the bursting shrapnel and high explosive of the barrage, which lifts and moves forward in 100 yard jumps every three minutes. Jardine reports that the barrage is very good until the railway line and then a number of rounds drop short and land among the advancing soldiers particularly on the left flank.[35]

In the centre A Company is almost immediately held up by machine gun fire from the high ground straddling the railway line at the left-hand angle of the railway triangle. A carefully sited German machine gun annihilates the right-hand platoon. The supporting platoon comes forward to outflank the gun and suffers similar casualties. Sergeant John Grubb in the left forward platoon leads his section forward and suppresses the two machine guns to his front. Rifleman Charlie Birch of the Stokes mortar team attached to the battalion brings mortar fire down onto the machine gun

Deaths 2 Rifles
ARNOTT, Robert Henry 53995 Rifleman
AYLING, Frank 64982 Rifleman
BATES, George Ronald 24/345, 2nd Lieutenant
BROWN, Robert 53312 Lance-Corporal
BURGESS, John 65339 Rifleman
DANIELS, James Edward 44259 Rifleman
DOUGLAS, Percy Osmond 52970 Rifleman
EVEREST, Thomas Daniel 48822 Rifleman
FLEMING, John Samson 71106 Rifleman
HILLS, Charles Francis Robert 47888 Rifleman
HOPE, Thomas Alexander 42666 Rifleman
JOHNSON, Ewart Gladstone 59208 Rifleman
MANCER, Albert Edward 24/835 Rifleman
PERCY, Andrew 49168 Rifleman
ROSS, Samuel 41888 Rifleman
SCULLY, Peter Alphonsus 24/1189 Company Sergeant-Major
SINCLAIR, Andrew James 72427 Rifleman
WATSON, Thomas 56891 Rifleman
WATSON, Walter Harold 65006 Lance-Corporal
WILLIAMSON, James 71309 Rifleman
WILSON, William Archibald 65644 Rifleman
WOOD, Alan Carruthers 4/178a, 2nd Lieutenant

post, then he and team member Rifleman William Ferguson charge the position, capturing three machine guns and their garrison of an officer and 27 men. This allows the advance to continue. All three men are awarded the Distinguished Conduct Medal for their actions.[36]

Lieutenant Leslie Denniston in B Company sees the problem and immediately moves his company through the remnants of A Company to fill the gap. On the left Jamieson's C Company reaches the Blue Line at 6.20 a.m. "without any great resistance and taking a fair number of prisoners". It clears the railway triangle, and then swings to the east to clear toward the Orsinval–Le Quesnoy road. The regimental history records that: "Several enemy posts were dealt with in succession, but, fortunately in nearly every case resistance was so slight that the garrison surrendered on closer approach."[37]

One post along this road shows resistance. This is attacked by Sergeant William McGillan who, with his Lewis gun, causes the defenders to hastily retire to a house further back, which McGillan immediately rushes, killing five defenders and taking 14 prisoner.[38] McGillan, a 25-year-old farm labourer from Temuka, has already shown his leadership qualities in defending an isolated forward post against German counterattacks on 26 October 1918. This is evident in his rapid rise through the ranks. Promoted corporal on 12 September, he was made sergeant on 26 October, and becomes company sergeant-major with the rank of warrant officer on 1 January 1919. It also reflects the attrition among both officers and non-commissioned officers in the constant fighting of 1918. McGillan receives the Distinguished Conduct Medal for his actions on 26 October and 4 November.[39]

McGhie's D Company on the right also meets increasing resistance after it crosses the railway line, particularly in the area of the sunken road circling the town's ramparts, immediately east of the railway line. The brick factory on the extreme right of the triangle is occupied by a German garrison of some 75 men and despite being surrounded holds out until 9.30 a.m. before it surrenders.[40]

At 8 a.m. a four-man patrol from B Company probes forward to see if the walls are still defended and manages to cross the moat and get onto the inner rampart. They capture a machine gun and throw it into the moat but German fire forces them to withdraw. Jardine's battalion has taken the Blue Line and has closed up to the outer ramparts, but for the moment can get no further.

BARROWCLOUGH'S 4 RIFLES REACH THE OUTER RAMPARTS

In the centre facing the maze of ramparts on the western side of the fortress, 24-year-old Dunedin law student, Captain and temporary Major Harold Barrowclough's 4 Rifles advances with three companies forward: 22-year-old Hawera medical student Lieutenant Selwyn Kenrick's A Company on the right, 22-year-old Parnell land agent Lieutenant Valentine Maxwell's B Company in the centre and Lieutenant Clarence Rabone's C Company on the left.[41] All three companies follow up the barrage and reach the railway line with little difficulty. Lieutenant Selwyn Kenrick has left us his impressions of the attack. He writes:

> it was an amazing spectacle to see German machine gunners dancing round on top of the high ramparts silhouetted against the flames of the burning drums of oil fired by Livens Projectors onto the ramparts.

After capturing our section of the railway, "A" Company paused momentarily to attend to casualties, send back prisoners and also, I confess, to collect souvenirs. When we later continued the advance under the cover of the smoke barrage and fog, my batman walked beside me carrying a sugar-sack full of German pistols, binoculars, compasses and range finders — our shared loot. The smoke suddenly cleared and we came under heavy machine gun fire. My batman was shot through the hand, dropped the souvenirs, and beat it towards the rear muttering "They won't stop me till I get to Blighty." Together with the rest of my men I ran forward to get cover behind one of the bastion islets, and I did not see my batman again until some years later he greeted me loudly and warmly in a tram in Dunedin.[42]

Barrowclough later writes to the divisional historian:

The attack on the Battalion's objective had been quite successful and comparatively easy. The task of exploiting our success was next proceeded with. Under cover of the excellent smoke barrage patrols worked their way up to the outer ramparts and soon established themselves there so strongly that both the right company (Lieut H.S. Kenrick) and centre company (Lt V.F. Maxwell) were able to advance to the protection of the high tree-covered banks. The left company under Lieut. C.N. Rabone after doing very good work on the railway and in the vicinity of the houses near the level crossing were held up at the sunken road which runs round the North-western part of the fortress. Here they were subjected to such an accurate machine gun and minenwerfer fire that they were practically isolated for the rest of the day.[43]

Captain Henry Thompson(?), D Company, 1 Rifles, 3rd Rifle Brigade, with two of his platoon commanders discussing the 3-inch mortar shell he is holding. The Stokes mortar gun crew is on the right, in the sunken road near Le Tilleul on the Beaudignies–Le Quesnoy road on 4 November 1918. NZ RSA Collection, Photographer: Captain H.A. Sanders, NZEF Official H Series H1309, Ref: 1/2-013799-G, Alexander Turnbull Library, Wellington, New Zealand

51

H1146

Second Lieutenant Valentine Hunter, DCM, commanding A Company in 1 Rifles, 3rd Rifle Brigade, on 4 November 1918, tells Battalion Headquarters that the objective has been taken. Note the sunken road, hedgerows and poplar trees that are characteristic of the close orchard country to the south and east of Le Quesnoy. NZ RSA Collection, Photographer: Captain H.A. Sanders, NZEF Official H Series H1246, Ref: 1/2-013699-G, Alexander Turnbull Library, Wellington, New Zealand

At this point, Barrowclough finds himself at an impasse. As the brigade history records: "Streams of machine gun bullets and even shell-fire from the 77 mm guns posted on the ramparts, were a sufficient indication that the garrison had no intention of quitting the town, and that our attempts to enter it would be strenuously resisted."[44]

1 RIFLES SECURES THE SOUTHERN FLANK

Securing the Blue Line south of the town was the task of 1 Rifles commanded by 37-year-old Lieutenant-Colonel Robert Allen, DSO, a farmer from Piako, one of the redoubtable Allen brothers, both of whom command battalions of the Auckland Regiment on the Western Front.[45] Robert Allen is transferred from 1 Auckland to command 1 Rifles and immediately makes his presence felt.

As the attack diagram on page 39 shows, Allen's battalion leads with A Company on the right and B Company on the left. Second Lieutenant Valentine Hunter, DCM, commands A Company. Hunter's rank belies a great deal of experience. The 27-year-old baker from Takaka joined the Canterbury Mounted Rifles with the 10th Reinforcements. He transferred to 2 Canterbury in Egypt as an infantry private. In France he advanced rapidly through the ranks to warrant officer class one and was awarded the Distinguished Conduct Medal in early June 1917. Commissioned as second lieutenant on 4 May 1918, he is posted to 1 Rifles.[46]

Hunter's junior rank and those of three of the four company commanders in this attack indicates the heavy losses in officers suffered by the brigade in 1918. Captain Ernest Harding commands B Company on the left. Following on were C Company commanded by the recently commissioned Second

Lieutenant L.M. 'Curly' Blyth with Captain Henry Thompson's D Company in reserve.

The riflemen advance in their company formations, two platoons leading with individual soldiers widely dispersed to minimise casualties. They hug the barrage to get as close as possible to the exploding shells in front of them as they go forward knowing that as soon as the barrage lifts they will be under German machine gun and artillery fire. As it is, German machine guns firing on fixed lines send streams of bullets through the mist and smoke of the barrage and German artillery fire bursts behind them. The riflemen speed up to get through this killing ground and walk into their own barrage and this causes casualties.

Securing the railway line involves heavy fighting and each platoon in the leading two companies winkle their way forward by fire and movement with section Lewis guns giving covering fire. Hunter's A Company is held up by machine gun fire. Corporal Michael Mulvaney in B Company, on A Company's immediate left, breaks the stalemate. Mulvaney, a 23-year-old roadman from Mahitahi, is one of the non-commissioned officers who are the bedrock of the division's professionalism. He was awarded a Distinguished Conduct Medal for his bravery in the fighting at Crevecour on 8 October 1918.[47] He again comes to the fore with his Lewis gun section, ordering his No. 1 gunner to keep the German machine gun team's heads down. Mulvaney worms his way round to the flank and single-handedly rushes the post capturing the four-man crew and the machine gun. For this he is awarded the Military Medal.[48]

Similar initiatives occur in Hunter's A Company. Here Sergeant Robert Fergusson, an acting platoon commander, is pinned down with his platoon by machine gun fire from the railway line. He leads a small party to outflank the gun, killing the crew. He then leads his platoon forward onto the railway line capturing two machine guns and a number of prisoners. Fergusson, a 27-year-old farmer from the Halcombe district in the Manawatu, arrived in France as a soldier in 3 Canterbury Regiment, which was part of the now disbanded 4th Brigade. Fergusson was transferred to the 1 Rifles and was promoted to corporal on 12 September 1918 and then to sergeant on 8 October 1918.[49]

The Vickers machine gun section of the Otago Machine Gun Company, commanded by 28-year-old Lieutenant Arthur Reynolds, a surveyor from Te Kuiti, assists in the attack. As Reynolds reaches the railway, he notices that troops on his right are held up by machine gun fire from several German posts in the railway cutting. One of his guns fires on the German guns causing heavy casualties, "putting a swift end to the resistance in that quarter".[50]

Both rifle companies push forward beyond the railway line into the orchards south of Le Quesnoy. Hunter's A Company skirts the southern edge of the orchards and establishes a defensive line on the Ghissignies road. His riflemen deal with a number of machine guns and small parties of Germans, before consolidating a defensive line facing southeast. This covers any attempt to counterattack through the extensive maze of hedgerow-bordered apple orchards that is a feature of the landscape south of Le Quesnoy.

Twenty-one-year-old Lance-Corporal Stephen McDonnell, originally from Hurleyville in Taranaki, was a schoolteacher working in Wellington when conscripted into the 38th Reinforcements. He joined A Company on 14 October 1918 for the last hectic weeks of fighting. He describes the attack in a letter to his sister:

A Lewis gun team in a captured German fighting trench on the railway line before Le Quesnoy, 4 November 1918. The riflemen are from Second Lieutenant Lawrence 'Curly' Blyth's C Company of 1 Rifles. Photographer: Captain H.A. Sanders, NZEF Official H Series H1143, PH-ALB-420-H1142, v1, Auckland War Memorial Museum Tamaki Paenga Hira

We hopped off at 5.30 a.m. & the artillery opened up a terrific barrage; it was a dark morning but the shells bursting lit up the ground in front. It is simply marvellous what machine guns Fritz had on the railway we had to cross.

We made very rapid advance & soon put his machine guns out of action & before long the prisoners were to be seen coming in in great numbers. We advanced 2000 yards in an hour pretty quick eh? But quite long enough to be in it. You see we were in the first wave & consequently the first to pull out & so other battalions went through us & so the scrap went on, the day was particularly fine & divined in our favour. I saw that morning the first tank in action & very formidable things they look indeed.

McDonnell writes of the casualties in his rifle section:

The saddest news I have to tell you is the loss of my chum Stan Woods on Monday 4th Nov; in our big stunt we were very lucky but most of the casualties were inflicted by our own barrage our chaps advancing too quickly. We have reached our objective & were on the point of digging in when some of our shrapnel killed two & wounded two of our party of about nine of us. I was within arms [sic] reach of old Stan, in fact talking to him & when I heard the report of the burst thought he had ducked down but a moment later was sure of the worst. He never made murmur, death was instantaneous.[51] We had such good luck in our raid a few days previous & were intent on sticking together. Jones of New Plymouth was killed in the same fight — it is rather hard he had his brother killed just a month ago when he arrived in France with me. Jack Kelliher came through all right.[52]

Captain Ernest Harding's B Company ferrets out parties of German machine gunners in the hedgerows dividing the orchards. In contrast to the other company commanders, Harding is a veteran. A 25-year-old farmer from Dargaville and active in the Territorial Force before the war, Harding is one of the original officers who enlisted in the Rifle Brigade in 1915. This is indicated by his regimental number of 24/13. Initially a platoon commander in 2 Rifles, Harding was wounded in the trenches at Armentières in 1916 and transferred to 1 Rifles. He was appointed B Company commander during the Somme offensive in September 1916 and was awarded the Military Cross for his leadership in the Battle of Messines.[53] This leadership is again evident at Le Quesnoy on 4 November 1918. Reaching his objective Harding takes up a defensive line with part of the company facing toward the fortress and the remainder linking up with A Company to cover to the southeast in the event of a German counterattack.

C Company, commanded by Second Lieutenant L.M. 'Curly' Blyth, a 24-year-old farmhand, follows up the two leading companies. Its task is to mop up the German positions on the railway line and establish itself there as battalion reserve. As the riflemen of C Company approach the railway line, they come under fire from a German machine gun that has been overlooked by the leading companies. Rifleman Ernest Hallett, a Lewis gunner, instinctively responds by flanking the German gun, firing a long burst, before dashing in with his revolver, capturing the crew and shooting dead the one German who failed to comply. Hallett is awarded the Military Medal.[54] Blyth records:

> My company had taken the railway line and I was doing a little reconnaissance. [Blyth found the level-crossing mined and informed Battalion Headquarters.] While I was there I came under a certain amount of fire from the Germans in the town and I got down in a small trench to take cover. In two seconds time I found on my left hand side was a photographer busy turning on the handle taking snaps of the whole proceedings. I remember asking him how come he should be right up in the front line like this, and he said it was part of his job, and he proceeded on his way to keep turning the handle while we both took a certain amount of cover.[55]

The photographer is Captain Harry Sanders, and although we have this account of Sanders' filming, no film of the event is known to have survived but we have an impressive collection of official photographs, which includes pictures of Blyth's company on the railway line.

The Germans still hold the town itself and continue to fire from the ramparts.

> There was quite a lot of machine gun fire. They had positions well sited to bring in cross-fire.

Deaths 1 Rifles

AYLING, Arthur Bernard 23/58, 2nd Lieutenant
BUCK, Walter Henry 42030 Rifleman
CORMACK, Frederick Robert; 54472 Sergeant
CRAWFORD, Henry 72236 Rifleman
HAYTER, Arthur 54745 Lance-Corporal
HENDERSON, Edward Andrew Buick 45693 Rifleman
JOHNSON, Harry 47895 Corporal
JONES, Edmund Michael 65663 Lance-Corporal
KEILER, Wilbert Watson 63353 Private
KIDD, Robert David 74914 Lance-Corporal
LAUER, Thomas 34385 Corporal
LESTER, William Arthur 72109 Rifleman
McINTYRE, Walter 45610 Temporary-Sergeant
MacLACHLAN, Alexander 23/233 Corporal
MASSON, Roy Roland 67631 Rifleman
MORROW, Francis Richard 31134 Rifleman
O'BRIEN, Francis Trevor Laughlin 62601 Rifleman
POOLE, Samuel Joseph 46243 Lance-Corporal
RICHARDS, Dudley Charles 69727 Rifleman
RIDLAND, Alexander James 72271 Rifleman
SHEPHERD, Patrick John 41028 Rifleman
STREET, D'Arcy 40849 Corporal
TROTTER, Arthur Joe 69321 Rifleman
WARREN, Joseph 35136 Rifleman
WOODS, Lester Stanley 55576 Lance-Corporal
WOODWARD, Alfred John 18736 Rifleman

> They were able to fire down on us from these well-established places …
> My Commanding Officer [Allen, who was wounded in the action] He said
> to me, "If I hadn't got wounded Blyth, I was going to get your company
> to give them a leg over the wall." I said to myself, "Thank God you got
> wounded." It was pretty sticky. The 4th Battalion (who were on our left
> facing the main defences of the town) lost something like 50 men in that
> attack, which was quite a lot.[56]

Blyth found that 37th Division to the south has not kept pace with the New
Zealand advance. At 7.30 a.m., one of Blyth's patrols discover Germans
moving north along the railway line to counterattack. Blyth orders the recently
commissioned 31-year-old Second Lieutenant David Guthrie, an engineer
from Christchurch, to deal with the situation.[57] Guthrie's platoon quickly
corral the German party with Corporal Charles Taylor outflanking them with
his section and forces their surrender.[58]

As Blyth notes: "We stayed on the embankment. We were counter-
attacked from our right flank by about 150 Germans. We were able to deal
with them quite well."[59] The prisoners number more than 100 including five
officers and two machine guns. 'Ratting' the prisoners of valuables was a New
Zealand Digger trademark, Blyth recalls:

> We took all their damned souvenirs off them. It was part of the programme,
> everybody indulged in that. It was no avail to me because I had a whole
> sandbag of souvenirs when I got to England, but I had to go into hospital
> for a throat infection and that was the end of my souvenirs. I never saw
> another damn thing of them again.[60]

Captain Henry Thompson's D Company follows up behind Blyth's company
and passes through it on the railway line moving forward through A
Company's positions in the orchards to seize the battalion's objective on
the Blue Line between the Ghissignies and Louvignies roads. As soon as the
leading platoons reach the open ground beyond the orchards they come
under both machine gun and artillery fire. Thompson establishes that the
Germans occupy a number of houses on the far side of the Louvignies road.
With both the platoon commander and non-commissioned officers wounded,
Rifleman Jason Mason takes charge of the platoon, positions himself to the
flank of the house and opens fire with a Lewis gun. This allows Second
Lieutenant James Brown's platoon to clear the row of buildings along the
Louvignies road by coming in through the back doors. Shrouded in the
morning fog and smoke of the barrage, Brown and his men go from house to
house knocking out each German machine gun post in turn.

Meanwhile, Mason's men discover a German 77-mm field artillery
gun rapidly firing shell after shell toward the New Zealand positions.
Both Germans and New Zealanders see each other at the same time, but
Mason's Lewis gun opens fire first, killing the gun crew. A second artillery
gun is dealt with the same way and by the time Thompson's D Company
has secured the road, the two field guns and 40 unwounded prisoners are
part of the tally.[61]

Lieutenant Reynold's machine gun section is involved in this fighting.
"The section again went into action to bring converging enfilade fire on a
77 mm field gun and several machine guns that were still holding out

inside the orchard. The 1 Rifles with this assistance, quickly mopped up the orchard and secured the guns."[62] The 1 Rifle casualties for the day are reported as 15 killed, five missing, nine officers and 53 other ranks wounded. The list of dead grows to 26 as missing are found to be killed and some wounds prove mortal.[63]

3 RIFLES TIGHTENS THE NOOSE

Hart's brigade secures the Blue Line on schedule by 7.15 a.m. and now proceeds to invest the town. In the south this is the task of 3 Rifles, led by 37-year-old schoolteacher Major George Cockroft.[64] The war diary reports that 3 Rifles moves forward five minutes after the barrage: "dawn was just breaking the troops could be seen advancing in perfect order over the ridge line".[65] B Company has three casualties and C Company loses Second Lieutenant Beattie, all killed as they advance. There are 15 deaths in the battalion from the fighting this day.[66] The battalion is "advancing in splendid order". A Company on the right, D Company on the left followed by Battalion Headquarters, C Company supporting A Company and B Company supporting D Company. The war diary tells the story:

> At 7.29 a.m. the second phase of the attack commenced and the Bn went forward under barrage going [for] the Blue Dotted Line. During this time a heavy mist came down making it difficult to see more than 20 yards ahead. In this mist troops on our right allowed an enemy party of about 70 to come through them on our rear and the party was captured by the Intelligence Officer and a few personnel of Bn H.Q. just as they were seen getting their machine guns into action. This party yielded 4 officers and 70 men prisoners. Our barrage was too slow for our advance and the Blue Dotted Line was captured ahead of time.[67]

In his diary, 26-year-old Corporal Norman Coop, a coach-builder from Dargaville and a section commander in D Company, the left forward company, explains what getting there too soon actually means:

> Well over fences and through some we arrived at our first ejective [sic] safely. We went a little to [sic] far and got caught up in our own barrage and I tell you we had a job to get back through it again. We had a few men wounded getting back and we had to wait for 2hr. till the barrage lifted again.[68]

At 8.47 a.m. Cockroft's 3 Rifles advances to the Green Line as Coop describes:

> again we start on for another 3000 yds, having to go through orchards and bush clearing our way as we went when we got to the other side of the orchard our officer showed us our final ejective [sic] and told us to get there and dig in. So we had to go down a small hill and up the hill the other side. He was on the hill watching us with the O.C. [company commander]. We got down the hill with a few bullets at us, but [they] never got anyone.
>
> As soon as my section and I got at the bottom we noticed that we were well under machine [gun] fire and we also noticed that on both our flanks were held up by fitz.

Badly wounded German soldiers being brought by farm cart from the front line on 2 November 1918 to the Advanced Dressing Station established by Lieutenant-Colonel James Hardie Neil, commanding 3 Field Ambulance, at Pont-a-Pierres, west of Beaudignies. NZ RSA Collection, Photographer: Captain H.A. Sanders, NZEF Official H Series H1139, Ref.1/2-013694-G, Alexander Turnbull Library, Wellington, New Zealand

So the only thing left for us, was to try and find out, were [sic] the fire was coming from. So we crawled along the bottom and run across an open field in single file to a hedge the other side then we crawled up the hill, and we were about 75 yds from the top we noticed old fritz up there firing. So I got my Lewis gun into firing position while the remainder of the section opened up with their rifles. After we fired a few round [sic] old fritz came out with his hands up, So now the boys were able to carry on and we arrived at our final ejective [sic] and dug in now being 10.30.[69]

Coop is awarded the Military Medal for his actions. It is a classic description of fire and movement within a section and indicates once again the tactical skills of the New Zealand infantry. More important to Coop is that "My section came through without a scratch it was good luck than good management I think but san fairy ann."[70] There is now time for the Diggers' favourite pastime. "We stopped there till 1 o'clock and while we were there did a little ratting the dead and wounded fritz'es a[nd] got several things from them."[71]

At 10.20 a.m., 1st Brigade passes through on the fourth phase of the attack to seize the Red Line. Cockroft adjusts his defensive perimeter bringing one company to act as a reserve in the event of a counterattack from Le Quesnoy, which is now completely surrounded.[72] Rifleman Captain James Nimmo is a 21-year-old coal miner from Ngapara, North Otago, with a first name that must be a cause of confusion to military bureaucracy at the time and to historians ever since. He joined 3 Rifles on 27 September 1918 and leaves this account of the morning's work:

This is the scheme of the operations as far as I can see it. We were after an old French fortified town completely surrounded by water and having only two entrances. One mob of NZers went round one side, and another went round the other. In doing so they were to leave a triangle 1500 yards long untouched. This triangle was our real job. Up to where this piece started we were only in support. ... The whole of the 1500 yards proved to be a series of orchards. Fences through which holes had to be chopped were very numerous. We had no trouble until the finish and we struck a machine gun there. Had just about got into position to bomb them out when another mob of our boys came round from the other side of the town to connect up with us. They were right on Jerrie before he saw them and he surrendered immediately. That was our job finished and we moved back and took up a position outside one of the entrances. The position at this stage was that we had surrounded the town, gone miles past it and were still advancing. Jerrie was still in the town. He hadn't time to be anywhere else, as I suppose he was surrounded 2 hours after we started.[73]

The German defenders of the Herman Line are engulfed in an encircling wave. As the History of Reserve Infantry Regiment 83 later details:

The enemy is advancing with strong forces against the division's positions along the railway embankment. Worn down and exhausted by enemy fire, the weak companies are finally no longer able to repulse the enemy's attacks and they have to withdraw. Some of them are being taken prisoner; some of them are managing to withdraw to the Herman III position ...[74]

It seems that the majority of those not taken prisoner retire into the fortress and double or triple its combat strength.

Hart is keen to mop up Le Quesnoy, but he knows that Russell will not accept unnecessary casualties taking a town that is now invested and must eventually surrender. For the moment there is no option but to sit and wait while the war proceeds eastwards toward Forêt de Mormal. Hart summarises what his brigade has achieved in his diary:

The first effort yielded several hundred prisoners as the enemy was holding out in considerable strength. Each Battalion then proceeded steadily & surely to invest the town. It was completely surrounded by 8 a.m. & then our men manoeuvred forward from position to position, behind trees, mounds, outbuildings, anything that would give concealment from which fire could be brought to bear upon the garrison. The ramparts presented a vertical face of brickwork 50 feet high, having grass covered mounds on top, & completely surrounded by a wide deep moat, which fortunately was empty except for a small running stream. The enemy had field guns, minnenwerfer [sic], & dozens of machine guns mounted on in & around the ramparts and these had to be put out of action before the assault could be made.[75]

Deaths 3 Rifles
ALEXANDER, Frederick James 26/45 Corporal
BEATTIE, Percival Moore 38797, 2nd Lieutenant
BETTRIDGE, Walter 68104, Rifleman
DOHERTY, John William 23358 Rifleman
DOUGLAS, Kenneth 47127 Rifleman
HORSMAN, Arthur Frederick 51731 Rifleman
KEATING, Stanley Cecil 72406 Rifleman
MULVANEY, Thomas 72038 Rifleman
PARK, Thomas Joseph 51495 Rifleman
ROSE, Ernest Leslie 15846 Corporal
SHARP, Alfred 71285 Rifleman
SPEEDY, Alfred Lloyd 46398 Rifleman
STEWART, John Archibald 41041 Rifleman
THOMPSON, Joseph Lyons 44803 Lance-Corporal
TWIDLE, Vincent Stephenson 42231 Sergeant

Meanwhile the battle moves on.

Chapter 3

BEYOND LE QUESNOY

Brigadier-General Melvill's 1st Brigade is tasked to move through Hart's 3rd Rifle Brigade once the Blue Dotted Line is secured. 1 Auckland of Melvill's brigade is to pass through 2 Rifles, 3rd Rifle Brigade, and secure the Blue Dotted Line by moving north of Le Quesnoy. 1st Brigade is to then secure the Green Line with its two Wellington battalions: 2 Wellington on the right flank and 1 Wellington on the left. They both are to pass to the north of Le Quesnoy, through 1 Auckland and secure their sector of the Green Line. They will then take over that part of the Green Line held by 3 Rifles, 3rd Rifle Brigade, before advancing and securing the Red Line. This is the road on the western edge of Forêt de Mormal. Enemy resistance will then determine if Melvill's battalions are to able exploit into the forest as far as the Red Dotted Line.[1]

Supporting the brigade are mobile sections of field artillery to provide immediate fire support to knock out strongpoints or in the event of any German counterattack. There is machine gun support from the New Zealand Machine Gun Battalion, with a section of four guns from the Wellington Machine Gun Company attached to each battalion in the brigade. Two Stokes mortar teams from No. 1 Light Trench Mortar Battery, with additional infantry personnel from the battalions to carry ammunition, are also attached to each battalion.

The evening before, Brigadier-General Mevill goes forward with Brigade Major William Jennings and 30-year-old Gallipoli veteran Captain F. Stuart Varnham to Ruesnes where the brigade battle headquarters is established. Twenty-six-year-old Jennings is a regular officer of the New Zealand Staff Corps. A Royal Military College Duntroon graduate, he was one of the ten initial New Zealand entrants in 1911 and graduated as a lieutenant on 14 August 1914, first in his class. He was transferred to Otago Battalion, NZEF, on 14 September 1914. He was promoted captain in April 1916, and then to major in August 1916 as divisional machine gun officer. He is a general staff officer grade 2 (GSO2) in divisional headquarters in 1917 before being posted to brigade major, 1st Brigade. A superb staff officer, he is mentioned in

A smiling Major Hugh McKinnon inspecting the 2 Wellington field cookers close to the front line at Colincamps on 15 April 1918. A hard man who takes no nonsense, McKinnon commands 2 Wellington in the attack on 4 November 1918 and is killed by artillery fire that evening as he is moving forward to visit the leading companies of his battalion. NZ RSA Collection, Photographer: Captain H.A. Sanders, NZEF Official H Series H501, Ref: 1/2-013209-G. Alexander Turnbull Library, Wellington, New Zealand

despatches twice for his staff work and will receive the Distinguished Service Order for his work at Headquarters 1st Brigade in 1918.[2]

Captain Varnham, MC, a stock agent from Palmerston North, notes, they

passed all the Batt[alio]ns on the move up to the Assembly point for the attack at dawn the next morning. Very muddy, pitch dark & raining. A most uncomfortable ride up. Roads seething with men, horses, guns and waggons. Slept in my clothes in the cellar of a house. Went to Division Hdqrs & syncronised [sic] watches.[3]

1 AUCKLAND SEIZES THE BLUE DOTTED LINE

The war diary describes the move forward of 1 Auckland to seize the Blue Dotted Line. "Zero Hour was at 5.30am and the Battalion had orders to move at Zero plus fifteen minutes."[4] It is a fine morning with mist. Under the cover of "a splendid barrage the troops moved forward by platoons with 25 yards distance" in the following order: 6th Hauraki, 15th North Auckland, Battalion Headquarters, 3rd Auckland and 16th Waikato Companies.[5]

The battalion is commanded by 44-year-old Lieutenant-Colonel Walter Alderman, a regular officer of the Australian Commonwealth Force, who was on exchange with the New Zealand Military Forces on the outbreak of war. Alderman commanded 16th Waikato Company on 25 April 1915 and at various times commanded both Auckland battalions. He now commands 1 Auckland in its last battle. There is a wealth of battle experience in the men commanding the companies. Twenty-five-year-old acting-Major George 'Ditt' Dittmer, MC, commands 6th Hauraki. A masseur at the Rotorua Bath House, Dittmer enlisted in the Auckland Battalion as a private in August 1914. As the Auckland papers report, he "and Major George Holland, M.C. (killed in action) and Lieutenant Bob Tilsey, M.C … were the first three Rotorua boys to enlist. They sailed away with the Main Body as full privates, and all made thoroughly good."[6] Dittmer was commissioned as a second lieutenant on Gallipoli at the end of May 1915 and saw every major action on the Western Front. He was awarded the Military Cross for his leadership on the Somme in 1916.[7] "Anyone who has served in the Sixth Haurakis will know him for a fine hard-fighting soldier who never dodged strenuous work."[8] He will again make his mark in his raising of the 28 (Maori) Battalion in the Second World War and commands it in Greece, Crete and in the Crusader Operations of November 1941.[9]

Captain James McCarthy, formerly a clerk with New Zealand Railways, arrived in France with the 23rd Reinforcements and as acting major commands the 15th North Auckland Company. He is mortally wounded and dies this day, aged 29. The 3rd Auckland Company is commanded by 28-year-old Captain William Lang, MC, a farmer from Waipu. Originally a second lieutenant in the Auckland Mounted Rifles, he transferred to 1

Second Lieutenant James Henry Greenwood, MC, MM, MID, 1 Auckland. Greenwood was mentioned in Despatches for his bravery as a medical corps stretcher-bearer during the Gallipoli Campaign; was awarded the Military Medal for his action in evacuating patients under fire as a sergeant in the Medical Corps on the Somme in 1916, and receives a Military Cross for his actions at Le Quesnoy on 4 November 1918.
Archives New Zealand

Auckland. He was awarded the Military Cross in 1917 "for taking command of his company when he was the only surviving officer and captured his objectives with great skill and courage".[11] Captain Alexander Forbes, a 23-year-old Birkenhead bookbinder, commands the 16th Waikato Company. He was originally posted to 2 Auckland as a second lieutenant in early 1916 and was later posted to 1 Auckland. He was wounded in February 1917 and was awarded the Military Cross for his initiative that lead to the capture of ten German artillery guns in the advance to the Escaut Canal on 29 September 1918.[12]

Deaths 1 Auckland[10]
CORNISH, Wilfred Arthur 67960 Private
EDMONDS, James Frederick 12/3628 Corporal
FOLLETT, Hilary Leonard Charles 71617 Private
GRANDY, Richard 14421 Private
HEFFRON, William Thomas 70281 Private
KENNEDY, Robert Tannahill 71811 Private
McCARTHY, James Charles 33097 Captain (A Major)
MASON, Tom Allison John 76061 Private
MURPHY, Francis John 74112 Private
PURDY, Alfred William 50608 Private
THOMPSON, John Henry 12/2133 Lance-Corporal

The battalion crosses the Ruesnes–Le Quesnoy road as a German reconnaissance aircraft flies overhead. Almost immediately, German artillery open up and shell the route. This results in most of the casualties in the battalion on this day. It is here that Private John Bartle, a 32-year-old farmer from Devonport "did continuous and gallant work as a Company stretcher-bearer, under very heavy artillery and machine gun fire". Bartle remains behind and attends to the wounded while the shells rain down and after giving first aid, rounds up other men to assist him in carrying them back. "His conduct throughout was magnificent."[13]

The two lead companies, 6th Hauraki and the 15th North Auckland reach the Le Quesnoy–Orsinval road at 6.18 a.m. and move off again under cover of the barrage at 7.51. They meet pockets of fierce resistance in the village of Ramponeau. Lance-Corporal Clarence Black's platoon is pinned down. Black, with his platoon commander, Second Lieutenant James Greenwood, MM, MID, and another soldier take the initiative and despite heavy machine gun fire dash across 100 metres of open ground, firing and rushing while another provides covering fire, until they get in among the German gun teams. These immediately surrender and the guns are captured.[14]

Greenwood is an interesting character. He is mentioned in despatches during the Gallipoli Campaign for his work as a stretcher-bearer, and was awarded the Military Medal as a sergeant in the New Zealand Medical Corps for his bravery, clearing casualties at Armentières in 1916. However, he was court-martialled for drunkenness and as punishment was reduced to the rank of corporal. He transferred to infantry reverting in rank to private soldier and worked his way back up to sergeant. In the process of all of this, he was wounded three times.[15] Greenwood receives the Military Cross for his actions in Ramponeau and Black is awarded the Military Medal.[16]

The battalion war diary reports: "Ramponeau was in our hands at 08.36 and at 08.56 both the 1st and 2nd Wellington Battalions passed through [on their way to the Green Line] after which this Battalion wheeled to the right and reached its final objective at 10.10."[17]

The Aucklanders connect up with both 2 Rifles and 3 Rifles, 3rd Rifle Brigade, and tighten the noose. Le Quesnoy is now surrounded. The final dispositions see 2 Auckland headquarters establish in Ramponeau, 16th Company covering an arc to the northwest including the road running to Orsinval, 3rd Company covering the roads out of Ramponeau to the northeast, 15th Company covering the railway station and its approaches, and 6th Company linking with 3rd Battalion NZRB to cover an arc from the

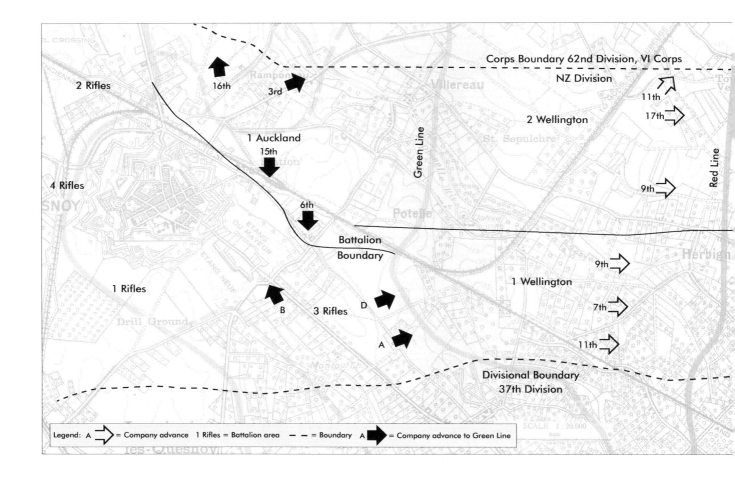

The advance of 1st Brigade to the Red Line.

crossroad on the north–south Villereau road running immediately east of Le Quesnoy linking to the railway junction east of the railway station.[18]

They take some 350 prisoners, 25 heavy and 29 light machine guns, six anti-tank rifles and one *minenwerfer*.[19] Officer casualties in 1 Auckland consist of Captain J.C. McCarthy[20] fatally wounded, Second Lieutenant J.J.C. Herzog, wounded, and nine other ranks killed and 37 wounded, one of whom will later die of wounds.[21]

1 WELLINGTON ADVANCES ON THE RIGHT

Anglican padre Clive Mortimer-Jones moves forward with Battalion Headquarters, 1 Wellington, and leaves this account of the securing of the Green Line and of the advance to the Red Line:

> On Monday at 5.30 a.m. we got up and had some breakfast; we paraded at 6 a.m. and then left for the "assembly point" a couple of miles away. But our wonderful barrage had commenced at 5.30 a.m. and by this time the 'Bosche' was putting a lot of stuff back. Our Headquarters cook, who was only a few yards from me was first to get hit. I picked him up and got the "Doc". He was only slightly hurt in the leg. We went through a wood and a swamp in extended order. It was just beginning to get light and it's a little less unpleasant when one can see where the shells are falling.
>
> Unfortunately the sunken road which was our "jumping off point" was evidently the Hun barrage line and the shelling there was intense. It was marvellous that our casualties were so light. The intelligence officer was hit [2nd Lieutenant P.G.H. Bennett]; our temporary aid-post (a newly made

Originally titled 'New Zealand soldiers in the front line', these are British soldiers of the 4th Company, 13th Battalion Royal Fusiliers of 112th Brigade, 37th Division, that are in support ready to advance through 111th Brigade to the Red Line. The man sitting down looking to the left and leaning on his elbow is Sergeant Harold Lee Spark. The man standing nearest to camera is Private Willoughby, 'a good boy who always stuck close to me. He always wore a steel waist-coat and we use to tease him about it.' [Source: Alan Holdaway] It seems the 13th Royal Fusiliers were on the continuation of the sunken road running southeast from Le Tilleul in the general direction of Ghissignies. The photo seems to have been taken by Captain H.A. Sanders, the New Zealand official photographer, on the morning of 4 November 1918. The glass plate negative has not survived, but the photo is part of the Album Collection of New Zealand official photographs, H1067–H1217. NZ RSA Collection, Photographer: Captain H.A. Sanders, NZEF Official H Series, Ref. PA1-f-103-1122, Alexander Turnbull Library, Wellington, New Zealand

shell hole which we quickly enlarged) was kept busy. We had to get the cases away as quickly as possible as the whole of that paddock was being heavily shelled.

Once I was sent head over heels and more than once got covered in mud. The ground was fortunately soft and the splinters were, therefore, not flying so far, otherwise our casualties would have been trebled. One of the most wonderful things and new to me was the smoke screen. We could by this time (8 a.m.) only see a few yards. The object of this was to hide us from the enemy garrison in Le Quesnoy only a mile away. Our plan was to go northward of the fortress and so surround the place. Before we left this spot we lost our adjutant [Lieutenant A.R. Blennerhassett]. He was about 20 yards from me at the time talking to the Colonel with a map when a shell landed at their feet. The C.O. [Lieutenant-Colonel Frank Turnbull, MC[22]] had a marvellous escape, being blown five or six yards but being unhurt. The adjutant was badly hit in the head and never regained consciousness. I helped to carry him the few yards to the R.A.P. [Regimental Aid Post], but he died after a quarter of an hour. The loss of the adjutant and the I.O. was a serious handicap so early in the attack.[23]

The Stokes mortar teams of No. 1 Light Trench Mortar Battery move up behind the leading companies of infantry, and are caught up in this barrage. Its chronicler 'Billy Popgun' is unknown, but this is his story.

We had orders to get away, later, with our company, and after a wait, off we lunged. The daylight came prettily; it developed into a light mist, of a slatey, smokey aspect; and the small woodland we were soon passing through would have delighted the eye of an artist. Then we passed down through long fields of cabbages of the blue, pickling variety which Fritz had planted for sauerkraut ... Then we reached a small passage-way, where we had a deal of delay and where his shells did not miss us by much. I could see for miles, the perfect artillery formation of the diggers coming up to go through the first waves [of 3 Brigade] when they shortly settled down.

Down we went, through a small brushland and creek, where everyone was wetted to the knees trying to jump the obstruction, and hereabouts we lost our sergeant — Jim Bain of Waikato — who was wounded, but is safe, I understand. Good old Jim. A true sport, and with the battery since December, 1916. Then we crossed the railway, and saw what a mess Fritz's answering barrage had here made. We had to diverge from the direct line of advance into the next big paddock, and make a wide detour to avoid a crest of which he was making a howling mess [with his artillery fire]. We had just crossed a sunken road when he landed a shell on a spot about thirty yards in front of us. Thinking to get past we went for our lives; but another shell came, exactly over the mark where the previous one landed and where we apparently had just reached. It killed Ewing Riddell[24] [sic] of the team, from Te Kuiti (a fine man and a great pal), and Ken Larking,[25] late of Victoria College, Wellington, and one of the [ammunition] carriers loaned by the [infantry] company. Ted Murray (corporal) our team's excellent five-eight was badly wounded in the leg; and I got mine in the groin. Finish Stoke's gun team!

After Jerry's barrage was over — a good one for about a further three quarters of an hour — they used all the Hun prisoners (four to a stretcher) to carry out our wounded. A great plan, this, Ehoa, as they took the boys out in great style … I believe another gun team covering Wellington was smashed up; Les. Mason,[26] of Masterton (a Ruahine Boy) was killed — He makes another fine threequarter gone from the rugby team — and a good soldier.[27]

1 and 2 Wellingtons pass through 1 Auckland at 8.56 a.m. 1 Wellington pushes forward though the hedgerows and apple orchards with 7th Wellington West Coast Company leading on the right, 9th Hawke's Bay Company on the left. When Lieutenant-Colonel Turnbull's battalion reaches the Green Line he moves 11th Taranaki Company further right to take over the frontage captured by 3 Rifles.

Lieutenant Arthur Reynold's machine gunners of the Otago Machine Gun Company support 3 Rifles of 3rd Rifle Brigade as they move forward to secure the Green Line. There are no tanks supporting the New Zealand attack, but one of the few tanks supporting the 37th Division loses its way and comes trundling in on the flank of the advancing New Zealanders.

On the Drill Ground beyond the orchard, one of our own male tanks, apparently mistaking the [machine gun] section for Germans in the smoke, opened on them with a 6-pounder Hotchkiss gun at a range of 50 yards. Although the section dropped its loads and "Kamaraded" in the approved German style, the tank did not cease fire until one of the machine gunners rushed the tanks and shouted unprintable remarks at the crew through a loophole. Fortunately, in spite of the point blank range, the tank failed to secure a single hit. The remainder of the section's advance to the Green Line was uneventful.[28]

At 10.20 a.m. both Wellington battalions begin their advance from the Green Line to the Red Line on the western edge of the forest. Supporting 1 Wellington is a section of 18-pounders of No. 13 Battery, New Zealand Field

Two officers of 1 Canterbury of 2nd Brigade inspect German 4.2-inch howitzers that were captured near Le Quesnoy in late October 1918. Losing guns like this in a withdrawal made the next battle more difficult for the German Army. This was the result of the speed of the advance and the toll it took on artillery horses. By 4 November there were four horses available for every three German guns. This resulted in some 100 German guns being captured on 4 November by the New Zealand Division in the area east of Le Quesnoy. NZ RSA Collection, Photographer: Captain H.A. Sanders, NZEF Official H Series H1119, Ref. 1/2-013676-G, Alexander Turnbull Library, Wellington, New Zealand

Artillery, commanded by 25-year-old Second Lieutenant James Baxter, MM, MID. The guns are limbered up and follow-up the advancing infantry ready to spring into action as needed. Baxter's war experience is typical of the many junior officers throughout the division. He was law clerk in Hamilton when he enlisted in 1915 and is mentioned in despatches for his work as a gunner in No. 1 Battery in 1916–17, not something that generally happens to a gunner private in the First World War. He was awarded the Military Medal for his work as a bombardier with No. 1 Battery, keeping the telephone lines working to brigade headquarters under two days of intense bombardment during the Battle of Messines. He attended an Officer Training Course (OTC) in England and was commissioned as a second lieutenant and returned to the front in March 1918. He was badly wounded in the jaw in April 1918 and returned to No. 13 Battery in July 1918. Now, after over three years' intense service, he leads his section of guns into action. He is active again in the Territorial Force after the war but takes his own life in 1931.[29]

A machine gun section of the Wellington Company of the New Zealand Machine Gun Battalion also supports 1 Wellington's advance. It is commanded by Second Lieutenant Frederick Mintrom, MM, a 26-year-old railway clerk from Waimangaroa, Westport. He was awarded the Military Medal for taking command of his machine gun section as a sergeant on 4 and 5 October 1917 at the Battle of Gravenstafel. He receives the Military Cross for his actions in command of his guns this day.[30]

Two guns of the New Zealand Light Trench Mortar Battery are also attached, but the concentration of orchards and hedgerows limit their effectiveness. A section of the 3rd Hussars report, but then ride off and work independently, feeding information back to Melvill's brigade headquarters. The role of these mounted horsemen becomes increasingly important as they move into Forêt de Mormal.

During the attack to the Green Line the artillery barrage is heavy and effective, but decreases in intensity as the New Zealand batteries cease fire and move forward. The barrage is fired by the four British artillery brigades but instead of the two separate barrages to coincide with the flanking divisions north and south of Le Quesnoy, it now becomes a single barrage moving at the rate of 100 yards every three minutes. The infantry move behind the barrage to scattered opposition from generally surprised parties of German soldiers. "The enemy was in considerable strength on our front and fought well at some places, but in many instances seemed only too pleased to surrender."[31]

Private Leslie Marfell is one of the 37th Reinforcements. He arrived in France in October 1918, one month before the Armistice.

> I was only in one stunt, Le Quesnoy ... we had very little opposition ... Fairly level country, orchards, and there were quite a few German gun pits in this orchard, but they were just absolutely caught completely unawares, having their breakfast, and they just surrendered to us. The only casualty our company had was the Company Sergeant Major [who] got a bullet in his tummy from a sniper, but he survived.[32]

The German divisional artillery are massed together in the orchards south of Le Carnoy. This is a question of necessity because the strain of the constant pulling back day after day kills the over-taxed horses, which cannot be replaced. German batteries are now reduced to one four-horse team for every three guns, instead of the standard six-horse team per gun. The speed of the New Zealand outflanking attacks places further pressure on the German gun lines. There is no obvious infantry protection on what is supposed to be the German second defensive line. Padre Mortimer-Jones captures the scene:

> At 10 a.m. we had taken our first objective (the green line marked on the map) and now the sun was shining and the worst was over. We had got right behind the enemy guns, the Huns were hiding in the villages ready to shout "kammerad" [sic] and by the afternoon though without food, everyone was enjoying the day's sport. There was plenty of sniping, prisoners were coming back in crowds, and souvenirs were plentiful.[33]

It is interesting to see that the padre is as relaxed as the Diggers in accepting and indulging in the universal relieving of prisoners' valuables for 'souvenirs'. The 1 Wellingtons sweep through the area where the German artillery is concentrated taking in turn the villages of Potelle and Herbignies. It is a day when the sergeants of the battalion, many of them acting platoon commanders, come into their own, mopping up the last pockets of German troops in the cellars and taking out machine gun posts and are rewarded accordingly in the generous lists of honours and awards that results from this battle.[34] Casualties are few, the Germans mostly being taken by surprise. Turnbull's Battalion Headquarters move forward on horseback in bounds to keep up with the speed of the advancing companies, establishing themselves in turn at Ramponeau, then Château de Potelle and finally in a farmhouse among the orchards south of Herbignies at 12.45 p.m.

The Red Line is successfully captured by 11.56 a.m. Companies re-organise and under the protection of patrols, the road on the western edge of Forêt de Mormal is secured, touch being established on the right with 1 Essex Battalion of 112th Brigade and 2 Wellington on the left.

At 2.15 p.m. patrols push on into the forest and encounter little opposition. Private Leslie Loveday, in 2 Wellington, patrols forward on his

The heroes return to Hawera. A frame enlargement of a film showing the welcome home to Lieutenant John Grant, VC (far right). Lieutenant Harry Laurent, VC, also of Hawera, is seen shaking hands with the mayor, while Sergeant Leslie Loveday, a local farmer and a crack shot who received the Military Medal for his patrolling forward on 4 November 1918, smiles at Laurent. Loveday won the King's Prize at the British Army's shooting competition at Bisley in 1919 — the first New Zealander to do so. *Civic Reception to Lieut. J Grant, V.C., 1919*, Cameraman: Unknown, Producer: A.M. Conroy, Opera House, Hawera, Ref. 500, 200, Archives New Zealand

own, skirting pockets of Germans withdrawing through the forest. Coming across a party of seven Germans in a clearing, he shoots three and takes four back as prisoners, including an officer. Loveday, a 28-year-old farmer from Hawera, is from a family of noted rifle shots. He competed at Bisley in 1911 and won the New Zealand Dominion Rifle Championship the following year. He spent the war training soldiers in musketry first in New Zealand and then at Sling Camp in England, rising in rank to sergeant. In 1918 he voluntarily reverted in rank to private, in order to get to the front. This is his first action, for which he is awarded the Military Medal. Loveday wins the King's Prize at the British Army's shooting competition at Bisley in 1919 — the first New Zealander to do so.[35]

The German defenders are caught off balance. A cavalry patrol comes riding unawares through the forest and runs into 1 Wellington dug in, covering the road. Leslie Marfell is on watch at the time.

> The Battalion had practically no opposition, so we dug in funk holes with a couple of us in each one with the machine gun in the best one covering the crossroads … This intersection was on the edge of the Mormal Forest and we were on duty there, coming dusk, and a jolly patrol of German cavalrymen, about half a dozen of them riding down the road in the forest towards us. So of course our Number 1 [on the Lewis Gun] opened fire on them. They got a terrific surprise and none of them were fatally wounded … and, of course, they surrendered straight away. They had no idea that the Allied troops were there.[36]

At 8.30 p.m. Hawke's Bay Company pushes through the forest to the Red Dotted Line while the Taranaki Company forms a protective flank on the right. One isolated German post is discovered and quickly captured. The Red Dotted Line is secured by 11.30 p.m. Meanwhile, the battalion's transport moves forward from Beaudignies to Ramponeau.[37] Padre Mortimer-Jones' account concludes the story of 1 Wellington on 4 November.

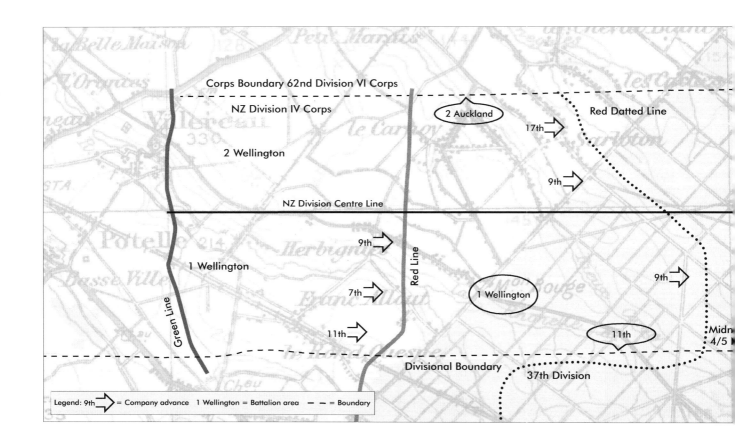

1st Brigade exploit to the Red Dotted Line. France: Sheet 12, Valenciennes, May 1915, Geographical Section, General Staff, War Office, 1:100,000

By six p.m. the front line was four or five miles ahead, if known at all. A curious feature of the battle was that the fortress of Le Quesnoy though surrounded was still holding out. We had gone 'through' the Rifle Brigade which was still behind this obstinate stronghold with its ancient double octagonal high walls … Yet up to mid-day I saw shells in front which were evidently fired from a gun inside Le Quesnoy, and in the afternoon it was still dangerous to get within range of the citadel from which the enemy was continually sniping — bullets seemed to whizz overhead from the most unexpected quarters. At one time I found myself in front of one of our outposts which faced the town, although the front line at the time was over a mile in the other direction.

It was amusing to see how all the guns, small and large, and machine guns were pointing in the opposite direction to the way we advanced — the Hun evidently expected the main attack from the south. Our captured were worthy of our success. This battalion accounted for 36 large and small guns, very many machine guns and nearly 1000 prisoners. The 4th Corps captured 6500 prisoners, of which 2500 were taken by the New Zealanders. That night we slept soundly at villages and in the forest four miles beyond the captured fortress and were relieved next day.[38]

The official losses to 1 Wellington on 4 November are an officer and seven men killed, and two officers and 20 men wounded. With those who later died of wounds, there are 12 deaths in 1 Wellington from this action.[39]

2 WELLINGTON

2 Wellington advance on the northern flank, on 1 Wellington's left. Private Monty Ingram is a runner attached to Commanding Officer Major Hugh

McKinnon's Battalion Headquarters. His published diary vividly captures 2 Wellington's day of battle.

> Suddenly the air is rent with the deafening thunder of artillery drumfire. The hour has struck! Popping of Vickers! Barking of field guns! Booming of heavies! Flashes in the greying dawn! Black smoke, red smoke, white smoke! Leaping earth, flying clods, and ripping steel! A tension of muscles and the first wave is off.

> For about 10 minutes we wait. Luckily we are on the extreme edge of the enemy barrage. Incendiary shells burst on high on the semi-light and burning matter, like blazing oil, rains down to earth, where it flames fiercely for a while before burning out.

> At last it is time for the second wave to move off. Away they go, and the C.O. [Major McKinnon] blowing his whistle, we scouts fall in behind as he strides off into the barrage. We do not proceed far before we observe prisoners running towards us with shambling gait through the crashing shells, their arms held high, faces deathly white, eyeballs protruding, and their whole bodies trembling with terror. They make an abject sight, running from one party of us to another, not understanding our commands to carry straight on rearwards, and completely bewildered. The appearance of the prisoners so soon is a good sign that the first wave is making satisfactory progress ahead of us.

> Reaching the railway line we get into a pretty hot corner, the Huns are shelling this area pretty severely and it is a relief when we traverse a potato field (a hot spot), and cross the railway line without a scratch.

> At about 9 o'clock we pass through the 1st Auckland Battalion and are launched on our own attack. The Huns are now mostly going for their lives rearwards, but here and there we encounter parties who put up stubborn resistance and their positions have to be rushed.[41]

The battalion's initial move forward is through the woods bordering the steep banks of Rhonelle River and there is little opposition. A small signals wiring party under Lance-Corporal John Griffiths, a 24-year-old driver from Auckland, comes across three 77-mm guns firing. They promptly drop their wire and charge the guns, capturing two of the gun crew, while the rest flee. The signallers then return to running out their telephone cable. Griffiths receives the Distinguished Conduct Medal for this action.[42]

The war diary notes that the speed of advance leaves pockets of Germans behind. This happens in the village of Villereau and it is Battalion Headquarters who has to clear out the cellars, "capturing 24 prisoners including two Officers".[43] Private Ingram is very much part of this action.

Deaths 1 Wellington[40]
ILLESDON, John William 72614 Private
BLENNERHASSETT, Arthur Reginald 23070 Captain
BROOKING, Arnold Whiddon 15677 Private
ELCOCK, Sidney J. 11852 Lance-Sergeant
FERRIS, Robert Alexander 46984 Private
HALL, Francis 68330 Private
HOWELL, Noah Albert 74051 Private
LARKING, Frank Campbell 48341 Private, I LTM Bty
MASON, Leslie Merton 10/4138 Private
RIDDLE, Ewing Stevens 32067 Private
THOMSON, Colin 44535 Corporal
WILLIAMSON, Matthew 14898 Corporal

DEATH OF A GISBORNE SOLDIER

The last mail brought a copy of the Shetland Times of January 11, which gives the following particulars of the death of Private Matthew Williamson, of the First Wellington Infantry, who prior to enlistment with the 14th Reinforcements, was resident at Tamarau, Gisborne. The paper states :—

"Dear Mr. Williamson.—Quartermaster-Sergeant of my company has just handed on your letter to me to answer, re Matthew's death. Poor old Mat. was killed on the morning of the 4th November, whilst walking along beside me at a place called Jolmitz, near Le Quesnoy. He was sniped through the right side. The poor chap only lived a minute, and died in the Sergt.-Major's and my arms. In consoling with you in your great loss, I would like to say that Mat. was easily the most popular and best-liked man in the company, and his loss was a grievous one to us all. As for myself, personally, Mat. was one of my strong men, and I had him on my personal Company Headquarters Staff, and that is how he came to be with me when he was hit. The things I have known him do for the boys would astound you; you know, of course, he won the Military Medal. The day he was killed our battalion did some good work, and my company did wonderfully well, but Mat.'s death robbed it of all the pleasures, and that night when all was over, we were a very silent crowd. Please convey to his relatives my sincerest sympathy, and that of his comrades.—Yours sincerely, E. WHITE, Capt. P.S. I forgot to say that Mat. was buried in the cemetery at Le Quesnoy, on 5th November. and a cross erected over his grave. All the boys attended the funeral."

Matthew Williamson was a son of Mr. and Mrs. Peter Williamson, who along with their family left Ollaberry for New Zealand some years before the war broke out. Matthew was home in Shetland on leave last New Year season, and visited his friends at Ollaberry and Lerwick. One of his brothers died on active service about a year ago, and his two other brothers are with the colors. Matthew was a nephew of Mr. Christopher Williamson, Alder Lodge, Lerwick.

'Killed near Le Quesnoy,' *Poverty Bay Herald*, 22 March 1919, p. 5

Dodging from tree to tree while advancing along the banks of the Rhonelle calls to my mind Fennimore [sic] Cooper's tales of fighting the Redskins, which I used to read in my young days. We are soon out of the woods and into a village, where bullets seem to arrive from all points of the compass. A party of us entering a house find a Frencie [sic] and his wife, wildly excited pointing to the cellar steps and crying, "Allemand. Allemand". A yell from one of us directed down the steps quickly brings forth the contents — eight terrified Jerries. These are put in a barn, under guard, and the party of eight are soon to be swelled to considerable numbers.[44]

McKinnon and his intelligence officer moves forward and sets up his headquarters in Villereau. Always keen to be in front, he then moves forward as Ingram describes.

After a short wait, the C.O. decides to push on to get in closer contact with the Companies, and off we stride, encountering in the road, the unusual sight of three enemy field guns, limbered up and driving back, the Hun drivers astride their horses and one of our boys sitting on the limber seat with a Hun Medical Officer beside him. These guns had been limbered up ready to gallop off rearwards but on driving out from their position to the road they ran into a party of diggers and it was a case of right-about-turn. Our advance was just a little too swift for them. Shortly after this we come upon a wounded Hun Major and several of his men on their way rearwards in charge of a digger. As soon as the Hun officer spotted the C.O. he sat down and refused to get up, while in a guttural voice he repeated "Ambulance. Ambulance." The C.O., Major McKinnon, has the reputation of being a 'hard' man, and he lived up to it on this occasion by booting the Hun in the stern and ordering him to get up and walk, as some of his men more badly hurt than he, had to walk. The look of wounded pride and disgust that spread over that Hun officer's face was a picture to see.[45]

McKinnon's headquarters moves to St Sepulchre and on hearing confirmation that the Red Line is taken, moves forward again to Ferme de Lion.[46] Ingram is

sent forward to locate the position of Taranaki Company. The advance has been so swift that it is almost impossible to keep track of the positions of the various Companies from time to time. At the present moment the C.O. has little idea as to their actual whereabouts. After some time spent in searching and suffering some sniping from a Jerry machine gun hidden among the thick hedges, I find Taranaki dug in, here and there, among the maze of thick hedges. The advance has now come to a standstill and the Huns are directing an obstinate machine gun fire from hidden positions. It is most difficult to locate them. As our advance has encompassed all the objectives laid down, and even progressed further than anticipated, the C.O. is satisfied to leave it at that for the present …[47]

McKinnon is ordered to push on into the forest to the Red Dotted Line. Ingram takes up the story.

In the evening we received orders to push on through the village of Le Carnoy up to a certain road. We advanced under a light barrage, during

A number of German prisoners captured at Le Quesnoy, awaiting examination at Divisional Headquarters in Pont à Pierres on 4 November 1918. NZ RSA Collection, Photographer: Captain H.A. Sanders, NZEF Official H Series H1117, Ref: 1/2-013674-G, Alexander Turnbull Library, Wellington, New Zealand

the early hours of darkness, and reached our objective, meeting with practically no resistance, the Huns having retired shortly before. We scouts went forward with our Companies and after we had searched the houses of the village two scouts were sent back to bring up the C.O. and Adjutant. It was a bit of luck for me that I was not sent back on this mission, for when the party was coming up a shell landed in its midst and killed the C.O. and Adjutant outright and fatally wounded the scouts. It was tough luck for the C.O., a Main Body man who had served on Gallipoli and had almost continuous service with the Regiment in France.[48]

Captain D.S. Columb takes over command and the leading companies, 9th Wellington West Coast on the right and 17th Ruahine on the left push on through the forest and secure the Red Dotted Line on the Sarloton road. "In yesterday's advance our Battalion took over four hundred prisoners and much booty, including 33 field guns and many machine guns …"[49]

There are four officers and 58 casualties in 2 Wellington including 15 killed in action or who later die of wounds.[51] Ingram sums up the day:

This was a great day and no mistake. Something like a War. Passing through the several captured villages during the advance, the wildly excited villagers, who had been sheltering in their cellars, poured out of their houses and fell upon our necks, kissing us, weeping, laughing, and madly wringing our hands. We were loaded with apples and wine in abundance was pressed upon us, needless to state we needed very little pressing …[52]

Deaths 2 Wellington[50]

BANKS, Henry Dunbar 33098 Lieutenant
CLOSE, Frank 69466 Private
CROTHERS, Frederick Cleveland 26998 Corporal
FLOOD, John William 5/244a 2nd Lieutenant
GIBSON, Llewelyn Guthrie 38010 Private
HARTLAND, Jack Wenham 64204 Private (Signaller)
HUNTER, John Joseph 49153 Private
HURST, Christopher John 22803 Sergeant
JENSEN, Ernest 39823 Private
Mc KINNON, Hugh Edgar 10/135 Major
MURRELL, Sydney Allan 1/557 Captain
NEILSEN, Alfred 39551 Private
QUILLIAM, Cecil Wilfrid 60294 2nd Lieutenant
RIGBY, Edward 38218 Private
WHITE, Leo Orton 64185 Private

THE GUNS MOVE FORWARD

The New Zealand Division has seven brigades of artillery providing fire support for the attack. These are the three New Zealand Field Artillery Brigades (1st, 2nd and 3rd); 210th and 211th Brigades of Royal Field Artillery from 42nd Division and the 72nd Brigade, Royal Field Artillery and the 14th Brigade, Royal Horse Artillery. Lieutenant J.D. Hutchinson of No. 5 Battery writes in his diary: "Barrage 5.30 to 6.30, then 7.51 to 10.50. Advance went well. Hun put good heavy strafe back, but we had no casualties."[53] The artillery history records that the German artillery fire was

> comparatively feeble but a good deal of hostile fire fell on battery areas. The 9th Battery had two guns put out of action, and "D" Battery of the 211th Brigade had five guns destroyed in succession and practically the whole of its personnel casualtied. Heavy shelling was also experienced at the waggon lines of 11th Battery, more than fifty horses having been killed and wounded.[54]

It is these casualties among the horses that have the greatest impact in the New Zealand batteries as they limber up to keep in touch with the infantry advance. Driver Ernest Looms is a 24-year-old farm labourer from Okaramio near Blenheim. On formation of the New Zealand Division in Egypt in March 1916, he was posted from the Canterbury Mounted Rifles to the New Zealand Field Artillery. In November 1918, Looms was a saddler in No. 11 Battery, 3rd Brigade New Zealand Field Artillery. He is in the wagon lines during the German bombardment and writes of its consequences: "When we moved out at midday the following day we were a very small Battery. Our first line wagons had to be left behind owing to the shortage of horses and even then the remaining teams had only four, instead of six horses each." Looms records that the battery suffers a further two men wounded and one horse killed on 4 November. "Out of the horses we had brought along with us with what were supposed to be slight wounds, thirteen had to be sent back again."[55]

Once the Blue Line is secured the attached British artillery brigades continue to fire in support of the advancing infantry while the New Zealand guns move forward to the east of Le Quesnoy where they can continue to support the infantry as they reach the Red Line and exploit forward into Forêt de Mormal. Headquarters New Zealand Artillery war diary notes that: "The artillery advanced well and helped greatly. There were no hitches."[56] One of the headquarters' staff records the scene the following day when the headquarters moves forward to Château de Potelle, describing where

> our guns got very effectively onto some Hun guns and men who lay dead in a group with a few other Bosches [sic] scattered about. The Guns, men and horses were lying in and near an orchard; the men looked as if they had been running away when caught by our fire.[57]

Hutchinson is with his battery commander, who, with the other battery commanders and brigade commander Lieutenant-Colonel Robert McQuarrie, move forward to establish the new gun positions. "Left with skipper and bde party to reconnoitre forward position 300 yds E[ast]. of Quesnoy at 9.30 a.m."[58] They cross the railway line about a mile northwest of Le Quesnoy, but are then held up by machine gun fire from the ramparts of the town. This

forces a detour north through the villages of Ramponeau and Villereau, and it is at midday before they site battery positions in the area of St Sepulchre. The batteries are then called forward, coming into action a couple of hours later. Hutchinson stresses how far the guns have come.

> Brought bty to position in afternoon 6000 yds as crow flies from this morning posy. And by nightfall 5000 [yards] from front which represents advance for day of almost 10,000 yds. 2 men wounded at new posy. Le Quesnoy entirely surrounded but some stout Hun machine gunners & a minnewerfer [sic] still hold the place. Early start again to-morrow. Us living in a cellar to-night.[59]

Reconnaissance parties of the 1st and 3rd Brigades then move forward. Those of 1st Brigade are also held up north of the town and make a major detour to the south. They eventually site their batteries in the area of Potelle, while 3rd Brigade goes into action in the vicinity of St Sepulchre. The advance artillery group now consists of the three New Zealand Brigades under the command of Lieutenant-Colonel McQuarrie. As Monty Ingram terms it, "Everything went swimmingly. A real good and successful battle, not unlike the battles of olden times."[60]

'Dumb victims of the war.' Horse casualties by bombing raids or artillery fire had a serious impact on the ability of horse-drawn artillery to keep up with the advance. No. 11 Battery, New Zealand Field Artillery, had 50 of its horses killed and wounded by German artillery fire on 4 November 1918. NZ RSA Collection, Photographer: Captain H.A. Sanders, NZEF Official H Series H1165, Ref: 1/2-013714-G, Alexander Turnbull Library, Wellington, New Zealand

244

Chapter 4

OVER THE WALL

JARDINE'S 2 RIFLES AT THE PORTE DE VALENCIENNES

By 9.30 a.m., four hours after the battle starts, Hart's 3rd Rifle Brigade has encircled Le Quesnoy. In the north the companies of Lieutenant-Colonel Jardine's 2 Rifles have worked their way in toward the sunken road that encircles the moat. Any attempt to get close is met with machine gun and sniper fire from the ramparts. Lieutenant Leslie Denniston's B Company gets a four- man patrol briefly across the moat before it is driven back, tries again with a platoon. The riflemen in the platoon are pinned down and unable to move for the rest of the day. A platoon from Captain George Jamieson's C Company seizes the road bridge over the railway line. The engineers clear it of mines, but German machine gun fire stops any further advance. A section from C Company secures the Orsinval crossroads and edge their way forward across the causeway leading to the Porte de Valenciennes — the northern gateway into the town. The defenders anticipate this and blow up the causeway arch nearest the gate. Nevertheless, one man gets across on a plank and shoots one of the garrison, but is forced back. This happens to be one of the Maori Pioneer Battalion working with the engineers, Private Winiata Tapsell, a 26-year-old drainlayer from Maketu in the Bay of Plenty.[1] According to Malcolm Ross, the official New Zealand war correspondent, Tapsell is assisted by the divisional salvage officer. Ross's report gives it a little more gloss.

> One of the first men, if not the first man, up the ramparts was a Maori from the Pioneer Battalion, and his rifle was thrown up after him by a salvage officer. Neither man had any business in the fight. The Maori was met with bombs, and the officer was seen later riding back with his arm in a sling and beaming with delight.[2]

Tapsell is not given any accolades for this. It seems from his personal file that wandering off to see what else is happening is one of his quirks and instead of a medal, he is in front of his commanding officer and collects 14 days' Field Punishment No. 2.[3]

The western walls of the inner rampart of Le Quesnoy showing the effects of New Zealand 18-pounder shells fired over open sights to suppress German machine gun and sniper fire while Barrowclough's 4 Rifles closed up to the walls. NZ RSA Collection, Photographer: Captain H.A. Sanders, NZEF Official H Series H1244, Ref: 1/2-013791-G, Alexander Turnbull Library, Wellington, New Zealand

Lieutenant-Colonel Jardine's 2 Rifles attempts to enter Le Quesnoy.

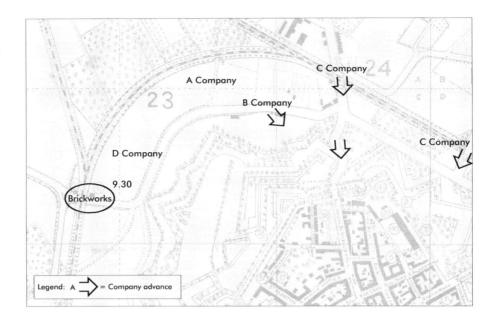

Below: Lieutenant Leslie Denniston commands B Company, 2 Rifles, on 4 November and is awarded the Military Cross for his actions in the attack on 4 November 1918. Archives New Zealand

Jardine's riflemen continue to apply pressure with Lewis guns and Stokes mortar on the northern gate and ramparts waiting on any opportunity to break in. It is late in the afternoon when the intensity of German fire drops and the riflemen move forward across the causeway and through the gate, only to find 4 Rifles there before them.

COCKROFT'S 3 RIFLES AT THE PORTE DE LANDRECIES

In the south Major Cockroft's 3 Rifles are also trying to enter the town. At 11 a.m. Cockroft sends patrols onto the hornwork toward the inner gate.

Porte de Landrecies is the gate that opens onto the island and leads to Porte Fauroeulx that leads through the inner ramparts into the town itself.[4] The hornwork is a fortified island surrounded by two lakes separated by a moat from the steep brick-lined inner ramparts. There are houses either side of the main road on the island "but machine guns sweeping down [from] the bridge [at the inner ramparts] caused casualties and as instructions had been issued to avoid casualties once the town was surrounded no offensive action was adopted".[5]

Rifleman James Nimmo is in one of the patrols.

When we got to the gate [Porte de Landrecies], a Corp[oral], another chap and myself were sent into the village [the houses on the island or hornwork surrounded by the lake] to try & find out where a patrol which had gone in earlier in the day was. How I am alive to write this today I don't know, or at the very least I should have been in Blighty. We got into the town and were simply overwhelmed by Civies. Laughing,

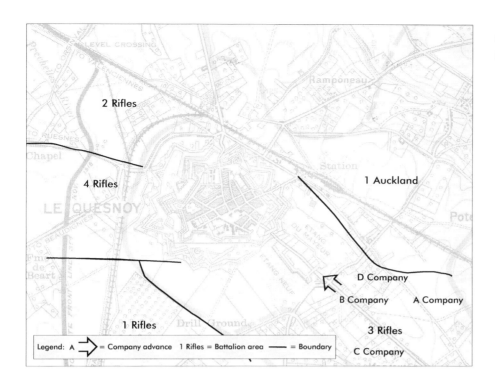

Cockroft's 3 Rifles at the
Porte de Landrecies.

crying, and just about mad with joy. It was ten minutes before we could
get away from them. Then two of us searched everywhere near the gate but
found no Jerries. We then found out by the aid of a word or two of French
& by signs that one of our boys was down the street wounded. The Civies
reckoned there were no Jerries round that part so we decided to go and get
him. We expected to find out something about the patrol from him.

A civie took the lead, and we started off getting a pancake each on
the way. Had just got a mouthful when the old boy opened out from 50
yards down the street. The civie got one through the hand. One of my
mates got one through the leg and one in the arm. There was no shelter
and there was nothing for us to do but run for it. A good hundred yards.
Could see the bullets hitting the cobbles in front of us, and were getting
pieces of brick from behind, but neither of us got hit. Half way along I saw
a doorway and decided on a spell. I bounced into it in such a hurry that I
bounced out again like a ball. I took it gently next attempt and had a few
minutes in which to get my wind. Then it was a case of go again, and he
opened as soon as I appeared and helped me along the final stretch. One
poor little dog ran after us barking like blazes and had his leg blown clean
off. Lucky! Yes the Corp & I were very lucky.

We got our mate out later on, & they also brought out the chap we had
gone down to get. The civies had treated them very well. I can tell you I
wasn't sorry to get out of the village again though.[6]

Brigadier-General Hart, having sent his 25-year-old brigade major, Major
Eric Bremner of the New Zealand Staff Corps and Royal Military College
Duntroon graduate, north of Le Quesnoy to take any measures necessary to
assist Lieutenant-Colonel Jardine to mop up the town, similarly despatches
Major Inglis "to go round the south side and do anything that seemed
useful".[7] Taking a sergeant with him, Inglis goes on horseback to carry out
this mission.

Looking over the lake from the area held by Major Cockroft's 3 Rifles to the southwestern walls of the Basse ville or hornwork that was explored by patrols who were pinned down by machine gun fire from the Porte de Fauroeulx (cut of picture to the left) and driven back on the Porte de Landrecies (out of picture to the right). NZ RSA Collection, Photographer: Captain H.A. Sanders, NZEF Official H Series. H1238, Ref: 1/2-013785-G, Alexander Turnbull Library, Wellington, New Zealand

On the Ghissignies–Villereau road not far west of the point at which it joins the Louvignies–Villereau one, we found a company of riflemen lining the low north bank of a cutting, who told us that machine guns fired from the ramparts on any movement in this locality. The enemy also had a 77 mm field gun with which they fired from the walls on any traffic south of the town. I sent Coster (my Sergeant) back with an order for [Second Lieutenant] Arthur Billington to move his section forward on packhorses. In the interval I set about drawing the fire of the machine guns by walking about on the top of the road bank, quaking inwardly in case the whizz-bang gun joined the chorus at what was for it point blank range over open sights. My belief that I was outside the arc to which it was paying attention was happily confirmed but flashes as it fired on a mounted battery staff advancing further west enabled me to locate the shielded gun quite clearly. With the glasses I also got the flashes or smoke of three machine guns and, by the time Billington arrived with his guns, had sorted out a well screened fire position within close range of the ramparts and with a covered approach to it.

Immediately the guns arrived they went into action with effect; and there was no more annoyance from the southern ramparts. When we examined the field gun later, we found its shield well spattered with bullet splashes.[8]

Inglis moves further east to check on his guns and meets with Major Cockroft to see if his guns can assist. Cockroft "sent an English-speaking German officer in to the Commandant of Le Quesnoy garrison informing him that he was surrounded and cut off". Later in the afternoon two German soldiers are sent in with a message in German drafted by Inglis. An aircraft also drops a message requesting surrender and this too is ignored. Word comes back that the soldiers are ready to surrender but that their officers refuse.

> My runner and I then went in through the [outer] suburb [on the hornwork] with the intention of getting into communications with the German post at the east gate of the town proper [Porte Fauroeulx].
>
> A rifleman who had been into the suburb on patrol earlier in the day told us that the street was swept by a machine gun from the ramparts. One of his patrol had been hit by it, but he, himself had got back by the south side of the street, which he thought the machine gun could not hit, so we proceeded on the side that he recommended and had almost reached the far end of the street when some French people called to us from a house on the other side of the street. We went over to them to be received with great excitement by a party of two men and four women, who insisted that we must wait till they produced something that they had been keeping "till the English came." One of the girls ran out of the room to return in a few minutes with a bottle of cognac and a bundle of rags from which she unrolled a small tin of Peak Frean's [sic: Peek Freans] fancy biscuits. These treasures had been safely concealed, they told us, throughout the war. In cups of cognac we drank each other's healths.
>
> They showed us the abominable bread and scanty allowance of lard on which they had been existing. I asked the runner if he had any bread in his haversack, and, when he replied that he had half a loaf, told him to give it to them. Passed from hand to hand, it was examined appreciatively.
>
> "This is not bread. It is cake," said one of them.
>
> Protests met my assurance that it was British Army bread and a daily ration. Shepherd also gave them a tin of butter that he had — more astonishment.
>
> At this stage a clatter of rapid fire accompanied by the detonations of bombs broke out on the far side of the town. Harold Barrowclough's battalion was making its entry by scaling the wall with ladders on the west side. Shepherd and I had missed our chance of being first in to interview the commandant.[9]

BARROWCLOUGH'S 4 RIFLES GO OVER THE WALL

Major Barrowclough's three companies, A, B and C, in this order from right to left, have closed up to the outer ramparts, each looking for a way in. On the left 25-year-old Lieutenant Clarence Rabone's C Company under cover of the smokescreen moves into the sunken road with 2 Rifles on their left. Rabone is a serving soldier and member of the New Zealand Permanent Staff. He was a quartermaster sergeant and warrant officer when he was posted to the Rifle Brigade when it is formed in Trentham in 1915. He served in France in 1916, then commissioned and served as an officer instructor in the UK in 1917–18. He was posted to 4 Rifles in France in September 1918 and appointed company commander.[10] In the sunken road his company comes under fire with his forward platoon pinned down and unable to move.

Frederick Avery, a 22-year-old salesman from Motueka, is a rifleman in C Company. He enlisted in October 1916 and sailed with 24th Reinforcements. He was wounded in April 1918 and has just come back to the battalion.[11] He is one of a Lewis gun team that clambers up on one of the outer bastions to give covering fire.

81

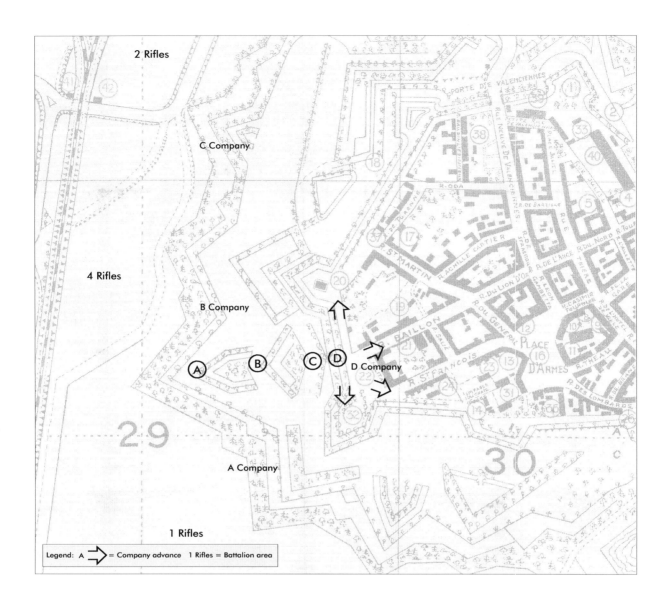

2 Rifles

C Company

4 Rifles

B Company

Ⓐ   Ⓑ   Ⓒ Ⓓ   D Company

29

A Company

30

1 Rifles

Legend: A ⟹ = Company advance   1 Rifles = Battalion area

Map of Barrowclough's
4 Rifles' route to the inner
ramparts.

We went up there and Corporal Tait turned round and said, "I think the officer's right, there's no sign of life here." And all of a sudden — zzzzzzz. I wasn't hit, but I fell on my rifle.

The Germans had stopped. I said to the fellow behind me, "Andy — you all right? For Christ's sake, don't move." After a while the Germans were back again and went to the dead ones. We were protected somehow.

They stopped firing machine guns. I said, "Now!" We ran back and over the wall — and the Germans — zzzzzzzzzzzz all down on top of us. If they had come over the top, some of our boys would have shot them, so they couldn't come over. An officer came along later and said, "Christ, I thought all you fellows there had been wiped out."

We went along the next morning to attend to our mates and the Germans had ratted them, taken their watches, money and water bottles. They were stone dead. Two good men that had been out there a long while too, quite young. And in only four days' time the war finished.

That gave me the shivers, that place, because I should have gone [been killed]. What saved me, I don't know. But I'm a Catholic, and my sister always asked me to say a night and morning prayer, and I did say them, in the trenches and anywhere, so I think I was protected a bit.[12]

View from top of outer rampart, looking west toward the motorway in the middle distance and ground over which the riflemen of 4 Rifles attacked on 4 November 1918 (A on map). Christopher Pugsley

At the base of the demi-lune or ravelin (B on map) protecting the western side of Le Quesnoy. Averill's ladder party scaled this face to establish a Lewis gun at the top before pulling up the ladder and proceeding onto the inner ramparts. Christopher Pugsley

View back toward the inner side of the demi-lune or ravelin showing how it was open to fire from the inner ramparts. Note the carponier or covered way that also serves to divide the attackers. Averill's party moved down the right of the carponier (C on map). Christopher Pugsley

View of inner rampart and water gate, which was blocked by timber on 4 November. Second Lieutenant Frank Evans and his batman were shot and killed as he tried to extricate his party, in the area where the photo was taken. The small group of survivors had to lay low until Averill's group moved forward (D on map). Christopher Pugsley

Second Lieutenants Leslie Averill and Phillip Lummis capture a German machine gun crew in the outer defences of Le Quesnoy on 4 November 1918. The early morning mist and thick smoke limits observation to 5–10 metres allowing Barrowclough's 4 Rifles freedom of movement forward to the inner ramparts. George Edmund Butler, 'Jumping a machine gun in the moat at Le Quesnoy', 1919, Ref: AAAC 898 NCWA Q170, Archives New Zealand

Having secured the Blue Line and with his rifle companies closed up to the outer earthworks of the fortress of Le Quesnoy, Barrowclough and his intelligence officer Second Lieutenant Averill reconnoitre the maze of defensive outworks between the outer earthworks and the steep brick-lined inner ramparts. Twenty-one-year-old Second Lieutenant Leslie Averill came with the 34th Reinforcements. He was awarded the Military Cross for exceptional gallantry as a platoon commander during the fighting around Bapaume in August 1918.[13] On 4 November he is Barrowclough's intelligence officer and accompanies him as part of the battalion tactical headquarters. Observation is limited to five to ten metres in the mist and from the thick smokescreen. They capture a couple of Germans, who they coerce as guides, but after blindly meandering in the maze, Barrowclough is aware that there is strength in numbers. They retrace their steps for more men but this is at the cost of losing the cover of the smoke which, as it thins, allows the German machine guns on the ramparts to open fire. Nevertheless, Averill working with the recently commissioned Second Lieutenant Phillip Lummis, a carpenter from Christchurch, overpowers a German machine gun team in position on the low ground. Barrowclough believes: "This little success gave us complete freedom of movement in the low broken ground lying between the outer wall and the series of more-or-less-connected angular bastions which protected the salient of the inner wall."[14]

At this point the advancing infantry of 1st Brigade have still to reach the German artillery positions. Barrowclough writes: "At this stage the Boche artillery … shelled us fairly heavily and made things very unpleasant. A few shells must have fallen among the enemy posts at the tops of the island bastions, for ... a number of light signals were fired, and the artillery fire ceased."[5]

As the map shows, Vauban's outer works that lead to the inner ramparts are designed to break up and channel any attacker into carefully designed killing zones that work equally effectively for modern rifles and machine guns as they did for smoothbore musket and muzzle-loading cannon. Barrowclough decides to sit tight and wait for the German surrender.

> At this stage of the operations I decided to give up the attempt to force an entry. Our orders had been to capture the railway line and if enemy resistance weakened to exploit our success. We had already done more than was asked of us in the operation order, and I judged it wiser not the run the risk of further casualties in a frontal attack when the enveloping movements of the 1st Brigade and of our 3rd Battalion had already settled the ultimate fate of the fortress. During the morning however I was constantly meeting artillery officers who were anxious to use the road running round the north of the town in order to move up guns and ammunition. This was impossible while the German machine gunners remained on the walls of the town. So I decided to make another attempt.[16]

Major Harold Barrowclough, a 24-year-old Dunedin law student, commanding 4 Rifles. *Otago Witness Illustrated,* 20 June 1917, Toitū Otago Settlers Museum

While the moat is dry in this sector, it is obvious that ladders will be needed to scale the wall. These have been collected by the field engineers and stockpiled on the Ruesnes road. The three field companies of engineers do sterling work this day and two later feature in the honours and awards for this battle, as stated in the engineer history. "For conspicuous gallantry and devotion to duty while carrying and controlling the indispensable ladders, Lance-Corporal A.J. Randall received the D.C.M and Sapper J. Hodgson the Military Medal."[17] However, as we will see, both Barrowclough and Averill are adamant that there were no engineers with the actual ladder party when the wall is scaled. Stewart, in his divisional history, decides that this is a topic better not addressed so close to the event, and so, even though the engineers initially bring the ladders forward and are involved in clearing mines and fighting fires once the town is taken, the truth — or at least the details — of the engineers' part in the scaling of the walls remains unresolved. The weight of evidence suggests that the engineers under Lance-Corporal Randall got the ladder forward and then the job was done by the riflemen of 4 Rifles.

> I then sent back two scouts who brought up one of the 30 foot ladders which I had told the engineers to carry down to the point where the Ruesnes–Le Quesnoy road crossed the railway line. The scouts returned with the ladder — (The two sappers were never there — of that I am positive) by means of the ladder we were able to get a footing on the

bastion [B on map] … We had first "straffed" it with rifle grenades there being no Stokes available at the time. This post was then occupied by 2/Lt F.M. Evans and a platoon of the Centre Company. By a bold stroke Evans and a few of his men got right forward … where the wall was low and broken down [C on map]. The little party then rushed forward again to a hollow midway … here they were discovered by the German machine gunners on the wall and were heavily fired on. In a very gallant attempt to find a way out, Evans and his batman were both killed. They were both buried where they fell. The remainder of the party were compelled to remain in this isolated position for about 6 hours till they were relieved by our advance in the afternoon.[18]

Second Lieutenant Leslie Averill takes up the tale.

The time was approximately midday and we still had not gained entrance into Le Quesnoy. We were, however, making progress and the German fire-power from the walls had lessened. There were two outlying bastions … Fortunately the possibility of wall climbing had been foreseen and a ladder had been provided by the engineers … The CO [Barrowclough] was anxious that these bastions should be explored and so, with 5–6 men, I put the ladder against the wall, we climbed it and drew up the ladder behind us … We took the ladder down on the … sloping grassy side of this first bastion only to find a similar fortification straight ahead of us. The wall climbing of this second bastion had to be repeated and from the top of this outlying rampart I could see that we could now approach the main and final wall of this well-fortified town … The 30-foot ladder was too short to reach from the bottom of the moat to the top of the final wall but there was one place where the ladder could be placed to reach the top. This was on a narrow stone bridge, about a foot wide, which spanned the moat and was connected with a sluice-gate … After crossing this bridge and sluice-gate a narrow ledge ran for some 10 yards beside the wall to an arched opening, giving entrance to the town, but which — needless to say — had been completely blocked by the enemy to deny us access through the wall. It was only on this narrow wall above the sluice-gate that the ladder could reach the top.[19]

After a council of war with his battalion commander, Averill returns to the spot with an assault party. Barrowclough brings up all available firepower and engages the Germans on the ramparts. He writes to Stewart:

One after the other we attacked the salient positions … First they were subjected to a heavy Stokes mortar fire … and also a miniature barrage of rifle grenades. We got possession of the whole of the line of bastions. On these commanding positions I placed every available Lewis gun in the battalion and developed a tremendous covering fire on the inner walls completely driving the enemy from the parapet on top. Thus we were able to exploit in safety the ground and moat at the foot of the inner walls …[20]

Barrowclough commits Lieutenant Birch's D Company, his reserve company for the assault, and Birch details Second Lieutenant Harold Kerr, a 23-year-old teacher from Palmerston North, to use his platoon for the task and to accompany Averill, who knows the ground.

The point selected for scaling the walls … was selected by necessity rather than by choice, for it was the only spot where our 30 foot ladder would reach to the top of the wall. For this last venture I decided to use a platoon of my reserve company which had hitherto not been engaged. No. 14 Platoon under 2/Lt H.W. Kerr were soon in position and told off into three parties — one to hold the "bridge-head" at the top of the ladder and the other two to secure the positions A & B [at each of the flank bastions on the inner wall] these two salient being of course of vital importance. Meanwhile the ladder was being raised into position ag[ain]st the wall. At the first attempt the little party was greeted with such a fusillade of German stick bombs that they had to withdraw very hurriedly. A further dose of Stokes shells and a burst of fire from the covering Lewis guns … materially reduced the hostility of Brother Boche. The ladder was raised without further difficulty. No. 14 Platoon led by Averill & Kerr started off at once. The ladder was so flimsy that I would allow only three men on it at once. When Averill and Kerr got to the top and looked over the parapet we saw them fire a couple of revolver shots and by the way they hopped over the parapet I could see that the position was ours. At this stage the excitement was too much for me and I rushed up the ladder with my signaller and the field telephone. It was probably very unwise thus to interfere with the passage of the troops up the ladder but I wished to ring Brigade and establish the claim of the 4th Battalion as being the first troops to enter the town.

What Barrowclough does not say here is that he made a friendly wager with Lieutenant-Colonel Jardine of 2 Rifles on whose battalion would be first into the town, hence the keenness to stake his claim.

For the next quarter of an hour the whole battalion was busily scrambling up the ladder and as the platoons arrived on top I sent them off under their commanders to work down the various streets and "mop up" the town.[21]

Rifleman Bert Lee, a timber worker from Dannevirke, is a battalion runner and moves with Barrowclough's headquarters. "I was sent to the Headquarters as a runner, I was very pleased about it as it was much better than being in the front line."[22] His job is to take messages forward to the companies during battle when there are no telephones working.

I was a runner and was attached to Battalion Headquarters and took messages up to the companies. We had quite a gang of runners, there was always eight there and when a stunt was on of some kind, they would give us another lot, we have about 12 or 15 from the companies, they would come and join us. We had to run in pairs when we were in a battle, just in case one of us got killed or something, the other carried on …[23]

Lee follows Barrowclough up the ladder onto the ramparts.

We climbed up this ladder and got into this village, one of the old type fortified towns, had only three entrances and a brick wall … we just had to follow each other up … I think our Colonel went up first and the rest of them followed him and went into the town and everybody surrendered there.[24]

Averill, in his report of the battalion's activities writes:

> The Signallers came up the ladder with their telephone & very soon La
> Grande Place of Le Quesnoy was connected up with the outside world.
> Within ½ an hour of the entry into Le Quesnoy the Battalion cookers under
> Major B. McLeod MC, 2nd in Command came steaming into the town &
> the diggers settled down to a well earned feed.[25]

Averill recalls that the Germans soon

> threw up the sponge and some 15 minutes later the 2nd Rifles marched in
> through the Valenciennes Gate … After being under the heel of the Hun for
> four years, the delight of the people of Le Quesnoy on being free again knew
> no bounds. That their liberators had come from the other side of the world to
> help them in their hour of need impressed them very greatly and this battle
> … was a sacrifice which will never be forgotten.[26]

Accompanied by Captain John Greenwood, MC, who is attached to
Headquarters 4 Rifles, Averill is soon busy going from underground casemate
to casemate rounding up the German garrison.

> It was very funny to see the civilians, Greenwood & I walked round the
> walls collecting Huns & when we arrived in a street all would be quiet.
> Soon a head would poke out of a crack in the door & would immediately
> disappear again. A matter of a few seconds and half a dozen would rush out
> of the house & embrace us & shake hands, another few seconds the whole
> street was out till you couldn't move. The first thing they told us was how
> badly they had treated our prisoners. In one place we ran into a hospital
> with 200 Germans & about 50 cot cases. The cot cases were left under
> charge of a German doctor & were afterwards removed by our ambulances.
> The 200 joined the force in the Grande Place. The Brigadier arrived ½ an
> hour after the capture & was given a great reception by the populace.
>   With regards to the Engineers, I only saw one Engineer during the
> whole day & he was lost & didn't know what to do; as for putting up the
> ladder they never had anything to do with it.[27]

Captain Malcolm Ross, the official New Zealand war correspondent, writes:

> The inhabitants, realising that at last deliverance had come, rushed from
> cellars and houses and soon from every building the tricolour was flying in
> the breeze. Along the street, thronged with an excited cheering multitude,
> the diggers marched, embraced and kissed and showered with autumn
> flowers. Enthusiasm knew no bounds. Here and there a rifle still cracked,
> our men taking no risks when they saw a Hun who had not surrendered.
> The excited civilians stuck flowers in the men's tunics and in even their
> respirators and followed cheering to the main square where the German
> commander with a hundred men already drawn up, surrendered to a young
> captain, whom he formally saluted and to whom he handed his revolver.[28]

The Germans are rounded up and collected in the Place d'Armes, in the
shadow of the ruin of the town hall tower. As the German prisoners are

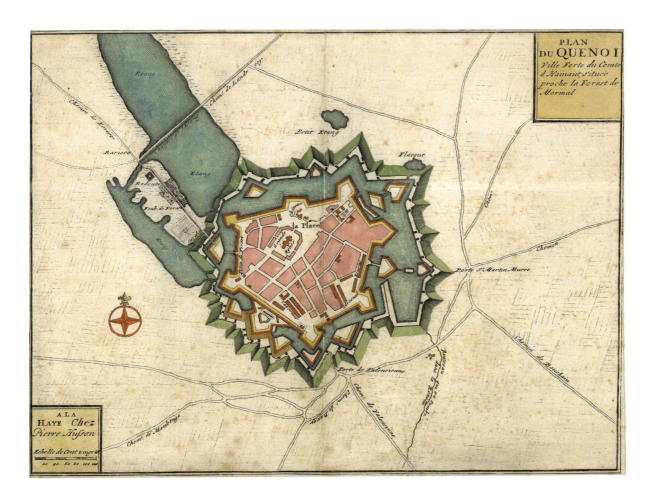

Plan du Quesnoi, Ville Forte du Comte d'Hainaut Situeé proche la Forest de Mormal, 17th century hand-coloured printed map. The plan is confusing because north is to the bottom of the map, and the axis of attack by Barrowclough's 4 Rifles is from the top right corner and one can clearly make out the series of outer defences that Averill's party scaled with their single ladder, one by one, before they finally reached the base of the inner ramparts. Note that the plan was drawn before the construction of outer defensive hornwork (so called because the bastions on each corner looked like horns) that leads to Forêt de Mormal. Author's collection

George Edmond Butler's careful recreation of the scaling of the walls, showing Second Lieutenant Leslie Averill on the grassed mound, with Second Lieutenant Harry Kerr about to ascend. The three riflemen are Privates Howden, Haxton and Peters from Captain Cyril Birch's D Company, 4 Rifles. It seems they followed Second Lieutenant Phillip Lummis up the ladder, (not in painting). After them came Major Harold Barrowclough, his signaller and then Lieutenant Selwyn Kenrick. George Edmond Butler, 'Capture of the walls of Le Quesnoy', oil, 1532 x 1220 mm, AAAC 898, NCWA 535, Archives New Zealand

French Tricolour embroidered in haste by the women of Le Quesnoy and presented to the 3rd Rifle Brigade on 14 November 1918 in the same ceremony that a New Zealand flag was presented to the town. Restored in 2005. National Army Museum, Te Mata Toa (1978.1364) Waiouru

Soeur Jean, the heroine of Le Quesnoy who cared for the malnourished population and British prisoners of war. She also hid and smuggled French citizens wanted by the Germans through Forêt de Mormal and across the border. George Edmond Butler, 'Soeur Jean, Le Quesnoy 14th November 1918', oil, 365 x 270 mm, AAC 898, NCWA Q00159, Archives New Zealand

Butler's sketch of the walls of Le Quesnoy shows that there was little in the way of recent defensive preparations, the German defenders relying on the natural strength of the fortress to provide protection with the main effort on the railway line defences west of the town. George Edmond Butler, 'The Walls of Le Quesnoy, Nov 9 1918', charcoal wash, 342 x 518 mm, AAAC 898 NCWA 443, Archives New Zealand

The exterior of the Gateway

F.W. Woodhouse
1922.

F.W. Woodhouse's painting looking from the hornwork to the gate in the inner ramparts on the approach taken by Major Cockroft's 3 Rifles to enter the town on 4 November 1918. F.W. Woodhouse, 'The exterior of the Gateway Porte de Fauroeulx, showing church tower on left', 1922, watercolour, 250 x 360 mm, AAAC 898 NCWA Q208, Archives New Zealand

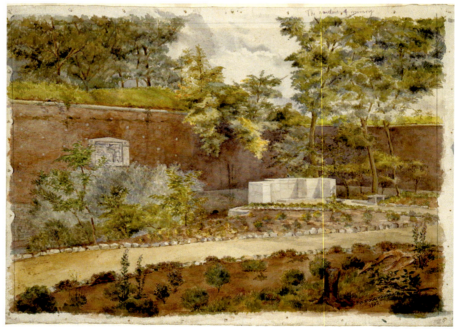

F.W. Woodhouse completed a series of watercolour paintings of the walls, principal gates and the memorial and its garden. These were most likely commissioned by the architect Samuel Hurst Seager. Initially New Zealand shrubs were planted but these did not survive the European winters. F.W. Woodhouse, 'The Garden of Memory, Le Quesnoy', 1922, watercolour/wash, 360 x 510 mm, AAAC 898 NCWA Q455, Archives New Zealand

Ngā Tapuwae New
Zealand First World
War Trails is a WW100
Legacy project that uses
an app incorporating
interactive mapping,
images and soldiers'
voices to link together
the New Zealand Western
Front experience.
This is the stand at the
Le Quesnoy New
Zealand Memorial
Gardens. Note the
marching soldiers
forming the Silver Fern,
New Zealand's national
emblem. This was
designed by Chris Hay's
team at Locales. WW100/
Chris Hay, Locales

Félix-Alexandre Desruelles and Alexander Roderick Fraser's sculpture for the New
Zealand Memorial, Le Quesnoy. The winged figure of Victorious Peace stands boldly
out on the right of the foreground: she breaks the sword of war beneath her feet, and
holds in her right hand the wreath of victory, in her left hand the palm of peace. At left
in the foreground, among rough rock, is a small cross in memory of those who fell in
the action. On the recessed background is the representation of the scaling of the wall
in low relief. Christopher Pugsley

The Memorial Window to the 3rd Rifle Brigade in the Battle of Le Quesnoy, 4 November 1918 in St Andrew's Church, Cambridge, New Zealand. Cambridge is twinned with Le Quesnoy. Richard Stowers

marched out of the town, there are many rueful glances by the watching 'Dinks' at the missed opportunity to rifle their pockets for 'souvenirs'. Rifleman Captain Nimmo reflects on this in a letter home.

> That night the whole garrison surrendered. I don't know how many there were, but I think it was about 2000. They went out the gate. That was the hardest part of the lot. What a crowd of watches a chap would have salvaged if only they had come our way.

It seems peace is about to get in the way of the New Zealanders' favourite pastime.

> A few souvenirs would have come in very handy especially as it appears there won't be any more prisoners. Peace looks very close now. The official news today is that the German fleet is out. Mutinied, & the German Peace Delegates meet Foch today, so it's quite on the cards that the war will be finished by Xmas.[29]

Barrowclough's 4 Rifles billet in Le Quesnoy that night and the following morning parade for their brigadier and are visited by Russell, the divisional commander. Lieutenant-Colonel Hardy Neil, commanding 3 Field Ambulance, moves the Advanced Dressing Station into the military hospital in the town. The modern or military wing is used as the German hospital with the civilians and British prisoners treated in the stables alongside. They are cared for by the Sisters of Mercy, one of whom, Sister St Jean, is seen as a heroine of the town

'Mayor, citizens and Sisters of Mercy — Le Quesnoy.' Group portrait taken in front of the hospital buildings showing the mayor of Le Quesnoy, with his councillors, soldiers and the nuns from the Sisters of Mercy who staff the civilian hospital. Sister St Jean, the heroine of Le Quesnoy, is the nun on the far right. The officers are from 3 New Zealand Field Ambulance who set up an Advanced Dressing Station in the former German military hospital and French military liaison staff. NZ RSA Collection, Photographer: Captain H.A. Sanders, NZEF Official H Series H1260, Ref:1/1-002084-G, Alexander Turnbull Library, Wellington, New Zealand

Major Harold Barrowclough, on horseback, parades with his battalion, 4 Rifles, on the morning 5 November 1918 in the Place d'Armes, Le Quesnoy, the day after the liberation of the town. The four companies of the battalion can be distinguished. The establishment strength is 1025 men, and the photo shows some 300 men on parade indicating the heavy losses over the previous months of fighting. NZ RSA Collection, Photographer: Captain H.A. Sanders, NZEF Official H Series H1152, Ref: 1/2-013704-G, Alexander Turnbull Library, Wellington, New Zealand

during the occupation, smuggling those wanted by the Germans through Forêt de Mormal and across the border to safety. She is angry at the treatment that the Germans meted out to British prisoners of war, telling the liberators that there was rarely a day that a prisoner did not die from lack of clothing and malnourishment, so that by the time they arrived into her care at the hospital it was impossible to do anything for them. She believed that the German officer in charge should receive swift justice and be shot.

All of this is watched by the attached official war artist, Honorary Captain George Edmund Butler, an established artist in Bristol who was raised in Aro Valley, Wellington. Butler does a preliminary study in oils of Sister [St] Jean. He talks to Averill and sketches the sluice gate entrance and the wall and gets the detail of how the ladder was climbed and who was where. He would change the detail to increase dramatic effect, showing Averill alone on top of the rampart with Harry Kerr still holding the ladder and yet to climb. His portrayal is of a small band of men and an unseen enemy, in stark contrast to the frenetic action portrayed in Fortunino Matania's illustration *The Storming of Le Quesnoy by New Zealand troops on November 4th, 1918* for *The Sphere*.

Butler also sketches and paints the walls of Le Quesnoy and imaginatively sketches Averill and Lummis taking out the machine gun post sited among the outer ramparts. These join his sketches and paintings of the journey forward of the New Zealand Division to this battle that are now part of the National Collection of War Art in Archive New Zealand.[30] In the same manner, Captain Harry Sanders and his team film and photograph the events of the battle.

On 5 November 1918, Captain Harry Sanders' team photograph Barrowclough's 4 Rifles on parade, its thinned ranks evident as it prepares to be inspected by Brigadier-General Hart, the brigade commander. He also captures the arrival of Major-General Sir Andrew Russell and his escort coming forward to see his brigadiers.

Hart first visits the town immediately after the German surrender,

and they gave a wonderful demonstration of welcome to our men. They cheered and laughed and wept for joy, clasping all and sundry around the neck, kissing and hugging them with joy at being liberated. I entered the town about that time and indeed it was a very stirring scene, one not to be appreciated and realised except by those actually taking part. One felt a great joy in having taken a part in the release of these poor people from the years of suffering they had endured at the hands of the Boche swine.

Next morning at the request of the *Maire* [mayor], I attended with two Battalion Commanders at the *Mairie* [town hall] — in impromptu but impressive ceremony — to receive on behalf of the Brigade, from the aged Mayor and his Council, the formal thanks of the town for their deliverance. During the morning I walked around the ramparts and saw from the enemy's viewpoint the country over which we had attacked. The position appeared so very strong I marvelled at what had been accomplished. The men showed great gallantry, keenness and determination throughout and their skill and cunning in using cover and concealment was equal to that one reads of in Red Indian warfare. Largely because of this, our casualties were remarkably small, an average of 77 per battalion, most of them I am thankful to say being machine gun bullets from which there will be a complete recovery. There were many enemy slain and we captured … [711] prisoners, 5 field guns, 8 *minnenwefer* [sic], 82 machine guns, 19 horses, 1 cooker and other war material.[31]

Russell is pleased with his division's achievements, recording in his diary: "Attacked this morning at 5.30. A very successful day. Rifle Bde, having surrounded Quesney [sic] it finally surrendered. 1st Bde continued advance and captured over 50 guns. 2 Bde then pushed on thro Forest."[32]

The 4th of November was probably the most successful day for the Division during the war. The net results of our operations were — an advance of six miles, the capture of LE QUESNOY, ROMPANEAU, VILLERAU, POTELLE and HERBIGNIES with nearly 2,000 prisoners, 60 field guns and several hundred machine guns.[33]

In Russell's eyes, the fall of Le Quesnoy is but one step in the journey — he is set on reaching the Sambre River, and once the fortress is successfully bypassed, his focus shifts to getting through the forest.

Deaths 4 Rifles

ANDERSON, Ernest 71546 Rifleman
BEAUREPAIRE, Louis Isidore 74852 Rifleman
BERNARD, Victor Raymond 21/42 2nd Lieutenant
CASSIDY, Frederick William 69681 Rifleman
DAW, Arthur Guy 26/757 Lance-Corporal
EVANS, Francis Meredith 26/67 2nd Lieutenant
GILES, Henry 74941 Rifleman
GRAY, George Cowie 26/448 Corporal
JONES, Roderick Leslie 33381 Rifleman
JURY, Vernon Richard 74874 Rifleman
KEAN, Peter 23/799 Rifleman
LESTER, Harry 23/190 Lance-Corporal
MORRISON, James Henry 26/315 Rifleman
SHARPIN, Robert Charles 26/254 Rifleman
SIMMONS, Gilbert John 70547 Rifleman
STOW, Edward John 35049 Rifleman
WILSON, Gladstone 13649 Corporal
WRIGHT, Everard Noel 46420 Rifleman

Chapter 5

5 NOVEMBER 1918 — TO THE SAMBRE

Forty-one-year-old Brigadier-General Robert 'Bobby' Young, married with eight children and a dental practice in Marton, commands 2nd Brigade. The four infantry battalions of his brigade concentrates early in the morning of 4 November in the fields to the southwest of Beaudignies with Brigade Headquarters in the village. It stays there until 2 p.m. when it is ordered to move up to Herbignies and be ready to pass through 1st Brigade the next morning, 5 November. There is a certain amount of shelling during this period with some casualties in the battalions. Le Quesnoy is still holding out, so the brigade faces a long detour to the south through Ghissignies and Louvignies to avoid German machine gun fire from the ramparts.

At 8.30 p.m., Young receives orders directing his 2nd Brigade to pass through 1st Brigade at dawn on 5 November and secure the eastern edge of Forêt de Mormal and if possible to exploit to the Sambre crossings. Two battalions are to lead the advance: 2 Otago on the right and 1 Canterbury on the left. A section of the Canterbury Machine Gun Company is attached to 1 Canterbury and 2 Otago. On reaching the Brown Line at the eastern edge of the forest, Young's remaining two battalions, 1 Otago and 2 Canterbury, are to follow-up and each is to be prepared to pass two companies through to maintain pressure but to avoid getting drawn into action against determined resistance.[1]

The fighting on 4 November has destroyed the combat effectiveness of the German 22nd Division. Army Group Rupprecht reports that the heavy fighting has "led to a massive consumption of forces" and that the front-line units "whose fighting power had been low already before the battle, have been weakened to the extreme". Withdrawal is recommended and this starts the night of 4/5 November. The German defensive structure rapidly falls apart, "units often failed to fight coherently. Their backbone, the artillery has to leave its guns behind in every new withdrawal due to a lack of horses. The fighting strength of the battalions was down to less than 150 men."[2]

Major James 'Jimmy' Hargest, commanding 2 Otago, escorts the Prince of Wales as he inspects his battalion at Beauvois, 14 October 1918. Following behind is Brigadier-General 'Bobby' Young who commands 2nd Brigade, which is made up of the four South Island battalions: 1 and 2 Canterbury and 1 and 2 Otago. NZ RSA Collection, Photographer: Captain H.A. Sanders, NZEF Official H Series H1049, Ref: 1/2-013613-G, Alexander Turnbull Library, Wellington, New Zealand

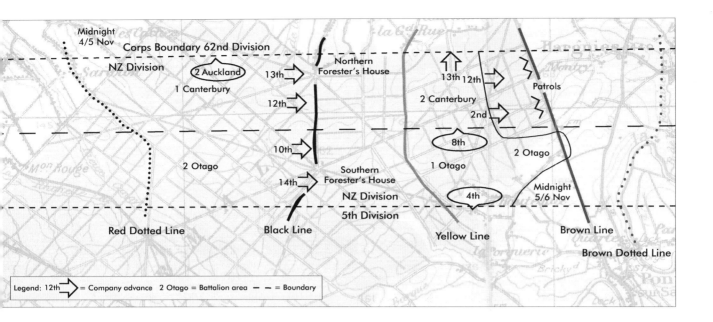

Legend: 12th ▷ = Company advance   2 Otago = Battalion area   — — = Boundary

2nd Brigade's advance through Forêt de Mormal, 5 November 1918.

Young is given a series of objectives for his brigade. His start line is the road though the forest that runs north to the village of Sarloton. Zero hour is 5.30 a.m. There are three objectives set for Young, each are on roads running north to south through the forest. The first is the Black Line two miles to the east on the north–south road to Obies, with each battalion having a forester's house at key track junctions within their boundaries. (There are foresters' houses featured on the map all through the forest — to the confusion of future historians and visitors wanting to see for themselves.) The Yellow Line is a mile further east where the forest is bisected by the road north to the hamlet of La Grande Rue. The third objective, or Brown Line, is the Bavay road marking the eastern edge of the forest. The line of exploitation is the high ground on the western banks of the Sambre River, designated the Brown Dotted Line.[3]

Young moves forward with the divisional commander, Major-General Russell, to Headquarters 1st Brigade where Brigadier-General Melvill briefs them on the situation. Young then returns to Brigade Headquarters and briefs his commanding officers.

At Russell's direction, Melvill provides 2 Auckland to assist Young's operation. The battalion is commanded by Gallipoli veteran and original member of the Auckland Infantry Battalion, 37-year-old Major W. Courtney Sinel, a shipping clerk in a family firm in Auckland. His battalion is tasked to cover the northern flank, which is still open as 62nd Division of VI Corps has not yet reached this far. On the southern flank, the 37th Division has been replaced by the 5th Division. The three New Zealand artillery brigades provide the fire plan and No. 1 Battery gives close support to 2 Otago and No. 12 Battery to 1 Canterbury. A section of 6-inch guns from 90th (Heavy) Brigade, Royal Garrison Artillery, are also in support to Young's advance. It is a simple fire plan that acknowledges the infantry's difficulty in moving through the forest. At 5.30 it will fire on a fixed line 500 yards ahead of the advancing soldiers for 30 minutes and then jump forwards 500 yards and fire for ten minutes, before doing the same again, and then stop. After this the battalions will call on their close support batteries.[4]

The 2nd Brigade attack on 5 November is carried out across the whole divisional frontage with 2 Otago and 1 Canterbury, each advancing on a frontage of some 1500 yards [1372 metres]. The battalions move forward in the dark to assembly positions on the Bavay–Englefontaine road on the edge of Forêt de Mormal. Much of the forest has been milled to provide timber for German defences, but the once cleared woodlands are covered in very tall and dense undergrowth interspersed with thick blocks of tall trees, criss-crossed by muddy forest rides.

1 CANTERBURY ON THE LEFT

1 Canterbury is temporarily commanded by Major Alan Stitt. Ashburton-born, Stitt enlisted as a 20-year-old second lieutenant, having served as an officer in the Territorials. Wounded on Gallipoli, he was adjutant of 1 Canterbury on the Somme and commanded the battalion in the heavy fighting for Gird Trench on 27 September 1916, for which he was awarded the Military Cross. He commanded the battalion at Messines and in the fighting at Warneton in June and July 1917 and was awarded the Distinguished Service Order. At the age of 24 he is a very experienced officer who knows his trade and is highly regarded as a fighting commander.[5]

1 Canterbury halts for tea at Moulin Goffart, northwest of the village of Jolimetz, then continues to Herbignies, where it spends the night. A young Canterbury platoon commander describes his view of the events in a letter to his father.

> We stayed there for a few hours, but had no sleep at all, for we had to have a conference. While we were in a house there, a shell hit the roof, and down came part of the place about us. At about 3 a.m. on Tuesday we moved on to a fresh assembly place, where we hopped off at dawn with a very light barrage to give us direction.[6]

The tactical formation is for the two leading companies to advance side-by-side: 12th Nelson on the right and 13th North Canterbury West Coast on the left. In support is 2nd South Canterbury Company and then behind it again is 1st Canterbury Company in reserve.

As on the previous day, the attack begins at 5.30 a.m., behind an artillery barrage. There is little German resistance; the major difficulty is for the files of soldiers to struggle through and keep contact with each other and with flanking platoons in the dense undergrowth. A section of machine guns supports each leading battalion. Second Lieutenant Ivor Griffiths commands one of the sections. It is delayed by mines and destroyed bridges in their move into position.

> Nevertheless we arrived in good time but very tired. We have had no sleep for three days and nights. Our march from Solesmes to the Forêt de Mormal is about 18 miles of which 9 was in action … Very little artillery fire after the first hour — then up to and especially the Forêt de Mormal M[achine] gun fire was the principal fire.[7]

The problem is discerning friend from foe and in the forest contact is at close range. "Two of my gun teams, also myself had wonderful luck — we encountered heavy M.G. fire but all missed." They have a close call with their infantry flank protection. "A platoon of infantry from 2nd AIB [Auckland] also missed."[8]

The first serious resistance is at the northern forester's house at the road junction on the Black Line. There is heavy fighting. The young officer tells his father:

> I pushed on with my platoon as hard as I could, and soon reached the edge of the wood, where we were confronted by a nest of four machine guns and snipers in houses. By the time I got there two sections of my platoon were lost in the wood, and, as there was not time to waste, it meant rushing the machine guns. I grabbed a rifle and let drive at a Hun, who fell dead — the first man I have ever shot. I felt very queer, but let fly again and got another. I had only five men with me and a sergeant. By this time my men were at it and I had a machine gun too. The Huns ran for it.[9]

The battalion is held up until the leading companies outflank the house and take it from the rear. It is "occupied by an old couple, who were absolutely dazed with the fighting".[10] It is here that Sergeant Laurie O'Dell of 12th Nelson Company goes forward with his Lewis light machine gun to deal with the German machine gun posts holding up the advance.

> Well, it was a bit of a mix-up … and we were held up on several occasions by German machine guns … I said to the RSM, "Look, I would like to have a go ahead, go up there and see if I could stop these blokes." So I went out there by myself, with a [Lewis] machine gun. He [the RSM] said, "Do you want to commit suicide?" I said. "Not necessarily, I want to try and stop the casualties.[11]

Sergeant Laurie O'Dell, 12th Nelson Company, 1 Canterbury Battalion, who was awarded the Military Medal for his actions at the northern forester's house on 5 November 1918.
Archives New Zealand

This is achieved by 9 a.m., with the attackers taking five machine guns, one *minenwerfer* and numerous prisoners as part of the spoils. At this point the units of 62nd (2nd West Riding) Division to the north are still some 2300 metres behind the leading elements of Stitt's 1 Canterburys. The 2 Otagos are also held up on the right. However, Stitt's companies push on another 1400 metres toward the final objective. Stitt occupies the forester's house as his headquarters and this and the forest itself are subject to intense shelling by German artillery who have no means of taking back unused ammunition dumped by their guns and fire off what they have.

It is easy to get lost in the trees. Private Joel Hislop, a 22-year-old clothes presser from Sydenham, Christchurch, is a member of 13th Nelson Company in 1 Canterbury.[12] He is the last New Zealander to be taken prisoner in the First World War.

> I was taken prisoner in a wood near LE QUESNOY about 10.30 o'clock on the morning of November 6th. We had

gone through the wood and we were all scattered in twos and threes. I found myself alone, but I kept going on. In front of me was a heap of logs and I saw no Germans about, though when I got up to the logs about ten Huns jumped up and grabbed me.[13]

Deaths 1 Canterbury
GALPIN, George Henry 63596 Private
HEMSLEY, Albert Henry 62309 Private
HENDERSON, David 66167 Private
KELLY, Robert Dyson 38290 Lance-Corporal
LUCAS, Charles 62350 Private
McALLISTER, George Benjamin 15583 Private
McGEADY, James 4/1684 Private
PUTNAM, Philip Stanley 32378 Lance-Sergeant
WARD, Thomas Frederick 38324 Private

Hislop gives 6 November as his date of capture, however, it is more likely to have been 5 November. It is not reported to Headquarters NZEF in London until 27 November after his arrival with a batch of former prisoners in Dover on 23 November 1918 and it is now that his battalion is informed that he is alive. Hislop says he was sent under escort to the small Belgian town of Lobbes where he met with other New Zealanders. "The Germans gave us bread and barley water, and the Belgians gave us soup. I did not have to work. Three days later the armistice was signed, and, with others, I marched back to the British lines. I was treated alright."[14]

The 1 Canterburys advance to the Yellow Line as our young Canterbury officer records.

We had to fight for every yard of the way. Rushing from tree to tree, we kept the Hun going back and back. It was a wet day, and we were all soaked. The undergrowth was very hard to get through, especially in the face of machine gun and rifle fire. My word it was hard going! … It rained like fun — and so cold! I have never spent such a time — frozen to the bone, and not a dry stitch.[15]

On the western edge of a large clearing they are held up by German machine gun fire from both flanks and in particular from the edge of a large stand of trees on the right in the Otago sector. The 2 Otagos are advancing through the forest but are not yet up with 1 Canterbury. Stitt is conscious that his battalion is increasingly exposed on his northern flank as German infantry are reported massing to the north in 62nd Division's area and there are sounds of fighting to the south in 2 Otago's area.

2 CANTERBURY JOINS THE FIGHT

2 Canterbury is commanded by 30-year-old Waimate-born Major Newman Wilson, DSO, MC. A Gallipoli veteran, Wilson commanded an infantry company at Messines where he was badly wounded. He was awarded a Distinguished Service Order in the fighting around Bapaume in August 1918. He has been wounded five times and is regarded as a brave and skilled leader.[16]

On 4 November, Wilson's 2 Canterbury marches cross-country from Louvignies to the Le Quesnoy-Jolimetz road and through Jolimetz to its bivouac area west of Herbignies. Both battalions recall this march as one of the worst days of the war, and are exhausted when they finally halt for the night.

2 Canterbury follows up Stitt's battalion. Private John McFarlane is a 22-year-old clerk from Blenheim who, before enlisting, worked for New Zealand Loan and Mercantile. He arrived with the 24th Reinforcements and was posted to 12th Nelson Company on 25 October 1917.

A 6-inch howitzer of 90th (Heavy) Brigade, Royal Garrison Artillery, firing in support of the New Zealand Division in the final offensive. NZ RSA Collection, Photographer: Captain H.A. Sanders, NZEF Official H Series H540, Ref: 1/2-013155-G. Alexander Turnbull Library, Wellington, New Zealand'

[O]ur front was in an immense forest which is about 30 miles long and about half that distance wide. It is called the forest of "Mormal" and it is quite near the Belgian & French border. Our troops were about three parts thro it and we had to do the rest. Many machine guns were in it and the bullets flying about and striking the trees produced a very unpleasant feeling. He used a good many shells and they used to hit the trees and split them to pieces, so it was flying wood and iron. About 10 a.m. it came on to rain and it continued all day it turned the ground which the autumn leaves had covered into quite a bog.[17]

At 2 p.m. Brigadier-General Young, having had no word from Stitt, orders Wilson to pass through 1 Canterbury and continue the advance. However, Stitt has advanced almost to the Brown Line, reaching the last clearing before the eastern edge of the forest. The leading companies of 2 Canterbury face the same difficulties as its sister battalion. Contact is lost with Wilson's Battalion Headquarters. Indeed, they find Stitt established on the objective and initially place themselves under his command. Wilson moves forward and the two commanding officers arrange that 2 Canterbury will pass through with Stitt leaving one company on the northern boundary with 62nd Division.

This is achieved by 4 p.m. and Wilson's battalion is now holding the western edge of the large clearing with 2nd South Canterbury and 12th Nelson companies and 1st Canterbury on the northern edge of the wood. The remaining 13th Marlborough West Coast is further back. Patrols are sent forward to the eastern edge of the forest but it is evident that there are scattered German parties within the forest and as it is now dark, no further advance is attempted.

Private John McFarlane in 12th Nelson Company is on the left flank on the divisional boundary.

Deaths 2 Canterbury
AITKEN, John 6/3979 Private
BASHFORD, Herbert (served as Alfred MARTIN) 72075 Private
HOOD, William Roland Errol 73502 Private
McCLUNG, Gilbert Edward 70176 Private
PAINTER, Percival Ernest 73445 Private

We were held up several times with M[achine] Guns but about 11pm we got our objective. [I]t got pitch dark on us about 4 p.m. and one couldn't see a yard in front of him. It was the most disagreeable and worst stunt I have yet been in. The reason we did not get our objective earlier was that we had to wait for the tommies on our left flank who were unable to get forward owing to stronger opposition … However I can have the satisfaction of saying that I was in the last stunt the New Zealanders done in France.[18]

Young's brigade is relieved during the night by 126th Brigade of the 42nd Division. Stitt's 1 Canterbury marches at 8 p.m. direct to the barracks at Le Quesnoy. The young Canterbury platoon commander vividly recalls the march back to Le Quesnoy.

At last at 9.45 p.m. we were relieved, and we started off back on about a seven-mile march. The night was black and the forest made it worse. Up to our knees almost in mud, we trudged on and on. Oh that march! We had frequent spells and just flopped down where we were on the side of the road despite the mud. Eventually we reached our destination, Le Quesnoy, at about 5 a.m. The last two or three miles were cobbled roads, and our feet being wet the cobbles just tortured us. We got billets in the big barracks here, and soon were off to sleep — the first sleep for 48 hours![19]

Wilson's 2 Canterbury is not relieved till after midnight, and so halts at dawn at Herbignies for a hot meal. McFarlane describes the march out in his letter to his mother.

We got relieved by the tommies about midnight that night and we trekked our weary footsteps homeward. Hungry, wet, covered in mud, and far from home. We marched all the early hours of the morning and I for one was pretty well walking in my sleep. At daylight 6 a.m. we caught sight of the cooker with a hot feed of stew & tea. A N.Z. mail and above all a nice tot of rum. The last mentioned being most appreciated.[20]

The Canterbury regimental history sums it up.

Altogether the 5th/6th is one of the most exhausting days of the last phase of the war; for the advance in the rain all day — long though it was — was shorter than the march back to Le Quesnoy, but there they found comfortable billets, with fires to warm themselves and dry their clothes.[21]

Casualties in the Canterbury battalions since 23 October 1918 are: 1 Canterbury: two officers and 25 other ranks killed in action or died of wounds, nine of which result from 5 November, eight officers and 116 other ranks wounded (a total of ten officers and 141 other ranks); 2 Canterbury: two officers and 24 other ranks killed in action or died of wounds, five of which

The southern forester's house at the Carrefour du Cheval Blanc. Lieutenant-Colonel Hargest was standing in the doorway when he was stunned by an exploding shell. Barely had his men got him into the cellar when a shell blew down the wall of the house. It is now Auberge du Coucou. The road to Obies is the Black Line. Photograph: mapio@mapio.net

result from 5 November, two officers and 100 other ranks wounded (a total of four officers and 124 other ranks).[22]

2 OTAGO ADVANCES ON THE RIGHT

At 1.30 a.m. on 5 November the 10th North Otago and 14th South Otago Companies of Lieutenant-Colonel James 'Jimmy' Hargest's 2 Otago march from their overnight bivouac at Herbignies to take up positions 200 yards in rear of the front line of 1 Wellington along the general line of the road from Sarloton running south through Forêt de Mormal. Hargest is regarded as one of the outstanding battalion commanders in the New Zealand Division. He joined as a sergeant in August 1914, and was commissioned as a second lieutenant before embarkation. Badly wounded on Gallipoli, he returned to action as a company commander on the Western Front. Idolised by the men for his constant presence in the front-line trenches, he is heedless of danger. Edward Bibby is a company runner attached to Battalion Headquarters, 2 Otago.

> I used to go along the front line with Hargest, he was then a Major … he was acting Temporary CO in our Battalion. The runners didn't like him, he got in all sorts of little holes and in [situations] that might draw fire. He was popular … We didn't find him [too] severe.[23]

An Otago veteran recalls how the war has changed from earlier days.

> Very early in the November morning, which was fairly cold, the various battalions moved off to their "jumping off places" to wait for "zero" hour. It was the beginning of winter —the fifth winter of the war — and the

ground was damp and heavy. As we approached the forest it appeared dark and gloomy and we little knew what fate we might meet in its shade. The war had not been so hard of late — quite different from the early days of La Bassee Ville, Ploergsteert, and Passchendaele — and the Hun was not showing so much tenacity in his defence. His artillery was weak and he relied mostly on machine gun fire. There were few of us, however, who thought that this was to be our last fight. The war had gone on for so long that we had given up thinking of the finish. Yet, in our innermost self, we knew that some day we would win through, and the possession of this confidence —which, by the way, the New Zealand soldier always had in a very large measure — went a long way to keep up our spirits.[24]

Deaths 1 Otago
HAWLEY, William 47525 Private
HURLEY, Charles George 35023 Private
MATHERSON, Charles 9/1580 Private

Deaths 2 Otago
BLACKBURN, James Joseph 29728 Sergeant
FARQUHARSON, William Alexander 49366 Private
FIELD, Thomas Lucas 73576 Private
FLYNN, Michael 27870 Private
MARWICK, John Robert 46753 Private
NORTHAM, Robert Rowan 8/3724 Private
REID, John 71134 Private
RUSBATCH, Hubert 72193 Private
SALISBURY, Charles Arthur 41630 Private
SAVAGE, Richard Attlesey 8/727 2nd Lieutenant
TODD, George Johnston 39358 Private
WALKER, Allen Richard 59766 Lance-Corporal
WILLIAMS, Samuel; 11762 Private

At 5.30 a.m. it all starts with the artillery barrage exploding some 500 yards ahead of the leading troops. It fires until 6 a.m. to enable the Canterburys, who are on the left with further to go, to come up. The barrage jumps twice every ten minutes and then stops. The battalions go on without it, moving forward — each company with two platoons up, each with a section patrol with Lewis guns out in front. If they strike trouble, it allows the platoon commander to respond by moving the rest of his sections round to a flank and attack. The first difficulty for the quietly cursing infantry is the dense scrub three to four metres high instead of the cleared ground they expect. The Otago chronicler records:

> In groups of sections we moved slowly forward, fully prepared for instant action with a foe we had got to know well. We went slowly forward, and by the time we had gone about a mile the darkness had lifted and it was fairly light. Then, about a mile ahead of us, we saw some German cavalry — the first most of us had seen in the war — galloping at top speed along a road. Our Lewis guns spat at them and made them ride faster. A loud explosion explained their mission. They had been laying mines in the road to delay our advance, and in some instances the holes made were over 20 ft deep. The cavalry went quickly out of sight and we were unopposed for another mile.[25]

The first opposition is encountered at what becomes known as the southern forester's house. "Suddenly … some Germans ran out from some undergrowth at the side, quickly put a machine gun in position, and opened fire. To make matters worse rain fell heavily, and soon everyone was very wet … we outflanked the guns and dealt with the crews.[26]

It was here that the Hargest confirms again his battle leadership, moving on horseback from company to company to assess the situation and to keep the movement going forward. Sixty years later his former adjutant Colonel Bill Murphy tells of his exploits, stating he is the finest leader he has ever served under, one with an instinct for knowing where things were going wrong and where he needed to be.[27]

SAVAGE.—Lieut. R. A. Savage (Dick), Main Body, Otago Regiment, killed in action Mormal Forest, Le Quesnoy, 6th November, 1918.

Lieutenant Dick Savage was killed in the fighting for the southern forester's house on 5 November 1918. *Evening Post,* 6 November 1919

The two leading companies — 10th North Otago on the left and 14th South Otago on the right — outflank the house and the German positions on the higher ground behind it. A 10th Company patrol led by Second Lieutenant Dick Savage gets to within 46 metres of the house but is driven back by machine gun and rifle fire. Savage, a Main Body Gallipoli veteran, and one of his patrol, are killed. Both companies attack the German position from the rear, capturing two machine guns and 30 prisoners.[28] By now it is 11 a.m. The companies reorganise and the advance continues. Hargest establishes his headquarters in the forester's house, which is heavily shelled. One bursts at the front of the house near to where Hargest is standing and stuns him. His men quickly bustle him into the cellars. A following shell then destroys the front of the house.

"The advance was continued, despite some gas and other shells fired by the enemy, and by the afternoon we were clear of the forest."[29] It is in this section and platoon-level manoeuvre and skirmishing that the quality of the junior leadership within the battalion stands out. Lieutenant Fraser McIntosh, a 30-year-old farmer from Fairfax in Southland, commands the two leading platoons of 8th Southland Company. A member of the 27th Reinforcements, McIntosh arrived in France on 2 November 1917. In 12 months of active service he was three times wounded in action, but accepts that this is the price of being a platoon commander. On 5 November when the troops on his flank are held up, he pushes his platoons forward "with great dash" as the citation for his Military Cross states. "Later he encountered five enemy machine guns in succession, and after skilfully outmanoeuvring them he led the charge on each occasion and so captured four machine guns and twenty-six prisoners."[30]

Similarly in 14th South Otago Company, Gallipoli veteran Sergeant Leonard Dickinson, MM, a 30-year-old shipping clerk from Remuera, Auckland, charges forward with his platoon against a German position, killing a number and capturing 26 prisoners. He attacks a second group, disperses them, but is wounded in the fighting.[31]

The Brown Line, the road running south from Bavay, is reached. Patrols push forward to the western bank of the Sambre River. Two companies of 1 Otago move up to provide protection on each flank — 4th Otago Company on the right and 8th Southland Company on the left. The Germans are being thrown back in a rush by the speed of the advance, as our Otago chronicler records.

Coming in view of a small village, a number of Huns ran down the main street, and were followed by bullets. Little French boys who had been under German oppression since 1914 ran into the road and jumped into the air for sheer joy. The joy of deliverance made their eyes glisten. They could hardly constrain themselves as they cried: "Vive la Francais, Vive la Angleterre," and waved their arms. Women and old men came out of the houses on either side of the road, and gazed upon the khaki, for the sight of which they had waited patiently for so long.[32]

The soldiers are overwhelmed by the civilian response.

In the village of Pont de [sur] Sambre a Corporal rushed into a house in search of any Germans who might be hiding. A half-eaten meal on the kitchen table testified to the hurried exit of the enemy. Hearing a noise in the house, the Corporal listened attentively, and came to the conclusion that it was someone sobbing down in the cellar of the house. It was French women in terror as to what would happen next to them. Using his best French, the Corporal called out that he and his comrades were "Soldats de Anglaise", and at once three tear-stained French girls rushed up and threw their arms around his neck in a paroxysm of joy.[33]

Bobby Young's 2nd Brigade achieves its objectives: 2 Auckland is picketing the northern flank; 2 Canterbury and 2 Otago are on the Bavay road with patrols forward overlooking the Sambre River. Lewis gunners meanwhile make havoc on German soldiers withdrawing back to the river.

At midnight 5/6 November the New Zealanders are relieved by 42nd Division. Young is forward with his brigade signals officer, the recently commissioned but very experienced Second Lieutenant James Sawers, and stays on to assist the incoming brigade. That same evening, the adjutant of 2 Auckland, Boer War and Main Body Gallipoli veteran Captain George Tuck, writes in his diary:

I am sitting writing this in a French farm house on the north-western edge of the Forêt de Mormal. Le Quesnoy is many miles [7 kilometres as a fact] to the west & in front lives Bavay, about 5000 yards [4572 metres] east & 19000 yards [17,374 metres] east of here is Mauberge. The Division has done extraordinarily well & a large number of prisoners has been taken, also many M.G.s & field guns ... In the operations the Rifle Brigade took a definite line running on the west of Le Quesnoy; they then advanced past the South of the Town while the 1st Brigade — 1st Auckland on the right — advanced past the north of the place. 1st Auckland then finishing on their right wheeled right round to the south east & met the Rifles Brigade. Le Quesnoy was surrounded. The 1st Brigade then pushed on due east at a rapid pace, while the 3rd Brigade mopped up the town. Our Brigade were advancing six miles east of Le Quesnoy while a few deluded Bosch were still firing M.G.s in the place. It was not completely subdued until evening. By night our men had advanced further than the line laid down as being the limit of exploitation. We were far past the flank divisions.[34]

2 Auckland too have casualties on this day. One of these is Private John Raynor, a 34-year-old Australian bridge builder. He was working at Kawhia when he enlisted in March 1916. He sailed with the 14th Reinforcements and on arrival in the UK was immediately in trouble. He was court-martialled at Bulford Camp in September 1916 for being absent without leave, resisting arrest, drunkenness and, to cap it all off, conduct to the prejudice of good order and military discipline in telling the military police that they can go and "fuck themselves".[35] Given the weight of evidence the cards are stacked against him and Raynor pleaded guilty and gave this plea in mitigation of sentence. "My trouble has been caused

FOR THE EMPIRE'S CAUSE.

IN MEMORIAM.

HURLEY.—In loving memory of Charles George Hurley, who was killed near Le Quesnoy, November 5, 1918, second son of James and Alice Hurley, Wendonside; in his 31st year.—Inserted by his loving parents, brothers, and sisters.

MATHEISEN.—In loving memory of my dear brother, Charlie, who was killed in action at Le Quesnoy, France, on November 5, 1918.
He gave his life—it was his all—
    That Freedom still might live;
No greater love, no greater gift
    Hath any man to give.
    Nobly fighting, nobly fell.
—Inserted by his loving mother and brother.

REID.—In loving memory of our dear son and brother, 71134—Private J. Reid (35th Reinforcements), who was killed in action near Mormal Wood, November 5, 1918.
One year has gone since that sad day
    When our dear son was called away;
It was God's will, it must be so,
    At His command we all must go.
Could I, his mother, have clasped his hand,
    The son I loved so well;
To stroke his brow when death was nigh
    And whisper, "Jack, farewell."
Just when his life was brightest,
    Just when his hopes were best,
His Country called, and he answered,
    And now in God's hands he rests.
—Inserted by his sorrowing parents, sisters, and brother.

RIDLAND.—In loving memory of Bombardier William Thomas Ridland (5th Battery), who died at sea on November 5, 1915; aged 26 years.
When we see the boys returning
    Our hearts doth throb with pain,
To think that you're not there, dear Will,
    And will never come back again.
The war is really over,
    To some those words seem nice,
But, Oh! the sad, sad hearts of those
    Whose loved ones paid the price.
—Inserted by his loving mother, brother, and sister.

TODD.—In loving memory of Private G. J. Todd (22nd Reinforcements), who was killed in action at Forresters' House, Mormal Forest, November 5, 1918; aged 21 years.
While you rest in peaceful sleep
    Your memory I will always keep.
—Inserted by M. Vickers.

WARD.—In loving memory of Private Thomas Fredrick Ward, 21st C.I. Reinforcements, who was killed in action at Mormal Forest, November 5, 1918, youngest son of Edmund and Ruth Ward, Otekura.
He lies beside his comrades,
    In a grave we'll never see,
But as long as life and memory last
    We will remember thee.
—Inserted by his parents.

WARD.—In loving memory of our dear brother, Private T. F. Ward (Tom), No. 38324, C.I.B., who was killed in action in the Mormal Forest on November 5, 1918.
Time will heal the broken-hearted,
    Time may make the wound less sore,
But time can never stop the longing
    For our dear one gone before.
—Inserted by his loving sisters.

WARD.—In loving memory of Private Thomas Fredrick Ward (38324, 21st Reinforcements), who was killed in action in Mormal Forest on November 5, 1918.
True hearts that held you in fondest affection
Always shall love you in death just the same.
—Inserted by M. E.

WILLIAMS.—In loving memory of our dear sons and brothers— Rifleman W. D. J. (Billy) Williams (42nd Reinforcements), who died from pneumonia at Cannock Chase Hospital, England, November 5, 1918; aged 27 years; also, his dear brother, Thomas Robert (Tommy) Williams, who died at Hawera, North Island, July 6, 1904; aged 17 years.
Two precious ones from us have gone,
    The voices we loved are stilled;
Two places are vacant in our home
    Which never can be filled.
—Inserted by their loving parents, sisters, and brother.

Otago Daily Times,
5 November 1919, p. 4

Bringing in the last of the German wounded.
Photographer: Captain H.A. Sanders, NZEF Official H Series, ID: PH-ALB-420, Auckland War Memorial Museum Tamaki Paenga Hira

entirely by drink. I got drunk soon after breaking bounds and committed these offenses when I was badly under the influence of drink. I quite realise that I have done wrong and am prepared to take my sentence as a soldier ..."[36]

Raynor joined 2 Auckland in France and was constantly in trouble. In April 1917 he was sentenced to 90 days' Field Punishment No. 1 for insubordination and absence without leave. He was detached to the 3rd Canadian Tunnelling Company working underground on preparations for the Battle of Messines. He rejoined 2 Auckland after the battle and immediately went absent again on 12 June 1917. Seven weeks later Raynor was picked up by military police in Bailleul, without any ID discs or paybook. He appeared before a field general court martial convened by Brigadier-General Melvill commanding 1st Brigade on a charge of desertion. Raynor made no defence. His six absences without leave since arriving in France and now this seven-week absence spoke for itself. He was found guilty of desertion and sentenced to death. General Plumer commanding Second Army, perhaps mindful of the good work of the tunnellers at Messines and also that of the New Zealand Division, confirmed the sentence, but commutes it to ten years' penal servitude and suspends it, so that it remains as a sword of Damocles over Raynor's head. He remained with 2 Auckland but was wounded in November 1917. On recovery he was posted as storeman at the New Zealand Infantry and General Base Depot at Étaples. However, the quiet life is not for him, he got in constant drink-related trouble and was sent under escort to 1 Entrenching Battalion. He rejoined 2 Auckland and was again wounded on 1 September 1918. He joined his battalion again on 15 October, and receives a gunshot wound to the neck in Forêt de Mormal on 5 November. He is admitted to 3 Field Ambulance and transferred to 21 Casualty Clearing Station at Caudry where he dies of wounds on 7 November 1918.[37]

It is the end of active operations for the South Island brigade, and for the infantry of the New Zealand Division, but this will only be obvious in the days ahead. The New Zealand artillery remains forward and for the moment are the only artillery support available to 42nd Division.

Brigadier-General Bobby Young is the second territorial officer to command an infantry brigade in the New Zealand Division; Hart is the first. Now he hands over to the incoming British formation and brings out the last New Zealand battalions to see action in the First World War.[38]

Our chronicler in 2 Otago captures the mood.

> Before dark we "dug in" on the outskirts of the village and were not annoyed by the enemy. He was in full retreat. "Tommies" of the 42nd English Division arrived a few hours later to relieve us, and greeted us with "Where's Jerry Noo Zealand?" "He's gone chum," we answered; "He's had enough," as we marched away with the prospect of a few days rest in a comfortable village ahead of us before we would again be called upon to join in the chase. However, the Armistice was signed while we were resting in Le Quesnoy, and we saw no more fighting.[39]

A pleased Major-General Sir Andrew Russell summarises the day's events: "Attacked at daylight — not much resistance met and were able to reach outer edge of Wood before they handed over to the 42nd during the night."[40] Brigadier-General Bobby Young's 2nd Brigade advanced against little resistance until the forester's house and then working through the forest "fighting from tree to tree, until dusk, when our outpost line was established on the PONT SUR SAMBRE-BAVAI road … About 100 prisoners were captured during the day and the total distance covered was some 7,500 yards [6858 metres] over very difficult wooded country."[41]

IN MEMORIAM.

RAE.—In loving memory of our dear brother, Second Lieutenant T. H. Rae, killed in action at Le Quesnoy, November 4, 1918. To memory ever dear.
—Inserted by his loving brother and sister, Frank and Lottie Rae, Buckland.

RAE.—In sad and loving memory of our dear brother, Second Lieutenant T. H. Rae, who was killed in the attack on Le Quesnoy on November 4, 1918. Sadly missed.
—Inserted by his loving brother and sister-in-law, J. P. and G. E. Rae.

RAE.—In sad and loving memory of our dear son, Second Lieutenant Thomas Handley Rae, N.Z.R.B., aged 26 years, who was killed during the attack on Le Quesnoy on November 4, 1918.—A dutiful son. Sadly missed.
He bravely answered duty's call.
He gave his life for one and all;
His heart was true, his spirit brave.
His resting place a soldier's grave.
—Inserted by his sorrowing parents, Thomas and Annie Rae, Beresford St., Pukekohe.

STUART.—On November 5, 1918, killed in action at Le Quesnoy, Corporal G. Leslie Stuart, D.C.M., dearly-beloved and only son of Mrs. G. Stuart, Northern Wairoa.
Loved by all. Nobly done his duty.
—Inserted by his loving mother and sisters.

Each anniversary of the battle the papers carry their names.
New Zealand Herald, 5 November 1923, p. 1

Deaths 2 Auckland
JONES, Harold Hazelwood 57583 Private
LYONS, Pierce 70305 Private
RAYNOR, John 14864 Private
STUART, Godfrey Leslie 24076 Corporal

Chapter 6

THE GUNS REMAIN

"Dull day, rain slight moved off again, further forward, muddy roads, heavy traffic. Passed many dead horses and huns in field at Le Quesnoy, then went on to Le Carnoy billeted in barns, another trip to guns at midnight."[1]

This is the diary entry for 5 November 1918 by Driver Sidney Anton, a 21-year-old ironmonger from Brooklyn, Wellington. Anton's leather-bound diary has a series of cryptic entries. He joined No. 1 Battery, 1st Brigade, New Zealand Field Artillery, the day before, and finds himself pitchforked into his first and also his last battle of the Great War.[2] His job is to keep the guns fed with ammunition with his mule-drawn ammunition limber that carries 38 rounds of 18-pounder ammunition. His team of mules or 'donks' as he calls them, are more sure-footed than horses in the winter mud. Anton is based in the brigade wagon lines, which, with the rapid infantry advance, is constantly on the move to keep in touch with the guns.

In the early hours of the morning of 5 November the guns of the New Zealand Divisional Artillery are in position to support the attack by Young's 2nd Infantry Brigade through Forêt de Mormal. This began before dawn at 5.30 a.m. with No. 1 Battery firing in support of 2 Otago who encounter no opposition. The battery again comes into action and fire a barrage at 10.30 a.m. to assist 2 Otago take the southern forester's house. No. 3 and No. 15 Batteries of 1st Brigade move forward. As does 2nd Brigade, which consists of Nos 2, 5 and 9 Batteries of 18-pounder field guns and No. 6 Howitzer Battery. It is hard going for the columns of horse-drawn guns and limbers on muddy roads made worse by the drizzling rain.

The chronicler of No. 15 Howitzer Battery records that the forest "was quite a large pine forest and at the cross roads in the wood the road had been mined and blown up but it was not a big job to chop more trees down".[3] A section of the 2 Field Company New Zealand Engineers accompanies the artillery. Though much of the forest has been felled, thick undergrowth has grown in its place. A large number of trees have been deliberately dropped across the roads. "A champion axeman among the sappers had great opportunities of displaying his skill, and the speed with which he went through his blocks completely fascinated passing Tommies."[4] The Germans demolish the bridges over the boggy rides, some of which are mined.

A New Zealand 4.5-inch howitzer in action at Le Quesnoy, 29 October 1918.
NZ RSA Collection, Photographer: Captain H.A. Sanders, NZEF Official H Series, H1113, Ref: 1/2-013670-G, Alexander Turnbull Library, Wellington, New Zealand

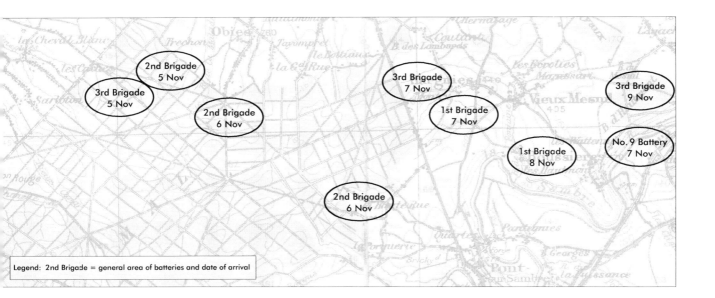

Legend: 2nd Brigade = general area of batteries and date of arrival

New Zealand Field
Artillery locations,
5–9 November 1918.

Engineers clear the trees and construct an improvised bridge of branches and pick handles to allow the guns to cross. This worked until "a clumsily driven waggon capsized into the stream and wrecked the makeshift crossing".[5]

James Hutchinson in No. 5 Battery, 2nd Brigade, writes:

> Stunt in morning 5.30 on. Moved about 8 a.m. Rendezvoused two or three times, finally came into action about 4 p.m. in centre of Forêt de Mormal 6500 yds as crow flies due E[ast]. of this morning's position. Enemy shelled us with whizz bangs from close range on left, which is not at all secure as we are well forward in a salient. Most unpleasant as we could not dig down at all, as whole place was water immed[iately] under surface. 3 men wounded, 1 gassed. Raining heavily all day. Beastly rotten day. Transport hampered by heavy going and shortage of horses.[6]

By the end of the day the guns are halfway through the forest supporting the infantry who have reached the eastern edge and are involved in bursts of fighting before securing the Brown Line. Patrols go forward to reconnoitre the villages on the Sambre River.

On this night 5/6 November Young's 2nd Brigade is relieved by the British 42nd Division, but, as usual, the guns remain forward in support, as the artillery columns of the relieving division are still negotiating their way forward. Hutchinson is on duty in the battery command post during the night. "Had control last night between two logs and slept fairly dry considering. Fortunately [German] battery that was shelling us captured soon after dark, and night was quiet."[7]

The following morning 6 November there are enough guns of 2nd Brigade to support the attack by 42nd Division as they cross the Sambre and advance on the important communications junction of Maubeuge. Hutchinson records:

> Stunt 6 a.m. Stood by till about 3 p.m. Waiting for makeshift bridge to be made. Raining incessantly still. Moved about 3 p.m. rendezvoused, going frightful. Finally came into action 7 p.m. in pitch dark on E[astern]. edge of Foret still in sodden ground, everybody wet and cold only half the

amm[unition]. Waggons up, no rations but still going strong.[8]

Finally that evening almost all of the guns of 2nd Brigade are through the forest and in action, and the remaining two New Zealand artillery brigades are moving forward. Driver Sidney Anton's ammunition limber of No. 1 Battery is part of this column. At one of the temporary bridges disaster strikes. His diary records: "Stuck at bridge for 2 hours 4 donkeys went over with me, landed out safe with a slight kick, had to shoot donk[s] and had to go back the next day for harness & waggon."[9]

The New Zealand Division also has 90th (Heavy) Brigade, Royal Garrison Artillery, with three batteries of 6-inch howitzers. If the field guns of the artillery found the roads through the forest difficult, the heavy batteries found moving the guns forward almost impossible. Captain Arthur Behrend, the brigade adjutant, writes of this day:

the roads which passed through it were so few and so poor that for the first time in our existence the guns of the brigade were unable to follow-up. Toc 2 [Second Battery] contrived to send forward two hows. [howitzers] which were in action in the middle of the Forest on November 6 and 7, and the Colonel himself helped to haul No. 2 into position, the last of the brigade's guns to fire a round in the war. The bridges over the Sambre had been destroyed, and no further advance proved possible.[10]

Deaths New Zealand Engineers
FRY, Raymond Thomas 4/1780 Sapper
O'BRIEN, Lawrence John 55114 Sapper

Deaths New Zealand Divisional Signals Company
CHAMBERS, Douglas Harvey 43581 Sapper
REDMOND, Jesse Thomas 59983 Sapper
TWEEDY, Glenholme Francis 36193 Sapper

New Zealand Engineers and Maori Pioneers manoeuvring one of the heavy 6-inch guns around a German mine crater. NZ RSA Collection, Photographer: Captain H.A. Sanders, NZEF Official, H Series H1074, Ref: 1/2-013637-G, ATL, Alexander Turnbull Library, Wellington, New Zealand

The unveiling of the roll of honour of the Mosgiel Volunteer Fire Brigade took place at the Fire Station on Sunday morning, in the presence of firemen, councillors, and the public. The unveiling was performed by the Rev. D. Calder, who spoke of the good record of service of firemen in the Great War, one having made the supreme sacrifice and others bearing the scars of battle. Part of the honour board consists of an enlarged photograph of the late Fireman D. S. Kennedy, who was killed in France two days before the armistice was signed. The Rev. Mr Weston offered a prayer, and the singing of 'God Save the King' concluded the service. The firemen afterwards fell in with the friendly societies' commemorative church parade, the service being held in the Mosgiel Presbyterian Church.

Top: Gunner Donald Stewart Kennedy, New Zealand Field Artillery.
Euan Kennedy

Above: *Otago Daily Times*, 16 December 1921, p. 10

On 7 November Hutchinson reflects on the work of the guns over the previous days.

> Last 2 days frightfully rough. Worked out stunt last night and got to bed 4.30 p.m. Stunt 8.15 a.m. Rations up in time for breakfast, amm. up too, and things generally pretty cheery, though still drizzling rain at intervals. Advance still going. Someone else going through us to-day as advance guard artillery. Our position about 5000 yds. in advance again of last one. Got a shave & a wash, and dried things up. Wrote home.[11]

THE LAST TO DIE IN ACTION

No. 2 Battery suffers its last casualties on 7 November. The battery comes under fire some hours before it withdraws into reserve on 7 November 1918. A shell burst alongside one of the guns kills three of the crew and wounds a fourth. Gunners Donald Stewart Kennedy and Frank Gardner and Driver Andrew Mather are killed and Gunner Stanley Ayling, a 31-year-old plasterer from Sydenham, Christchurch, is wounded by shell fragments to the left arm and hand.[12]

These are the last soldiers of the New Zealand Division to be killed in action in this war. Others will die of wounds received earlier in the fighting, by accident, or from the Spanish Flu that has started to cut its second swathe through all of the armies, but these are the last three New Zealanders to die in battle. Euan Kennedy wrote to me of the impact that the death of Donald Stewart Kennedy or Stewart, as he was known, had on his family:

> My grandmother never overcame her grief. She had received Donald Stewart's older brother home in late 1917. He had been very badly wounded on the Somme. No doubt her hopes of having her other son home had grown as news of the German retreat reached New Zealand. Donald Stewart's younger sister, my aunt, told me that her mother wore black for the remainder of her life and found images of him too painful to have in the house.[13]

Chaplain Alex Jermyn is the padre attached to 2nd Brigade. He writes to Mr Kennedy on 8 November 1918.

> Long before this letter reaches you, you will have received the sad news of your son's death. He was killed up at the guns on the 6th, this morning we brought his body back to the little village of Villereau, behind the line and we buried him in the shadow of the old village church.[14]

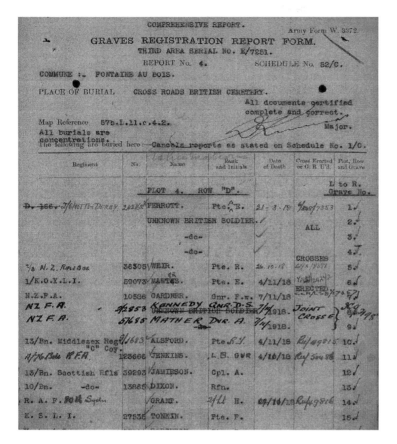

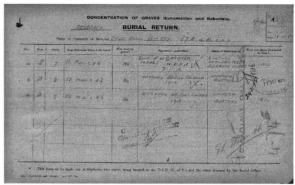

Left: Graves Registration Report Form, Cross Roads Cemetery, Fontaine-au-Bois, a cemetery formed from the many small cemeteries that dotted the route of the final advance. The stories of the New Zealand dead are told in the deletions and additions. Commonwealth War Graves Commission website

Above: Burial Return for the three New Zealanders exhumed from Villereau churchyard and reburied at Cross Roads Cemetery, Fontaine-au-Bois. The nature of the buttons may have been one of the clues in identifying Gunner Donald Stewart Kennedy and Driver Andrew Mather as New Zealanders. Commonwealth War Graves Commission website

The padre, with a list of letters to write to the next-of-kin of the brigade dead, got the date of death wrong; it applies to Gunner William Rutherford who was killed the day before. The bodies are wrapped in blankets and placed under a canvas tarpaulin in the wagon lines and then taken back through the forest. At the village church in Villereau the padre and burial party conduct a brief service for their dead, before moving back to the guns.

Donald Stewart Kennedy, a 25-year-old clerk from Mosgiel who enlisted in 1915, is buried together with Driver Andrew Mather, a 37-year-old bushman from Tasmania who was working in Wanganui.[15] Alongside lies Gunner Frank Gardner, a 28-year-old sheep farmer from Rakauroa.[16] After the war the bodies are disinterred and reburied in a concentration-cemetery at Cross Roads Cemetery at Fontaine-au-Bois. The cemetery is the site chosen to gather up and concentrate the scattered dead from the small cemeteries and churchyards that mark the route of the final advance. Gunner Frank Gardner is buried under his name, however, both Kennedy and Mather are initially listed as 'Unknown British soldiers' when they are disinterred. Whatever markings that were in place on the graves at the time of burial have been obliterated or vanished in the intervening years. The Kennedy family was shocked to hear that the location of Stewart's grave was lost. It is not until 13 August 1925 that cards are raised confirming the identities of the two soldiers who were buried in plot 4, row D, graves 8 and 9. The Grave Registration Report Form tells this story. Visit the cemetery today and Gunner Donald Stewart Kennedy and Driver Andrew Mather are identified by name in two adjoining graves, each with a separate headstone, but in 1925 the Imperial War Graves Commission staff are unable to identify which one is in each grave.

The headstones of Gunner Frank Gardner, Gunner Donald Stewart Kennedy, and Driver Andrew Mather, No. 2 Battery, 2nd Brigade, New Zealand Field Artillery, all killed by the same shell burst on 7 November 1918, the last New Zealanders of the New Zealand Division to be killed by enemy action. They lie alongside each other in Cross Roads Cemetery, Fontaine-au-Bois. Harakeke flax crosses have been placed at the foot of each grave. This was the initiative of Dolores Ho, Archivist National Army Museum, Waiouru. National Army Museum Waiouru

This is a glimpse into one family's story, but it reflects a universal agony in every home in every country on every side of this needless conflict. As Euan Kennedy concludes in his correspondence:

For me the need to know is very personal. Donald Stewart's death has a century-long reach into my understanding of my family and who I am. My brother too. Donald Stewart was the only one of the six Kennedy uncles we never got to meet. In my middle name, my father remembered the brother he had known for only eight years. One hundred years on, I am connected to the conflict through his service and loss. I owe it to him to care about what happened.[17]

The New Zealand artillery batteries of all three brigades remain forward. On 8 November it is still drizzling down and the wagon lines move up to the guns. The following day Hutchinson writes: "Final balance of W.L.'s [wagon lines] arrived, also our two waggons salvaged from creek. Glorious later autumn day, sun shining though still, of course, frightful under foot. Had a bath. The civiles here are still as pleased as they were the first day we arrived and do anything for us."[18]

The batteries of 1st Brigade carry out some harassing fire from the gun lines south of Hargnies on 7 November and move forward to Boussieres on 8 November where they fire their last rounds.[19] No. 9 Battery of 2nd Brigade remains in action until 9 November with its gun line on the outskirts of Hautmont, southwest of Maubeuge. Similarly No. 11 Battery, 3rd Brigade, is providing close support to the infantry until 3rd Brigade is relieved by 14th Brigade, Royal Horse Artillery. The New Zealanders go into billets at Hautmont.[20]

These are the last New Zealand guns in action on the Western Front. Fresh with a new team and wagon, Driver Sidney Anton is carting ammunition forward to No. 1 Battery, 1st Brigade. On 9 November he records, "Fine day. Grooming horses and shifting lines to drier spot and then all moved back to a bivvy near Hautmont. Fixed things up for a stay for awhile. Billeted in houses." These are easy days and the war has moved on. Anton has time to have a look around. "Went into Hartmont badly knocked about."[21] Hutchinson in No. 5 Battery records 10 November as being

Deaths New Zealand Field Artillery
GARDNER, Frank Warren *10586 Gunner*
KENNEDY, Donald Stewart *2/2853 Gunner*
MATHER, Andrew *57685 Driver*
RUTHERFORD, William *11/2217 Driver*

> Another glorious day, the first white frost of the season on the ground in the morning. The war seems to have rolled on and left us here in a backwash. Guns sounding very distantly on the front. It's pretty decent. Football the go to-day. 2nd beat 9th 6–3, 6th beat us 9–nil. We had pretty stiff luck, and were a weak team at any rate. Had another bath after the football. Parcel, sox & tin of tobacco dated Sept. 5 arrived. Marching orders for to-morrow back towards Le Quesnoy to Div.[22]

Driver Ernest Looms has set up his saddler's workshop for No. 11 Battery, 3rd Brigade, near Hautmont when the news of the Armistice trickles out.

> Next day Nov 11th proved eventually to be the day of days although at the time it was really not exciting. One of the Tommy soldiers came along in the morning and told us that the Armistice was to be signed at 11 o'clock. The news was received with as much enthusiasm as if he had said it was a fine day. Later, one of our officers repeated the news. Some believed it but the greater number didn't. We were getting ready to move out, going back this time for a spell and on a parade a few minutes before we moved off at 10.30 a.m. our Captain Todd gave it to us as official news that an Armistice would be signed at 11 o'clock. Half a dozen joyful souls performed a haka, but the remainder, for the most part took it with the same stolidity as if it had been an extra picquet.[23]

Bombardier Cyril Clark and his colleagues write in similar spirit in their informal history of No. 15 Battery. "On the 11th of November at 11 a.m., cease fire was enforced and the Armistice was signed so ended the conflict. But what a cold miserable day, no rum, little rations, and no cigarettes and little cheering."[24]

New Zealand 18-pounder battery in action in the open in 1918. This was typical of the New Zealand artillery experience in 1918. NZ RSA Collection, Photographer: Captain H.A. Sanders, NZEF Official H Series H1017, Ref: 1/2-013583-G, Alexander Turnbull Library, Wellington, New Zealand

Chapter 7

'I OWE IT TO HIM TO CARE ABOUT WHAT HAPPENED'

As soon as the German garrison surrendered, tricolours appeared at every window, and the French population flocking out of their shelters under the ramparts went joyfully hysterical. When the 4th Rifles band paraded in the square next morning and played the Marseillaise, the excitement was indescribable.[1]

As Major Lindsay Inglis' memoir details, the French civilians in Le Quesnoy do everything within their limited means that they can for their deliverers. After being feted on the evening of 4 November, Barrowclough's 4 Rifles parade the following day for brigade commander Brigadier-General Hart and divisional commander Major-General Russell in Place d'Armes. They then march out of the town and as Inglis happily records, "and for one night the Otago M.G. Company were the only troops in Le Quesnoy. What a night!"[2]

At 2 p.m. on 10 November, President Raymond Poincaré of the French Republic makes a ceremonial visit to the town. The New Zealand Guard of Honour is mounted by 2nd Brigade who are billeted in the town, "and the population went mad once more".[3]

The square is crowded with troops and civilians. New Zealand bands play "Le Marseillaise" and the crowds cheer. Allied flags flutter above the crowd, with the New Zealand flag most prominent of all. Planes fly overhead. Poincaré addresses the crowd and assures them that the Germans will pay for the damage they have done to France. As Malcolm Ross records, Poincaré adds, "Citizens of Quesnoy, you owe your liberty to the action of the Allied armies and notably to the New Zealand troops who are assembled here to-day."[4]

In this last week of the war the dead too are honoured. In the rain on 6 November the commanding officers, company commanders and 12 men per company from each of 1 and 2 Wellingtons attend the funeral of

Major-General Sir Andrew Russell commanding the New Zealand Division, entering Le Quesnoy, France, in the early morning on 5 November 1918, the day after its capture. The building on the left is the city hall that was destroyed by artillery fire. It is the only building deliberately bombarded to destroy its tower, which gave the Germans observation in all directions. NZ RSA Collection, Photographer: Captain H.A. Sanders, NZEF Official H Series H1157, Ref:1/2-013708-G, Alexander Turnbull Library, Wellington, New Zealand

The remaining inhabitants of Le Quesnoy crowd round the regimental band of Major Barrowclough's 4 Rifles as it plays the Marseillaise in the Place d'Armes on 5 November 1918, the day after its liberation. The three-storey brick building in the background is the former German Headquarters during the occupation. NZ RSA Collection, Photographer: Captain H.A. Sanders, NZEF Official H Series H1153, Ref: 1/2-013705-G, Alexander Turnbull Library, Wellington, New Zealand

the Adjt (Lieut, A.R. BLENNERHASSETT) and of Major H.E. MCKINNON, M.C. (Acting C.O. 2nd Wellington), Lieut. S.A. MURRELL (Adjutant 2nd Wellington), and two other officers and several men of 2nd Wellington, all of whom were killed on the 4th, and who were all buried in LE QUESNOY Cemetery.[5] A firing party from 2nd Wellington fired three volleys over the graves after the ceremony, which was conducted by the Rev. Mortimer-Jones (1st Bn), Rev. Brown (2nd Well) and Rev. Segrief (formerly 3rd Well). The Brigadier and Brigade Major attended the ceremony.[6]

Monty Ingram records the service.

Our C.O., Major McKinnon, and many other officers and men were buried this afternoon in Le Quesnoy cemetery with full military honours. Our padres spoke very strongly and feelingly about the desecration of our dead. When the body of the C.O. was brought in yesterday morning, the puttees and boots had been ratted and his pockets rifled. This was a beastly act and is decried by all. Though he was a 'hard' man and not loved by the men, he was a game soldier and as much should have been respected in his long last sleep. His death is a great loss to the Battalion.[7]

Had this been a German officer or soldier, the 'ratting' of the dead man's effects and the rifling of his pockets would not raise an eyebrow among the Diggers. They see this as the rightful spoils of war with the dead having no more use for them. Whoever did the deed had a life to lead and a paybook to nurse. It is an interesting perspective on the singularity of what is seen as fair. Given that the

Music written in honour of the New Zealanders who liberated Le Quesnoy. Chris Bourke

Townsfolk of Le Quesnoy to their Liberators
Translation by Raymonde Dramez
We all greet you with our songs of elation
Fourth of November O, Day that our hearts desire!
O, Day, when we saw in our stronghold
The victorious Allies jump up on over ramparts,
O, unforgettable day, when the town of Le Quesnoy
Spewing out from her breast the loathed enemy
After 50 months of Prussian invasion
Was given back to France and to Liberty

Chorus (twice)
Glory to our "poilus"
Glory to the French soul
Glory to the Tommies, to the American Nation
Glory to the New Zealand Fern
Which delivered the oak of Le Quesnoy

bodies lay within the area that the New Zealand Division controls then there is every possibility that a New Zealander or New Zealanders did the 'ratting', however, the immediate assumption is that it had to be a 'Hun'.

William McKeon is recovering at No. 2 General Hospital at Brockenhurst on the borders of the New Forest.

> We were home. For us the war was over. We could be sent back when we were well again, but we had ideas that there would be no necessity for this. We lay quietly in our beds, surrounded by comfort and kindliness, making up for all the sleep we had lost, all the fatigue and pain we had suffered.
>
> News of the Division came through; of its triumphant progress in the great advance; of the incredible capture of the fortress of Le Quesnoy by the Rifle Brigade, who had stormed the ramparts with scaling ladders and forced the surrender of the town. We heard of the death in action of Lieut.-Colonel H.E. McKinnon, a Main Body soldier who had taken over command of the battalion. From Gallipoli to this stage of the campaign he had been with the battalion as platoon officer, company commander and finally the commander of the battalion, only to be struck down within a few days of the cessation of hostilities. A tough commander, and many a West Coast Company soldier had reason to know this, he was nonetheless a fearless and skilful soldier who worthily contributed to the lustre of the Wellington Regiment.[8]

The German dead too are buried around Le Quesnoy and its surrounding villages. On 8 November Monty Ingram writes:

Arrival of President Raymond Poincaré of France (right of centre) in Le Quesnoy, 10 November 1918. The president was accompanied by the prefect of the Department of the North, and the local member of parliament. The visit marked France symbolically taking possession of the town liberated by foreign troops. It was also the first time that a president of France had visited Le Quesnoy. This visit was to be followed on 18 November by a visit of King George V of Britain. NZ RSA Collection, Photographer: Captain H.A. Sanders, NZEF Official H Series H1237, Ref: 1/2-013784-G, Alexander Turnbull Library, Wellington, New Zealand

Busy all day burying German dead. Their bodies lay thickly about this village [Villereau]. We simply dragged the corpses by their heels and threw them into any bit of trench that was handy. When the bodies reached to within a foot or so of the top we covered with a few shovelfuls of dirt. There they lie unhallowed and unsung.[9]

The New Zealand Division is to pull back on Beauvois where it can more easily be supplied by rail. Peace is on everyone lips. "Many are the rumours now floating about and we are all eagerly discussing the Peace which surely must soon come. I hope it comes before we have many more stunts as one must surely come to a sticky end if one keeps going over the top ad infinitum."[10]

The Diggers of 2 Auckland are billeted in Rompaneau, just north of Le Quesnoy, and are expecting a move at any time.

As peace talk was in the air, the diggers retired to roost with an expectant look on their faces. In these days a digger never expects to be able to wake up in the morning in the same place in which he first went to sleep the night before.

Late in the evening a sergeant poked his head into our possie in the dark and bawled out, "The Kaiser has abdicated." Sleepy Diggers wriggled and sighed and grumbled, and live ends of cigarettes soon marked out the spot where each man was lying. Asked one; "What was the Tommies doing to let him what do you call it?" The offence was laid at the door of the 42nd Division, who were then in the line.

The mean of the words abducted, adjudicated and abdicated was argued out and settled to the satisfaction of the disputants. "He's abducted

and fled" was the final word. The cigarettes went out one by one and silence reigned supreme for a while.[11]

The war has moved on but soldiers stoically live from day to day, sharing and mulling on rumour, and taking nothing as gospel until it happens. On 11 November Monty Ingram hears the news at a halt with 2 Wellington en route to Beauvois.

> While we were sitting on a bank at the side of the road enjoying our first halt on the march, an officer came down the road imparting the news that an armistice with Germany had been signed and would take effect at 11 a.m. There was not even a cheer raised. There have been so many rumours floating about lately that, I think, everyone thought this information but another false yarn. Although we all scouted the idea of an armistice being actually signed, in our inmost hearts we had a feeling of deep thankfulness and relief which could not be repressed. However no outward demonstration was made and the momentous news was most casually received.[12]

"In this hour for the first time since facing the enemy my mind allows itself to really believe that I shall see you all again."[13] So pencils Captain George Tuck, adjutant of 2 Auckland, to his parents on the day after the Armistice. A Boer War veteran at 18 and a carpenter by trade, Tuck immediately enlisted on the declaration of war and sailed with the Main Body of the New Zealand Expeditionary Force in October 1914. He first saw action in the Gallipoli landings on 25 April 1915 as a corporal in No. 7 Platoon of the 6th Hauraki Company, Auckland Battalion. Tuck was wounded on the

New Zealand soldiers, in their 'lemon squeezer' headdress, of 2nd Brigade parade through the streets of Le Quesnoy during the visit of French President Raymond Poincaré on 10 November 1918. The tower of the town hall destroyed by artillery fire is on the skyline to the right. The photographer is Captain Malcolm Ross, NZEF Official War Correspondent, who was forbidden from taking photographs as a condition of his employment as a war correspondent. Malcolm Ross Collection, Ref: 1/4-017543-F, Alexander Turnbull Library, Wellington, New Zealand

Somme in September 1916, saw action at Messines in June 1917 and before Passchendaele in October 1917. At the beginning of 1918 he was one of six original members still serving with his battalion.

Tuck's battalion is marching through the streets of Solesmes when "a message was shown to me which stated that hostilities would cease at the eleventh hour of the eleventh day of the eleventh month. So the end had come."[14]

At Headquarters 1st Brigade in Solesmes, Captain Stuart Varnham receives word at 8.45 a.m. that hostilities are to cease at 11a.m. — an Armistice. Varnham drives to Beauvois and finds billets for the Brigade Headquarters and the four battalions and is ready to receive them when the first battalion arrives that evening. "All cars & motor lorries have head lights burning tonight — quite strange."[15] He is equally busy the next day, issuing orders and instructions. "I can't realise that the war is practically finished."[16]

In Brockenhurst, Bill McKeon and his comrades keep abreast of the news from the front.

> Then suddenly it was all over. I had been allowed up for a few days to test my legs when the news came through. It was received quietly. The nursing staff staged a little party in each ward and expected us to warm up to some pitch of enthusiasm. We couldn't do it. We were too tired, mentally and physically, and too full of memories to let ourselves go. We remembered all those good comrades who would never return, the flower of New Zealand's youth cut down in its prime. No longer would we hear their cheerful voices and march with them along the straight French roads to the tune of "The Great Little Army".[17]

For 23-year-old Gunner Bert Stokes of No. 13 Battery, New Zealand Field Artillery, moving back with the guns through Forêt de Mormal on 11 November is a

> dull miserable day with misty rain and being in the Forest did not make it any more cheerful. On the way we were told that an Armistice was to be signed at 11.00 a.m. and the war was over. I wrote in a letter home it seems too wonderful to believe. There is no cheering or excitement, just a feeling of relief. Everything is going on as before, we still have the guns and horses to look after, but of course we miss the screeching shells screaming over from the enemy lines. We all have taken it in a very calm and subdued manner. No one seemed to want to cheer when we first heard the news. We realised that soon we shall see the home shores on the horizon and that is what the armistice means to us. For most of us tired in body and mind and with memories of the tragic field of battle this momentous announcement was too vast to be appreciated at that moment.[18]

Second Lieutenant Fred Cody, a 24-year-old clerk from Taihape, in 1 Canterbury, writes from Quievy:

> What a hell of a way to end a war. At least I suppose it's ended for I don't think Fritz could start up again if the Armistice broke down. We paraded this morning in full marching order and it was drizzling like it was the

day we did that show in the Mormal Forest. We were told that the Huns
had asked for an armistice and then we were marched to this empty
Godforsaken hole in a village. No civvies, no oeufs, no wine, not even a
drop of beer. And the billet leaks like a sieve. Still, why go crook? It's the
end of the penny section and a man is still alive.[19]

James Hutchinson writes in his diary:

11th Probably THE day in the world's history. Hostilities cease 11 a.m.
Only remains now to see what our terms to them are. We moved off at 11
a.m. to go back to division, now at Beauvois. Raw day. Halted for night at
RAMPONEAU just E. of Le Quesnoy. Got good billets. The news of peace
seems to be received most quietly. After all this time, nobody seems to
realise what it means.[20]

For Captain Arthur Behrend of 90th Heavy Artillery Brigade now about to
sever connections with the New Zealand Division,

Thus November 11 found the majority of us still at Salesches — ten or
more miles behind our infantry and at least twenty from the nearest
Germans — and a small group of officers assembled outside the Adjutant's
office and greeted eleven o'clock with a half-hearted cheer. We had no
beer, no gin, no cigarettes.

A day or two later General Russell sent the Colonel a farewell letter of
which we were so proud that I print it in full:

"All good things come to an end, and amongst others the association
of the New Zealand Division with IV Corps and consequently with
90th Brigade.

It has been, as times go, a long partnership and a successful one.
We shall carry away with us none but pleasant memories and sincere
admiration for the work done by you and your guns than at any time since
the Division has been in France.

I hope you will let your men know this, and that this expression on my
part is not merely a courtesy between one unit and another but the feeling
of every man in the ranks."

I went to say goodbye to General Russell myself, and he asked me why
I didn't come out to New Zealand to settle and told me to let him know
if I did. I have often thought how different my life would have been if I
had followed his suggestion; in the early nineteen-twenties there were
occasions when I felt sorry I had not.[21]

It is over the following days that the New Zealanders assess what it all means.
On 12 November Hutchinson's battery continues its move as part of 2nd
Brigade to join the division.

Sunny day but very cold wind. Moved off 9.30 a.m. and trekked via
Beaudignies, Romeries, & Solesmes to Quievy. Pretty fair billets again.
Believe we are to stay here for a week. All sorts of rumours, of course, but
nothing definite yet as to our terms to Germany, or as to the great question
of our future movements. It's alright to move back in perfect peace past the
places you got strafed going up.[22]

H 1240

New Zealand flag, presented to the town of Le Quesnoy by Brigadier-General Hart commanding 3rd New Zealand Rifle Brigade and his battalion commanders on 14 November 1918, flying from the town hall that was partly destroyed by artillery fire aimed at the tower. NZ RSA Collection, Photographer: Captain H.A. Sanders, NZEF Official H Series H1240, Ref: 1/2-013787-G, Alexander Turnbull Library, Wellington, New Zealand

Major-General Russell briefs all of the New Zealand Division's officers the following day. Hutchinson records:

He says we go to occupy the Rhinelands, that demobilisation will go on from there, leave to be as usual. On 14 November a Divisional church parade of thanksgiving was held in the fields between Beauvois and Quievy. Splendid to see the whole division together, but, needless to say, we did not hear one word of the service.[23]

There is grumbling and dissension in the ranks at the thought of going to Germany: all the men want is to go home. However, there is a job to be done and the division gets on with it. Russell puts his efforts into an education scheme to prepare his soldiers who for four years have known only war as their primary occupation.

Hutchinson later reflects on his war. "She has been a grand year again, 1915 and this year two of the greatest years a fellow could ever wish for. The next thing of course is to get back to N.Z., and then it's a case of settle down and work."[24]

On 3 February 1919 Fred Cody writes from Germany at what is the start of his journey home.

What is left of both battalions amalgamated today in our barracks and I am off to England tomorrow. One last lash tonight and I will begin to think about that new leaf that will need turning over before I get home and become a comparatively respected civilian again.

Been away so long that everything about home is a little blurred, but I suppose a man will settle down in time.[25]

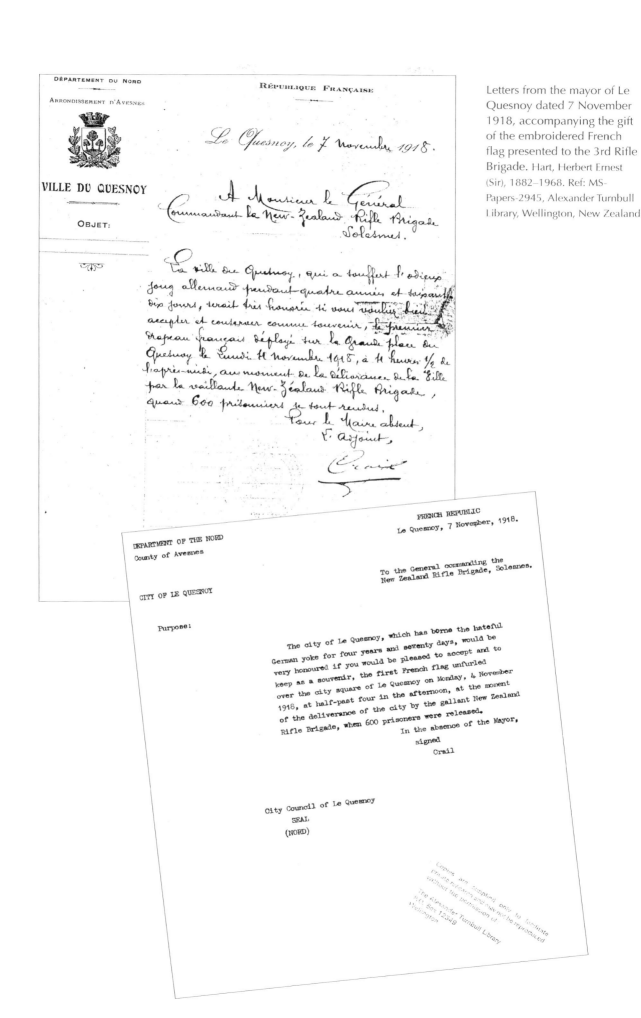

Letters from the mayor of Le Quesnoy dated 7 November 1918, accompanying the gift of the embroidered French flag presented to the 3rd Rifle Brigade. Hart, Herbert Ernest (Sir), 1882–1968. Ref: MS-Papers-2945, Alexander Turnbull Library, Wellington, New Zealand

Second Lieutenant Leslie Averill, MC, 4 Rifles, points out where the ladder was placed to scale the walls. From left to right: Colonel George Napier Johnston, CMG, DSO, former Commander New Zealand Divisional Artillery; Lieutenant William Lang, MC, 1 Auckland; Corporal Henry Thomas, MM, 1 Canterbury Regiment, and Corporal Jenner. The Central Press Photos Ltd, Ref: PAColl-6181-19, Alexander Turnbull Library, Wellington, New Zealand

REMEMBERING LE QUESNOY

In 1920 the New Zealand government approves the proposal to erect six battlefield memorials on the sites of the major New Zealand battlefields: Messine and Gravenstafel in Belgium, the Somme and Le Quesnoy in France, Chunuk Bair on Gallipoli and a memorial in Palestine.[26] A sum of £5000 is approved for each memorial. One of New Zealand's leading architects, 65-year-old Samuel Hurst Seager of Christchurch, is commissioned to produce designs for each site. He spends much of 1920 to 1925 abroad. "The memorials, designed in 1921 and executed in the following years include those at Longueval and Le Quesnoy in France, Messines (Mesen) in Belgium and Chunuk Bair at Gallipoli. Each is distinguished by careful siting and austere simplicity of design."[27]

He writes to the government on his plans for Le Quesnoy. "At Le Quesnoy it is proposed to utilise part of the wall on which should be placed a memorial in marble depicting the scale of the walls by New Zealand troops, and to make an appropriate approach and platform."[28]

In his illustrated report the architect introduces his proposal with the statement that:

Le Quesnoy is an exceptional town in that it has its original mediaeval walls surrounded by the low-lying land which once formed the moat. The scaling of these walls by the New Zealanders at the capture of Le Quesnoy is a unique incident in the whole of the war, and it appears to me that this may be commemorated by a large stone sculptured panel let into the ancient wall, representing the scaling. In front of this monument the ancient moat might be retained and laid out as a sunk garden, separated from a terrace garden at a higher level from which the sculpture could be well seen. This would, I submit, be an appropriate form of memorial, and one which I think would be appreciated by the people of Le Quesnoy.[29]

Seager bases his concept for the carving of the scaling of the wall on Fortunio Mantania's vivid but fanciful drawing published in *The Sphere* in January 1919.[30] Seager proposes a formal walk from the square through a new opening in the ramparts that is to lead to the monument. He also stresses the importance of maintaining a close relationship with the local community.

> I would suggest that estimates for all the work in France should be obtained from French contractors, and that this sculpture should be executed by an eminent French sculptor. It would, I think, be in accord with the spirit of the Entente Cordiale, and give greater satisfaction to the French people and greater value to the Memorial in their eyes.[31]

The town council of Le Quesnoy give him their approval being "very proud of it, and expressed their pleasure that the incident should form the subject of the memorial".[32]

Seager's final concept for the sculpture is the joint effort of Valenciennes-born Félix-Alexandre Desruelles, regarded as one of France's leading sculptors, and Scottish-born Alexander Roderick Fraser (1877–1953). A sculptor and stonemason, Fraser arrived in New Zealand in 1901 to teach sculpture and modelling at Wellington Technical College and he became a New Zealand member of the Royal Society of British Sculptors. He returned to England in 1910, and served as a draughtsman with the British Flying Corps 1916–18.[33] Fraser is commissioned by Seager to do a series of scaled plaster models that reflects Seager's evolving views on the Le Quesnoy sculpture. There are important changes as Seager becomes more familiar with the events of the battle and the relative importance of the act of the scaling of the walls.

> I realised that this scaling of the walls, although unique in the whole of the war, was only a small incident in the action of the battle, and I therefore came to the conclusion that it would be better to treat this as a subordinate feature in the monument, and to have a purely symbolic figure of Victorious Peace as applying to the whole action of the army. As completed the winged figure of Victorious Peace stands boldly out on the right hand of the foreground: she breaks the sword of war beneath her feet, and holds in her right hand the wreath of victory, in her left hand the palm of peace. On the left hand of the foreground — among rough rock — is a small cross in memory of those who fell in the action. On the recessed background is the representation of the scaling of the wall in low relief.[34]

Desruelles's finished sculpture is carved in a block of Nabresina marble 3.48 metres long, 2.13 metres high and 48 centimetres deep, and weighs nine tons (9144 kilos). It comes in under budget and there are sufficient funds to

The Viscount Milner, Sir James Allen, New Zealand High Commissioner to London, Marshal Foch and dignitaries at the unveiling of the New Zealand battle site memorial at Le Quesnoy on 15 July 1923. The Central Press Photos Ltd, Ref: F- 53834-1/2, Alexander Turnbull Library, Wellington, New Zealand

commission Fraser to produce a full-scale plaster cast of the sculpture at a cost of £200 to be shipped to New Zealand for display in the proposed War Memorial Museum.

The War Memorial Museum never eventuates and the plaster work of the Le Quesnoy memorial is never displayed in New Zealand. Few New Zealanders travel to Le Quesnoy in those years and the subtlety of the images of peace, war and its price in Desruelles and Fraser's work would never be appreciated by the New Zealand public. On 31 August 1941 the under secretary for Internal Affairs writes to the district engineer of the Public Works Department.

I have to confirm the advice given over the telephone that there is no objection to the plaster cast which has been stored at the old Base Records Building, Buckle Street, since 1922, being broken up as it is necessary to get it out of the way owing to demolition work being in progress and the

Director of the Dominion Museum having advised that it has no value for museum purposes.[35]

The Le Quesnoy memorial is unveiled on 15 July 1923 by Viscount Milner, in the presence of Sir James Allen, New Zealand's high commissioner to London, Marshal Ferdinand Foch, commander-in-chief of the Allied Forces in 1918, Lieutenant-General Sir Alexander Godley, former commander of the New Zealand Expeditionary Force, and among the many New Zealanders were a number of former soldiers who took part in the battle, including Colonel George Napier Johnston, the former chief of Royal Artillery of the New Zealand Division, who continued in the British Army and reverted to his substantive rank of colonel after the war, and Leslie Averill who was first up the ladder.

In his speech, Milner builds on the mythology in saying that

the New Zealanders in scaling the high ramparts of the fortress, which were considered unscalable, reached the final turning point in the war and achieved the pinnacle of their wonderful record. It was a most daring act for a mere handful of New Zealanders to place a flimsy ladder against the great wall and mount in single file, and its success had a great moral effect on the Germans.[36]

Godley talked to the men he commanded.

No general ever commanded finer fighters than those of the "Silent Division," who have earned the greatest of all reputations, because they are known to the world as the men who always attained their objective at the exact moment, in accordance with plans. They were models of efficiency in all respects and in all ranks.[37]

But perhaps the most valid statement comes from the mayor of Le Quesnoy, who "gave feeling expression to the people's joy when they stealthily peered out of their places of refuge, and saw not the Germans, but deliverers from a strange land which they then knew little. The thought of New Zealand would always create a warm glow in their hearts."[38]

Le Quesnoy itself treasured its memorial. In 1924 the Imperial War Graves Commission took over the contract for the maintenance of the New Zealand memorials and its report for that year stated that on 11 November

A Procession was formed, headed by the Town Band, composed of ex-soldiers, Civilian Prisoners of War, Fire Brigade, Gymnastic Club, School Children, Conscripts 1924 and general Public. The Ex-soldiers' Organisation placed a large wreath in the recess of the stonework on the "Island" in honour of the New Zealand Soldiers who delivered the Town of Le Quesnoy in 1918.[39]

The New Zealand Division is the only Dominion division to take part in the Battle of the Sambre on 4 November 1918, and it continued to exploit the success of this day in the fighting on the following day, 5 November. The New Zealand Field Artillery continued to fire their guns until 9 November. As the story of this battle shows, this division, made up in the main of

Left to right: Corporal F.T. Jenner, NZ Provost, Lieutenant L.C.L. Averill, MC (son of the Bishop of Auckland, and the first man to enter the town over the walls), Lieutenant-General Sir Alexander Godley, Lieutenant F.W. Lang, MC, 2 Auckland, the Rev. M. Mullineux (Chaplain to the Division), Colonel G.N. Johnston, CMG, DSO (Commander Royal Artillery of the NZ Division), Corporal E. Thomas, and Sergeant Harry Moscroft, MM, 4 Rifles. The Central Press Photos Ltd, Ref: PAColl-6181-19, Alexander Turnbull Library, Wellington, New Zealand

citizen soldiers who honed their professionalism by trial and error, were very good at the business of war. They stoically did the job demanded of them, grumbled when they believed, as with the Cologne deployment, that it was time to go home, but made the best of it. New Zealand never saw the professionalism of its two wartime divisions on the Western Front and in the Mediterranean in the two world wars, but each, under superb commanders, were ranked with the very best divisions in the British armies of their day. We and they rightly questioned what war achieved, but at the time few questioned the need that the war had to be fought. Although New Zealand did not make the decision to fight, the division believed it to be justified and that the world would be a better place for their efforts. And the final advance of 1918 and the liberation of the villages and towns of northern France that climaxed with the taking of Le Quesnoy confirmed that belief. Our soldiers "from the uttermost ends of the earth" spared a town and freed its citizens. That act is still remembered — especially in Le Quesnoy — and a 'warm glow' remains a century on.

I have made a point in this story to highlight the age and occupations of our citizen soldiers. Gunner Donald Stewart Kennedy's death on 7 November along with Gunner Frank Gardner and Driver Andrew Mather have a certain poignancy because they are the last of the New Zealand Expeditionary Force to be killed in action, and I have taken Euan Kennedy's words for why he is researching his uncle's war to title this final chapter. Their deaths are no more dreadful than the impact of 12,855 officially confirmed New Zealand dead on the Western Front, who lie buried in France, Belgium and the United Kingdom. As Ian McGibbon points out in his conclusion to *New Zealand's Western Front Campaign*, add this to the 600 or so New Zealanders who died serving with Imperial units and the 500 who died of wounds, in training or from sickness while in the United Kingdom or during repatriation to New Zealand, then New Zealand's dead approaches 14,000, "18.9 per cent of the estimated 74,000 New Zealanders who served on the Western Front".[40] It is New Zealand's costliest campaign in its history and that cost continues to reverberate with succeeding generations. The Battle of the Sambre and the taking of Le Quesnoy is one of New Zealand's least costly battles, but that does not make the 189 known dead from 1–7 November 1918 and those who later died of wounds any less distressing.

We owe it to them — everyone who fought at Le Quesnoy, those who remain buried there, those who brought their memories back to New Zealand, and to the people of Le Quesnoy who have never forgotten — to understand and care about what happened in this corner of France. A century on, it is high time to reassess our appreciation of the story of our New Zealanders on the Western Front, and thereby reaffirm our association with the locations of some of our greatest collective national achievements and disasters.

One tangible way of increasing our understanding of the war is to support the initiative of those who have purchased the property in Le Quesnoy for the express purpose of creating a New Zealand Memorial Museum. Their collective vision looks to the future by building something permanent in the present, a transformative memorial that is only limited by imagination. It seems the logical progression of the approach taken by Major-General Sir Andrew Russell of the New Zealand Division in 1918, in not seeing Le Quesnoy as an end in itself, but as one more step toward a larger objective: for New Zealanders and the French to marry an understanding of our shared past in war with a shared future, based on the gift of liberation so willingly given and accepted on 4 November 1918.

The aged town crier of Solesmes in France reading war news of Allied successes to local people on 9 November 1918. Note that the group is of women, children and old men. NZ RSA Collection, Photographer: Captain H.A. Sanders, NZEF Official H Series H1108, Ref: 1/2-013666-G. Alexander Turnbull Library, Wellington, New Zealand

Endnotes

INTRODUCTION

1. Letter from W. Jack to Eleanor Hunt dated 17 November 1918, MS-Papers-7483-01, ATL. Jack, William James — WW1 25/645 — Army, ANZ.
2. *The New York Times*, 7 November 1918, p. 7.
3. *Grey River Argus*, 8 November 1918, p. 3.
4. 13/2002 Captain James Evans, 2 Auckland, 9 November 1918, 1916–1918 World War I diaries, MSX-2936-2939, ATL, quoted in Matthew Wright, *The New Zealand Experience at Gallipoli and the Western Front*, Oratia Books, Auckland, 2017, p. 280.
5. *Grey River Argus*, 16 November 1918, p. 3.
6. Quoted in 'The Division,' *Chronicles of the N.Z.E.F.*, Vol. 5 no. 57, 22 November 1918, p. 199.
7. Colonel H. Stewart, *The New Zealand Division 1916–1919: A Popular History Based on Official Records*, Whitcombe and Tombs, Auckland, 1921, pp. 618–619.
8. Brigadier-General Sir James Edmonds with Lieutenant-Colonel R. Maxwell-Hyslop, *History of the Great War, Military Operations France and Belgium 1918. Volume V: 26th September–11th November, the Advance to Victory*, HMSO, London, 1947, p. 483.
9. Major A.F. Becke, *History of the Great War, Order of Battle, Part 4: The Army Council, G.H.Q.S, Armies, and Corps 1914–1918*, HMSO, London, 1945, pp. 98 and 159.
10. Jeffery Williams, *Byng of Vimy: General and Governor General*, Leo Cooper, London, 1983, p. 253.
11. J.P. Harris with Niall Barr, *Amiens to the Armistice: The BEF in the Hundred Days' Campaign, 8 August–11 November 1918*, Brasseys, London, 1998, p. 278.
12. Jonathon Boff, *Winning and Losing on the Western Front: The British Third Army and the Defeat of Germany in 1918*, Cambridge University Press, Cambridge, 2012, p. 34.
13. Ian Beckett, Timothy Bowman and Mark Connelly, *The British Army and the First World War*, Cambridge University Press, Cambridge, 2017, p. 374.
14. Stewart, *The New Zealand Division 1916–1919*. Lieutenant-Colonel W.S. Austin, *The Official History of the New Zealand Rifle Brigade*, L.T. Watkins, Wellington, 1924. Major N Annabell, *Official History of the New Zealand Engineers During the Great War 1914–1919*; Evans, Cobb & Sharpe, Ltd, Wanganui, 1927, pp. 216–222. Lieutenant A.E. Byrne, *Official History of the Otago Regiment in the Great War 1914–1918*; J. Wilkie & Co., Dunedin, nd, pp. 373–379. Lieutenant J.R. Byrne, *New Zealand Artillery in the Field, 1914–1918*, Whitcombe &Tombs, Auckland, 1922, pp. 289–302. Lieutenant-Colonel A.D. Carbery, *The New Zealand Medical Service in the Great War 1914–1918*; Whitcombe & Tombs, Auckland, 1924, pp. 444–448. James Cowan, *The Maoris in the Great War*; Maori Regimental Committee, Whitcombe & Tombs, Auckland, 1926, pp. 152–154. W.H. Cunningham, C.A.L. Treadwell, J.S. Hanna, *The Wellington Regiment, NZEF, 1914–1919*; Ferguson & Osborn Ltd, Wellington, 1928, pp. 320–328.
15. Captain David Ferguson, *The History of the Canterbury Regiment NZEF, 1914–1919*, Whitcombe & Tombs, Auckland, 1921, p. 282.
16. Second Lieutenant O.E. Burton, *The Auckland Regiment: Being an Account of the Doings on Active Service of the First, Second and Third Battalions of the Auckland Regiment*, Whitcombe & Tombs, Auckland, 1922, p. 259.
17. Ian McGibbon, *New Zealand's Western Front Campaign*, Bateman, Auckland, 2016, pp. 344–353. John H. Gray, *From the Uttermost Ends of the Earth: The New Zealand Division on the Western Front 1916–1918: A History and Guide to its Battlefields*, Willsonscott Publishing, Christchurch, 2010, pp. 354–374.
18. Glyn Harper, *Johnny ENZED: The New Zealand Soldier in the First World War 1914–1918*, Exisle, Auckland, 2015, pp. 468–472; Jane Tolerton, *An Awfully Big Adventure: New Zealand World War One Veterans Tell Their Stories*, Penguin, Auckland, 2013, pp. 247–249.
19. N.M. Ingram, *Anzac Diary: A Nonentity in Khaki*, The Book Printer, Maryborough, Victoria, nd, pp. 131–137; a new edition was published as *In Flanders Fields: The World War 1 Diary of Private Monty Ingram*, David Ling Publishing, Auckland, 2006, pp. 144–150; Laurie Barber and Cliff Lord, *Swift and Sure: A History of the Royal New Zealand Corps of Signals and Army Signalling in New Zealand*, New Zealand Signals Incorporated, Auckland, 1996, pp. 53–60; Julia Millen, *Salute to Service: A History of the Royal New Zealand Corps of Transport and its Predecessors 1860–1996*, Victoria University Press, Wellington, 1997, pp. 125–136; Alan Henderson, David Green and Peter Cooke, *The Gunners: A History of New Zealand Artillery*, Raupo (Penguin), Auckland, 2008, pp. 145–156.
20. Nathalie Philippe with Christopher Pugsley, John Crawford and Matthias Strohn, *The Great Adventure Ends: New Zealand and France on the Western Front*, John Douglas Publishing, Christchurch, 2013, p. 9.
21. Sally Blundell, 'Les Kiwis,' *Listener*, 26 May 2018, pp. 24–25.
22. Christopher Pugsley, All Blacks' Visit Diary, unpublished ms, November 2000.

1. PREPARING FOR ARMAGEDDON

1. Huntly Gordon, *The Unreturning Army*, J.M. Dent, London, 1967, p. 124.
2. Arthur Behrend, *As from Kemmel Hill: An Adjutant in France and Flanders, 1917 and 1918*, Greenwood Press, Westport. Connecticut, 1963, pp. 117–118.
3. Lieutenant-Colonel John Studholme, *New Zealand Expeditionary Force. Record of Personal Services During the War of Officers, Nurses and First-Class Warrant Officers*, Government Printer, Wellington, 1928, pp. 18, and 168.
4. Chief of General Staff, Headquarters New Zealand Military Forces, *War 1914–1918, New Zealand Expeditionary Force, Its Provision and Maintenance*, Government Printer, Wellington, 1919, pp. 3–9.
5. Studholme, *Record of Personal Services*, p. 18.
6. Quoted in Boff, *Winning and Losing on the Western Front*, p. 57.
7. Studholme, *Record of Personal Services,* pp. 15–18.
8. 2 Brigade Strength States as at 31 October 1918, Headquarters — 2 NZ Infantry Brigade — War Diary 1 August 1918–28 February 1919, WA 76/119, ANZ.
9. Russell Diary, 1 October 1918, The Russell Saga, Volume III, World War 1, extracted and compiled by R.F. Gambrill, qMS-0822, ATL and Russell Family.
10. Russell to Allen dated 12 August 1918, Sir James Allen. Miscellanous files and papers — Correspondence with Colonels Birdwood and Russell, December 1914–April 1920 and copies of personal letters, 1920 [Loose papers] (R22319674), ANZ. See also, Jock Vennell, *The Forgotten General: New Zealand's World War 1 Commander Major-General Sir Andrew Russell*, Allen & Unwin, Sydney, 2011, pp. 201–213.
11. J. Bryant Haigh and Alan J. Polaschek, *New Zealand and the Distinguished Service Order*, Haigh & Polaschek, Christchurch, 1993, p. 172.
12. John Crawford (ed.), *The Devil's Own War: The First World War Diary of Brigadier-General Herbert Hart*, Exisle, Auckland, 2008.
13. Haigh and Polaschek, *New Zealand and the Distinguished Service Order*, p. 293.
14. Studholme, *Record of Personal Services*, pp. 6–11.
15. Major N. Annabell, *Official History of the New Zealand Engineers During the Great War 1914–1919*. James Cowan, *The Maoris in the Great War*. Christopher Pugsley, *Te Hokowhitu A Tu: The Maori Pioneer Battalion in the First World War*, Oratia Books, Auckland, 2018.
16. Roy Finlayson Ellis, *By Wires to Victory*, 1st Signal Company War History Committee, Auckland, 1968.
17. 'The Changes in the Composition of a British Division on the Western Front During the Great War, 1914–1918, Appendix 1,' in Major A.F. Becke, *History of the Great War, Order of Battle of Divisions, Part 1: The Regular British Divisions*, HMSO, London, 1931, pp. 126–127.
18. Stewart, *The New Zealand Division 1914–1919*, p. 566.
19. NZ Division, 'Report on Operations for November and December 1918.' Reports of operations by the New Zealand Division, Hugh Stewart Papers, MS-Papers-9080-07.
20. Stewart, *The New Zealand Division 1916–1919*, p. 565.
21. Brigadier-General Herbert Hart Diary, 1 November 1918, Diary 22 August 1918–18 May 1919, KMRL, NAM.
22. Becke, *History of the Great War, Order of Battle, Part 4*. pp. 153–160,
23. 'Le Quesnoy,' Wikipedia, https://en.wikipedia.org/wiki/Le_Quesnoy#, cite_note-39. Accessed 21 June 2018.
24. Russell Diary, 14 September 1918.
25. Ibid.
26. Russell to Allen dated 16 September 1918.
27. 1st Battalion Wellington War Diary, 1 November 1918, WA73 108, ANZ.
28. Ibid, 2 November 1918.
29. Ingram, *Anzac Diary*, p. 131.
30. 1st Battalion Wellington War Diary, 3 November 1918, WA73 108, ANZ.
31. Ingram, *Anzac Diary*, 131–132.
32. 1st Battalion Auckland War Diary, 1–2 November 1918, WA71 102, ANZ.
33. Ibid, 3 November 1918.
34. Annabell, *Official History of the New Zealand Engineers During the Great War 1914–1919*, pp. 215–217.
35. Trooper George Ewan Soutar, Otago Mounted Rifles, 6th Reinforcements [later Maori Pioneer Battalion], 3 November 1918, 'A Diary Kept from 10 November 1915 until Return to NZ in April 1919,' London Papers, copy in author's possession. George Ewan Soutar — WW1 7/1525 — Army, Personal File, ANZ.
36. Soutar Diary, 30 October 1918.
37. New Zealand Engineers — Divisional Signal Company 1–30 November 1918, 2 November 1918, WA 65/93, ANZ.
38. New Zealand Engineers — Divisional Signal Company 1–30 November 1918, 3 November 1918, WA 65/93, ANZ.
39. Ibid.

2. THE 'DINKS' ENCIRCLE LE QUESNOY

1. Brigadier-General Herbert Hart, 4 November 1918, Diary 22 August 1918–18 May 1919, KMRL, NAM. Crawford, *The Devil's Own War*, p. 264.

2. Austin, *The Official History of the New Zealand Rifle Brigade*, p. 443.

3. Hart Diary, 4 November 1918.

4. 48456 Cpl N. Coop, M.M. 1st N.Z.E.F., Diary and Postcards, entry 4 November 1918, No. 2002.266, KMRL, NAM, p. 49.

5. Hart Diary, 4 November 1918.

6. Major-General Lindsay Merritt Inglis, World War 1 Memoirs, MSY-5455, ATL, pp. 182–185.

7. In addition to the three New Zealand artillery brigades, this consisted of 42nd Divisional Artillery and two additional RFA brigades. Stewart, *The New Zealand Division 1916–1919*, p. 571.

8. Haigh and Polaschek, *New Zealand and the Distinguished Service Order*, p. 163. Wayne McDonald, *Honours and Awards to the New Zealand Expeditionary Force in the Great War 1914–1918*, Richard Stowers, Hamilton, revised 2nd edition, 2009, p. 169.

9. Austin, *The Official History of the New Zealand Rifle Brigade*, p. 437.

10. Ibid, p. 441.

11. Inglis, World War 1 Memoirs, pp. 182–185.

12. D.V.G.S, 'The Guns Bark in their Last Action,' *Chronicles of the N.Z.E.F.*, Vol. 5 no. 58, 6 December 1918, pp. 224–225.

13. 42915 Gunner William Jamieson, No. 3 Battery, 1st Brigade NZFA, interview by Jane Tolerton and Nick Boyack, WW1 Oral History Archive, ATL.

14. Ibid.

15. Byrne, *New Zealand Artillery in the Field, 1914–1918*, p. 290.

16. HQ 2nd NZ Infantry Brigade to Headquarters New Zealand Division dated 13 September 1918. Lessons from Recent Operations, WA1, Box 10/3/3, ANZ.

17. Ibid.

18. CRA NZ Division to Headquarters New Zealand Division dated 19 September 1918, WA1, Box 10/3/3, ANZ.

19. Cyril Clarke, 'History of 15 Howitzer Battery,' NZFA, 1914–1918, RV6627, KMRL, NAM.

20. See details in appendix.

21. Inglis, World War 1 Memoirs, pp. 182–185.

22. Tweedy, Glenholme Francis — WW1 36193 — Army, Personal File, ANZ.

23. Ayling, Claude Roy — WW1 23/59 — Army, ANZ.

24. Inglis, World War 1 Memoirs, pp. 182–185.

25. Carbery, *The New Zealand Medical Services in the Great War, 1914–1918*, pp. 445–447.

26. See appendix for details.

27. Austin, *The Official History of the New Zealand Rifle Brigade*, p. 566.

28. 18926 CQMS Harold Green, Diary No. 1997.817, 4–7 November 1918, KMRL, NAM.

29. Ibid.

30. Beckett, Bowman and Connelly, *The British Army and the First World War*, p. 371.

31. Quoted in Matthias Strohn, 'Defending Le Quesnoy,' in Nathalie Philippe et. al., *The Great Adventure Ends*, p. 328. See also, Isabel V. Hull, *Absolute Destruction: Military Culture and the Practices of War in Imperial Germany*, Cornell University Press, Ithaca and London, 2005, pp. 303–319; Scott Stephenson, *The Final Battle: Soldiers of the Western Front and the German Revolution of 1918*, Cambridge University Press, Cambridge, 2009, pp. 19–35. Alexander Watson, *Enduring the Great War: Combat Morale and Collapse in the German and British Armies, 1914–1918*, Cambridge University Press, Cambridge, 2008, pp. 184–200.

32. Strohn, 'Defending Le Quesnoy,' in Philippe et. al., *The Great Adventure Ends*, pp. 327–328.

33. War Diary of the 2nd Battalion NZRB, MS-Papers-9080-32, ATL.

34. Haigh and Polaschek, *New Zealand and the Distinguished Service Order*, p. 134. Wayne McDonald, *Honours and Awards*, p. 130.

35. 2nd Battalion — 3rd New Zealand Rifle Brigade — War Diary, 1–30 November 1918, WA1 WA83 141 [83aa], ANZ.

36. Austin, *The Official History of the New Zealand Rifle Brigade*, p. 450. McDonald, *Honours and Awards*, pp. 23, 81 and 103.

37. Austin, ibid.

38. Ibid. McGillen, William Peter — WW1 36472 — Army, ANZ.

39. McDonald, *Honours and Awards*, p. 159.

40. Austin, *The Official History of the New Zealand Rifle Brigade*, p. 456.

41. Kenrick, Harry Selwyn [aka Kenrick, Selwyn] — WWI 14539, WWII 9384 — Army, Personal File, ANZ; Maxwell, Valentine Freke — WWI 33123, WWII 617135 — Army, Personal File, ANZ; Rabone, Clarence

Noel — WW1 23/29 — Army, Personal File, ANZ.

42. Dr H. Selwyn Kenrick's Memoirs, extract from 4 November 1918, copy in possession of Mrs Cynthia Brown (daughter).

43. H.E. Barrowclough to Colonel Hugh Stewart regarding the draft history of the New Zealand Division, Knox College dated 14 February 1920. Hugh Stewart Papers. Extracts from war diaries of Auckland Regiment and New Zealand Rifle Brigade relating to attack on Le Quesnoy in early November 1918. Includes correspondence relating to attack, Feb. 1920, MS-Papers-9080-32, ATL.

44. Austin, *The Official History of the New Zealand Rifle Brigade,* p. 449.

45. Haigh and Polaschek, *New Zealand and the Distinguished Service Order*, pp. 20–21. McDonald, *Honours and Awards,* p. 6.

46. Alan Polaschek, *The Complete New Zealand Distinguished Conduct Medal*, Medals Research, Christchurch, revised edition 1983, p. 115.

47. Ibid, p. 116.

48. McDonald, *Honours and Awards*, p. 189. Mulvaney returned to New Zealand in June 1919 and drowned in the Mikonui River, South Westland, 26 November 1921.

49. Fergusson, Robert Linton — WW1 37797 — Army, ANZ. His surname is incorrectly spelt as Ferguson in McDonald, p. 81.

50. Inglis, World War 1 Memoirs, pp. 182–185.

51. Ibid.

52. 65546 Lance Corporal Stephen McDonnell, A Company 1st Battalion, 3rd NZ Rifle Brigade, letter to his sister dated 7 November 1918, MS-papers -6993-4, ATL. See McDonnell, Stephen Joseph — WW1 65546 — Army, ANZ. 65663 Lance-Corporal Edmund Michael Jones, 1st Battalion, 3rd NZ Rifle Brigade, killed in action, France, 4 November 1918. 65664 Rifleman Francis Patrick Jones, 3rd New Zealand Rifle Brigade, killed in action, France, 8 October 1918. New Zealand Expeditionary Force, *Roll of Honour*, Government Printer, Wellington, 1924, p. 153. Note that the Jones boys have consecutive regimental numbers suggesting that they enlisted together.

53. Harding, Ernest Astley — WWI 24/13, WWII 20032 — Army, ANZ. See McDonald, *Honours and Awards*, p. 108.

54. Austin, *The Official History of the New Zealand Rifle Brigade*, p. 445. See McDonald, *Honours and Awards*, p. 104.

55. Lieutenant-Colonel L.M. 'Curly' Blyth interview with author, 5 June 1992.

56. Ibid.

57. Guthrie, David Carew — WW1 32319 — Army, Personal File, ANZ.

58. Austin, *The Official History of the New Zealand Rifle Brigade*, p. 449. 13824 Corporal Charles Semmens Taylor was awarded the Distinguished Conduct Medal for this action. See McDonald, *Honours and Awards*, p. 257.

59. Lieutenant-Colonel L. M. 'Curly' Blyth interview with author, 5 June 1992.

60. Ibid.

61. Austin, *The Official History of the New Zealand Rifle Brigade*, p. 448. See McDonald, *Honours and Awards*, p. 174. Captain Henry James Thompson is awarded the Military Cross for this action. See McDonald, *Honours and Awards*, p. 260.

62. Inglis, World War 1 Memoirs, pp. 182–185.

63. War Diary of the 1st Battalion NZRB, Stewart Papers, MS-Papers-9080-32, ATL.

64. Cockcroft George Walter — WW1 19/42 — Army, Personal File, ANZ.

65. War Diary of the 3rd Battalion NZRB, Stewart Papers, MS-Papers-9080-32, ATL.

66. Ibid.

67. Ibid.

68. Coop Diary and Postcards, p. 49.

69. Ibid. As the copy of the diary notes: "This is possibly where he collected the Luger revolver that his son still has."

70. Coop Diary and Postcards.

71. Ibid.

72. War Diary of the 3rd Battalion NZRB, Stewart Papers, MS-Papers-9080-32, ATL.

73. 72214 Rifleman Captain James Matheson Nimmo, 'Somewhere in France,' Marion M. Young (ed.), No. 2003.47, KMRL, NAM.

74. Quoted in Strohn, 'Defending Le Quesnoy,' in Philippe et. al., *The Great Adventure Ends*, p. 329.

75. Hart Diary, 4 November 1918.

3. BEYOND LE QUESNOY

1.   1st New Zealand Infantry Brigade Order No. 130 dated 2 November 1918, Appendix 1 to 1st NZ Infantry Brigade War Diary 1–30 November 1918, WA1 76/1, ANZ.

2.   Colonel J.E. Lee, DSO, MC, Duntroon, *The Royal Military College of Australia 1911–1946*, Australian War

Memorial, Canberra, 1952, p. 251. McDonald, *Honours and Awards*, p. 132.

3. Diaries of Frederick Stuart Varnham, 1915–1919, 3 November 1918, transcribed by Mrs Nancy Croad, youngest daughter, copy in author's possession.
4. 1st Battalion Auckland War Diary, 4 November 1918, WA71 102, ANZ.
5. Ibid.
6. 'Pars About People,' *The Observer*, 28 September 1918, p. 4. Studholme, *Record of Personal Services*, p. 100.
7. McDonald, *Honours and Awards*, p. 68.
8. 'Pars About People,' *The Observer*, 28 September 1918, p. 4. Studholme, *Record of Personal Services*, p. 100.
9. Christopher Pugsley, *A Bloody Road Home: World War Two and New Zealand's Heroic Second Division*, Penguin, Auckland, 2014, pp. 45, 47, 73, 79, 89.
10. See appendix for individual details.
11. Lang, William Robert — WWI 9/1884, WWII 1/23/1 — Army, Personal File, ANZ.
12. Forbes, Alexander McRae — WW1 12/3218 — Army, Personal File, ANZ.
13. McDonald, *Honours and Awards*, p. 17.
14. Ibid, p. 24.
15. Greenwood, James Henry — WWI 3/251 — Army, Personal File, ANZ.
16. McDonald, *Honours and Awards*, p. 102.
17. 1st Battalion Auckland War Diary, 4 November 1918, WA71 102, ANZ.
18. Ibid.
19. Ibid.
20. See appendix for individual details. New Zealand Expeditionary Force, *Roll of Honour*, Government Printer, Wellington, 1924.
21. 1st Battalion Auckland War Diary, 4 November 1918, WA71 102, ANZ.
22. Turnbull was awarded the DSO in December 1918. McDonald, *Honours and Awards*, p. 267.
23. Clive Mortimer-Jones letter dated 25 November 1918, *Cambridge Parish News*, Cambridge Museum.
24. New Zealand Expeditionary Force, *Roll of Honour*, p. 249.
25. Ibid, p. 165.
26. Ibid, p. 200.
27. Billy Popgun, 'On Towards Le Quesnoy,' *Chronicles of the N.Z.E.F.* Vol. 5 no. 57, 22 November 1918, p. 199.
28. Inglis, World War 1 Memoirs, MSY-5455, ATL, pp. 182–185.
29. Baxter, James Neil — WWI 2/2057 — Army, Personal File (two files), ANZ. McDonald, *Honours and Awards*, p. 18.
30. Mintrom, Frederick Harold — WWI 26363, WWII 3/1/5 — Army, Personal File, ANZ. McDonald, *Honours and Awards*, p. 182.
31. 1st Battalion Wellington War Diary, 4 November 1918, WA73/1, ANZ.
32. Interview with Leslie Marfell by Jane Tolerton and Nicolas Boyack. World War 1 Oral History Archive, ATL.
33. Clive Mortimer-Jones letter dated 25 November 1918.
34. Stewart, *The New Zealand Division 1916–1919*, p. 582.
35. Loveday, Leslie George Vivian — WW1 10/3938 — Army, ANZ. 'King's Prizeman,' *Evening Post*, 9 October 1919, p. 9. Christopher Pugsley, *The Camera in the Crowd: Filming New Zealand in Peace and War, 1895–1920*, Oratia Books, Auckland, 2017, p. 421. Stewart, *The New Zealand Division 1916–1919*, p. 583.
36. Interview with Leslie Marfell by Jane Tolerton and Nicolas Boyack, World War 1 Oral History Archive, ATL
37. 1st Battalion Wellington War Diary, 4 November 1918, WA73 108, ANZ.
38. Clive Mortimer-Jones letter dated 25 November 1918.
39. Stewart, *The New Zealand Division 1916–1919*, p. 583.
40. See appendix for individual details.
41. Ingram, *Anzac Diary*, pp. 132–133.
42. Griffiths, John Henry — WW1 38690 — Army, ANZ. McDonald, *Honours and Awards*, p. 103.
43. 2nd Battalion Wellington War Diary, 4 November 1918, WA74/1, ANZ.
44. Ingram, *Anzac Diary*, p. 133.
45. Ibid.
46. 2nd Battalion Wellington War Diary, 3 November 1918, WA74/1, ANZ.
47. Ingram, *Anzac Diary*, p. 134.
48. Ibid, pp. 134–135.
49. Ibid, p. 135.
50. See appendix for individual details.
51. According to his personal file Second Lieutenant C. W. Quilliam who is killed in action is serving in 2 Wellington and not 1 Wellington as listed in the regimental history; Quilliam Cecil Wilfred — WW1 60294 — Army, Personal File, ANZ. Cunningham et. al., *The Wellington Regiment*, p. 327.
52. Ingram, *Anzac Diary*, p. 134.

53. 3/203, 2nd Lieutenant J.D. Hutchinson, NZFA, 5th Battery, 2nd Brigade NZFA, 4 November 1918, Diary 1915–1919, RV3641, KMRL, NAM.
54. Byrne, *New Zealand Artillery in the Field*, p. 291.
55. Looms, Ernest Henry Thomas — WW1 7/2070 — Army, Personal File, ANZ; Driver Ernest Henry Looms, NZFA, Diary October 1915–February 1919 — Western Front — WW1, 1998.222, KMRL, NAM, p. 49.
56. Headquarters New Zealand and Australian Division — New Zealand Division — Divisional Artillery — War Diary, Narrative, 8 June 1917–18 March 1919, 4 November 1918, WA 50, 70/[50bs], ANZ.
57. Ibid, 5 November 1918.
58. Hutchinson Diary, 4 November 1918.
59. Ibid.
60. Ingram, *Anzac Diary*, p. 132.

4. OVER THE WALL

1. Tapsell, Winiata — WW1 16/135 — Army, Personal File, ANZ; Ross, 'First in Le Quesnoy,' *Te Puke Times*, 30 May 1919, p. 3. McGibbon, *New Zealand's Western Front Campaign*, p. 350.
2. 'Despatches from the Official Correspondent,' *Chronicles of the N.Z.E.F.*, Vol. 5 no. 57, 22 November 1918, p. 201.
3. Tapsell, Winiata — WW1 16/135 — Army, Personal File, ANZ.
4. Nimmo, James Matheson — WW1 72214 — Army, Personal File, ANZ.
5. War Diary of the 3rd Battalion NZRB, Stewart Papers, MS-Papers-9080-32, ATL.
6. 72214 Rifleman Captain James Matheson Nimmo, 'Somewhere in France,' Marion M. Young (ed.), no. 2003.47, KMRL, NAM.
7. Inglis, World War 1 Memoirs, pp. 182–185, MSY-5455, ATL.
8. Ibid.
9. Ibid.
10. Rabone, Clarence Noel — WW1 23/29 — Army, Personal File, ANZ.
11. Avery, Frederick William — WW1 45180 — Army, Personal File, ANZ.
12. Tolerton, *An Awfully Big Adventure*, p. 248.
13. After the war Averill qualified as a doctor of medicine and began a successful medical practice in Christchurch. In later life he achieved prominence as a medical administrator, and in 1961 he was appointed a CMG for outstanding services to medicine and the community. In 1968 the town of Le Quesnoy appointed him Citoyen d'honneur, and in 1973 the government of France appointed him a chevalier de la Légion d'honneur. He died in Christchurch on 4 June 1981.
14. Barrowclough to Stewart dated 14 February 1920, Stewart Papers, MS-Papers-9080-32, ATL.
15. Ibid.
16. Ibid.
17. Annabell, *Official History of the New Zealand Engineers During the Great War 1914–1919*, p. 219.
18. Barrowclough to Stewart.
19. L.C.L. Averill, *First Generation New Zealander*, no.1992.1215, KMRL, NAM, pp. 54–55.
20. Barrowclough to Stewart.
21. Ibid.
22. 26637 Rifleman, Albert Vivian Lee, 4 Battalion, 3rd New Zealand Rifle Brigade. Interview by Jane Tolerton and Nicholas Boyack, WW1 Oral History Archive, ATL.
23. Ibid.
24. Ibid.
25. L.C.L. Averill, Operations of 4th Battalion NZRB on 4 November 1918, Ref Map 51 A SE, Stewart Papers, MS-Papers-9080-32, ATL.
26. Averill, *First Generation New Zealander*, p. 56.
27. Averill, Operations of 4th Battalion NZRB on 4 November 1918.
28. 'Despatches, Great Days with the Division. From the Official Correspondent,' *Chronicles of the N.Z.E.F.*, Vol. 5 no. 58, 6 December 1918, p. 220.
29. Nimmo, 'Somewhere in France,' letter written on 7 November 1918, from 'Somewhere in France: World War 1 Letters,' compiled by Marian Young, 2001. 'Battle accounts, Private C.J. Nimmo,' New Zealand History, https://nzhistory.govt.nz/war/le-quesnoy/battle-accounts-private-nimmo, (Ministry for Culture and Heritage), updated 13 January 2016.
30. Caroline Lord, 'Painting the road to Le Quesnoy,' in Philippe et. al., *The Great Adventure Ends*, pp. 357–390.
31. Hart, 4–5 November 1918, Diary, KMRL. Crawford, *The Devil's Own War*, p. 265.
32. Russell Diary, 4 November 1918.
33. NZ Division, 'Report on Operations for November and December 1918'. Stewart Papers, MS-Papers-9080-07, ATL.

5. 5 NOVEMBER 1918 — TO THE SAMBRE

1. This is based on Byrne, *Official History of the Otago Regiment,* pp. 375–376.
2. Quoted in Strohn, 'Defending Le Quesnoy,' in Philippe, *The Great Adventure Ends*, pp. 331–332.
3. Stewart, *The New Zealand Division 1916–1919*, pp. 593–594.
4. Ibid, p. 594.
5. Polaschek, *The Complete New Zealand Distinguished Conduct Medal*, p. 45; McDonald, *Honours and Awards*, p. 252; Ferguson, *The History of the Canterbury Regiment*, p. 282.
6. 'Last Days of the War,' *The Sun*, 30 January 1919, p. 9.
7. Second Lieutenant Ivor Griffiths, Diary, NZ Machine Gun Battalion — Western Front — WW1, no.1993.973, KMRL, NAM, 5 November 1918.
8. Ibid.
9. 'Last Days of the War,' *The Sun*, 30 January 1919, p. 9.
10. Official Correspondent [Captain Malcolm Ross], 'Despatches: Great Days with the Division,' *Chronicles of the N.Z.E.F.*, Vol. 5 no. 58, 6 December 1918, p. 222.
11. Laurie O'Dell, MM, interview taped by Ngahura Stoupe, 28 June 1992, copy of transcript in author's possession.
12. Hislop, Joel Arthur — WW1 58530 — Army, Personal File, ANZ.
13. Statement by 58530 Pte J.A. Hislop prisoner of war captured near Le Quesnoy 6 November 2018, 1st Bn Canterbury Regiment, WA 10/3 ZMR 7/17/1, ANZ.
14. Ibid.
15. 'Last Days of the War,' *The Sun*, 30 January 1919, p. 9.
16. Polaschek, *The Complete New Zealand Distinguished Conduct Medal*, p. 285; McDonald, *Awards and Honours*, p. 286.
17. Letter to Mother dated 1–18 November 1918, Letters, John J. McFarlane, 1 Canterbury, no.1986.2602.1, KMRL. McFarlane, John James — WWI 44589, WWII 3/16/555 — Army, Personal File, ANZ.
18. Ibid.
19. 'Last Days of the War,' *The Sun*, 30 January 1919, p. 9.
20. Ibid.
21. Ferguson, *The History of the Canterbury Regiment*, pp. 284–285.
22. Ibid, p. 285.
23. 39937 Private Edward Stuart Bibby, Otago Regiment, interview by Jane Tolerton and Nicholas Boyack, WW1 NZ Oral History Archive, ATL
24. 'A Year Ago Today. The Last "Stunt". Through Mormal Forest', *Evening Star*, 5 November 1919, [by W. ML], p. 2.
25. Ibid.
26. Ibid.
27. Interview by author with Colonel W. Murphy, MC, 1979.
28. Byrne, *Official History of the Otago Regiment*, p. 377.
29. 'A Year Ago Today. The Last "Stunt". Through Mormal Forest,' *Evening Star*, 5 November 1919, [by W. ML], p. 2.
30. 'Deeds of Daring,' *Evening Post*, 24 February 1920, p. 7. Personal File, McIntosh, Fraser — WW1 44195 — Army, ANZ.
31. McDonald, *Honours and Awards*, pp. 67–68. Personal File, Dickinson, Leonard Ross — WW1 9/919 — Army, ANZ
32. 'A Year Ago Today. The Last "Stunt". Through Mormal Forest,' *Evening Star*, 5 November 1919, [by W. ML], p. 2.
33. Ibid.
34. Captain George Albert Tuck, MC, 2nd Auckland, NZEF, (1884–1980), 5 November 1918, Diaries 1914–1919, MS-2164-2166, ATL.
35. Proceedings of a District Court Martial dated 23 September 1916, 14864, Private J. Raynor, JAG 20/30/1312, quoted in Christopher Pugsley, *On the Fringe of Hell: New Zealanders and Military Discipline in the First World War*, Hodder & Stoughton, Auckland, 1991, p. 199.
36. Ibid.
37. Raynor, John — WW1 14864 — Army, Personal File, ANZ.
38. Young, Robert — WW1 10/451 — Army, Personal File, ANZ.
39. 'A Year Ago Today. The Last "Stunt". Through Mormal Forest,' *Evening Star*, 5 November 1919, [by W. ML], p. 2.
40. Russell Diary, 5 November 1918.
41. NZ Division, 'Report on Operations for November and December 1918,' Stewart Papers, MS-Papers-9080-07, ATL.

6. THE GUNS REMAIN

1. 72446, Gunner Sidney James Anton, NZFA First World War Diary, 10 July–30 September 1918, MSX-9134, ATL.
2. Anton, Sidney James — WWI 72446, WWII 2/18/42 — Army, ANZ.
3. Corporal Cyril Clark and others, History of 15th Howitzer Battery, NZFA RV6627, NAM, p. 52.
4. Annabell, *Official History of the New Zealand Engineers During the Great War 1914–1919*, p. 221.
5. Ibid.
6. Hutchinson Diary, 5 November 1918, RV3641, KMRL, NAM.
7. Ibid, 6 November 1918.
8. Ibid.
9. Anton Diary, 10 July–30 September 1918.
10. Behrend, *As from Kemmel Hill*, pp. 143–144.
11. Hutchinson Diary, 7 November 1918.
12. Ayling, Frank — WW1 64982 — Army; Personal File, ANZ.
13. Euan Kennedy correspondence with author, April–May 2018.
14. Rev. A.J. Jermyn to Mr J.S. Kennedy dated 8 November 1918, Kennedy Family.
15. Kennedy, Donald Stewart — WW1 2/2853 — Army, Personal File, ANZ; Mather, Andrew — WW1 57685 — Army, Personal File, ANZ.
16. Gardner, Frank Warren — WW1 10586 — Army, Personal File, ANZ.
17. Euan Kennedy correspondence with author, April–May 2018.
18. Hutchinson Diary, 8 November 1918.
19. 1st Brigade NZFA War Diary, 1–30 November 1918, WA 50/1, ANZ.
20. 3rd Brigade NZFA War Diary, 1–30 November 1918, WA 53/1, ANZ.
21. Anton Diary, 10 July–30 September 1918.
22. Hutchinson Diary, 10 November 1918.
23. Looms, Ernest Henry Thomas — WW1 7/2070 — Army, Personal File, ANZ; Driver Ernest Henry Looms, NZFA — Western Front — WW1, KMRL, NAM, Diary, p. 50.
24. Clark and others, p. 52.

7. 'I OWE IT TO HIM TO CARE ABOUT WHAT HAPPENED'

1. Inglis, World War 1 Memoirs, MSY-5455, ATL, p. 186.
2. Ibid.
3. Ibid.
4. Malcolm Ross, 'Despatches: Great Days with the Division: An Historic Ceremony in Le Quesnoy,' *Chronicles of the N.Z.E.F.*, Vol. 5 no. 58, 6 December 1918.
5. See appendices for individual details.
6. 2 Wellington Infantry Battalion War Diary, 1–30 November 1918, 6 November 1918, WA 74/111 [74ak], ANZ.
7. Ingram, *Anzac Diary*, p. 136.
8. William J. McKeon, *The Fruitful Years*, W.J. McKeon, Wellington, 1971, p. 204.
9. Ingram, *Anzac Diary*, p. 136.
10. Ibid.
11. L.V.M., 'About Turn! 2nd Auck Battalion,' *Chronicles of the N.Z.E.F.*, Vol. 5 no. 58, 6 December 1918.
12. Ingram, *Anzac Diary*, p. 137.
13. G.A. Tuck Diaries and Letters, 1914–1919, letter dated 12 November 1918, copy in author's possession. Also QEII Army Museum and Alexander Turnbull Library, MS140, 712-140, 714.
14. Ibid.
15. Diaries of Frederick Stuart Varnham, 1915–1919, 11 November 1918.
16. Ibid, 12 November 1918.
17. McKeon, *The Fruitful Years*, p. 204.
18. 25038, Bombardier Bert Oliver Stokes, 13th Battery, 3rd Brigade NZFA, '1914–1918 The Years of World War One,' unpublished memoirs, copy in author's possession, p. 60.
19. 6/2385, Second Lieutenant Joseph Frederick Cody, 1st Canterbury Company, 1 Battalion, Canterbury Regiment, 'Fred and Ita — Family History,' unpublished ms, copy given to author by Patricia Fry (daughter), p. 54.
20. Hutchinson Diary, 11 November 1918.
21. Behrend, *As from Kemmel Hill*, p. 144.
22. Hutchinson Diary, 12 November 1918.
23. Ibid, 14 November 1918.
24. Ibid, 'Last entry'.

25. 'Fred and Ita — Family History,' p. 57.

26. 'Battlefield Memorials,' J. Roache, Secretary NZEF War Graves Committee to Minister of Defence, 19 May 1920, War Graves — Le Quesnoy Memorial, IA 32/3/125.

27. Ian J. Lochhead, 'Seager, Samuel Hurst,' *Dictionary of New Zealand Biography*, first published in 1996, updated May 2002, Te Ara — the Encyclopedia of New Zealand, https://teara.govt.nz/en/biographies/3s8/seager-samuel-hurst, accessed 1 July 2018.

28. High Commissioner Sir James Allen in London to Prime Minister W.F. Massey dated 1 July 1921, War Graves — Le Quesnoy Memorial, IA 32/3/125.

29. 'Report on the Sites for Memorials in Le Quesnoy,' S. Hurst Seager, FRIBA, FNZIA, War Graves — Le Quesnoy Memorial, IA 32/3/125.

30. 'With the New Zealand Division in the Great War,' *The Sphere*, 16 January 1919, p. 69.

31. 'Report on the Sites for Memorials in Le Quesnoy,' S. Hurst Seager, FRIBA, FNZIA, War Graves — Le Quesnoy Memorial, IA 32/3/125.

32. Ibid, p. 9.

33. Louisa Horman, 'Mystery of Fraser's Bomber,' Te Ara — the Encyclopedia of New Zealand, https://blog.tepapa.govt.nz/2015/02/26/mystery-of-frasers-bomber/, accessed 1 July 2018.

34. S. Hurst Seager to High Commissioner Sir James Allen dated 6 July 1922, War Graves — Le Quesnoy Memorial, IA 32/3/125.

35. Memorandum: District Engineer from Under Secretary Internal Affairs dated 25 August 1941, War Graves — Le Quesnoy Memorial, IA 32/3/125.

36. 'General Godley's Tribute,' *New Zealand Herald*, 26 July 1923.

37. Ibid.

38. Ibid.

39. Imperial War Graves Commission No. 4 Area — Arras. New Zealand Monument — Le Quesnoy. Report on the Condition of the Memorial, with the work carried out during the period 22-9-24 to 31-12-24, War Graves — Le Quesnoy Memorial, IA 32/3/125.

40. McGibbon, *New Zealand's Western Front Campaign*, p. 359; see also Gray, *From the Uttermost Ends of the Earth*, pp. 373–374.

Bibliography

ALEXANDER TURNBULL LIBRARY, NATIONAL LIBRARY OF NEW ZEALAND (ATL)

Anton, 72446, Gunner Sidney James, NZFA First World War Diary, 10 July–30 September 1918, MSX-9134.

Evans, 13/2002 Captain James, 2 Auckland, 9 November 1918, 1916–1918 World War 1 diaries, MSX-2936-2939.

Hart, Herbert Ernest (Sir), 1882–1968. Ref: MS-Papers-2945.

Inglis, Major-General Lindsay Merritt, World War 1 Memoirs, MSY-5455.

Jack, William James, letter to Eleanor Hunt dated 17 November 1918, MS-Papers-7483-01.

McDonnell, 65546 Lance Corporal Stephen, A Company 1st Battalion, 3rd NZ Rifle Brigade, letter to his sister dated 7 November 1918, MS-papers-6993-4.

Russell, Major-General Sir Andrew Hamilton, The Russell Saga, Volume III, World War 1, extracted and compiled by R.F. Gambrill, qMS-0822, ATL and Russell Family.

Stewart, Hugh, 1884–1934: Papers relating to World War One, MS-Group-1704.

Tuck, MC, Captain George Albert, 2 Auckland, NZEF, (1884–1980), Diaries 1914–1919, MS-2164-2166.

World War 1 Oral History Archive (ATL)

Bibby, 39937 Private Edward Stuart, Otago Regiment, interview by Jane Tolerton and Nicholas Boyack, WW1 NZ Oral History Archive.

Jamieson, 42915 Gunner William, No. 3 Battery, 1st Brigade NZFA, interview by Jane Tolerton and Nick Boyack, WW1 Oral History Archive.

Lee, 26637 Rifleman, Albert Vivian, 4 Battalion, 3rd New Zealand Rifle Brigade, interview by Jane Tolerton and Nicholas Boyack, WW1 Oral History Archive, ATL.

Marfell, 72695, Private Leslie, 9th Hawke's Bay Company, 1 Wellington Battalion, interview by Jane Tolerton and Nicolas Boyack, WW1 Oral History Archive.

ARCHIVES NEW ZEALAND (ANZ)

Allen, Sir James, Miscellanous files and papers — Correspondence with Birdwood and Russell, December 1914–April 1920 and copies of personal letters, 1920, [Loose papers] (R22319674).

IA 32/3/125, War Graves — Le Quesnoy Memorial.

WA1, Box 10/3/3, Headquarters, New Zealand Division, Lessons from Recent Operations.

WA10/3 ZMR 7/17/, Statement by 58530 Pte J.A. Hislop, 1 Battalion Canterbury Regiment, prisoner of war captured near Le Quesnoy, 6 November 2018.

WA20/1, Headquarters New Zealand and Australian Division — New Zealand Division — General Staff — War Diary 1–30 November 1918.

WA 20/24, Headquarters New Zealand and Australian Division — New Zealand Division — General Staff — War Diary, Narrative — Chapters XI–XV, February 1918–April 1919.

WA 21 29/[21iii], Headquarters New Zealand and Australian Division — New Zealand Division — Intelligence — War Diary, 1 October–31 October 1918.

WA26/ 36, Headquarters New Zealand and Australian Division — New Zealand Division — Assistant Director of Medical Services (ADMS) — War Diary 1 January 1918–25 March 1919.

WA50 70/[50bs], Headquarters New Zealand and Australian Division — New Zealand Division — Divisional Artillery — War Diary, Narrative, 8 June 1917–18 March 1919.

WA50/1, 1st Brigade NZFA War Diary, 1–30 November 1918.

WA53/1, 3rd Brigade NZFA War Diary, 1–30 November 1918.

WA60 85/[60aj], Headquarters New Zealand Divisional Engineers — War Diary, 1–30 November 1918.

WA 65/93, New Zealand Engineers — Divisional Signal Company 1–30 November 1918.

WA71/102, 1 Auckland Infantry Battalion War Diary, 1–30 November 1918.

WA73/108, 1 Wellington Infantry Battalion — War Diary, 1–30 November 1918.

WA74/111 [74ak], 2 Wellington Infantry Battalion — War Diary, 1-30 November 1918.

WA76/1, Headquarters — 1 NZ Infantry Brigade — War Diary 1–30 November 1918.

WA76/119, Headquarters — 2 NZ Infantry Brigade — War Diary 1 August 1918–28 February 1919.

WA82 139/ 82 [82av], 1st Battalion — 3rd New Zealand Rifle Brigade — War Diary, 1–30 November 1918.

WA83 141 [83aa], 2nd Battalion — 3rd New Zealand Rifle Brigade — War Diary, 1–30 November 1918.

WA84 145/[84v], 3rd Battalion — 3rd New Zealand Rifle Brigade — War Diary, 1–30 November 1918.

WA85 147/[85aa], 4th Battalion — 3rd New Zealand Rifle Brigade — War Diary, 1–30 November 1918.

WA85 148/[85ad], 4th Battalion — 3rd New Zealand Rifle Brigade — War Diary, 1 July 1917–31 December 1918.

WA110 168 [110t], New Zealand Divisional Train — War Diary, 1–31 October 1918.

WA150 179/[150d], New Zealand Army Ordnance Corps — War Diary, Summary, 23 November 1918–9 June 1919.

WA180 196/ [180i], New Zealand Infantry & General Base Depot — Embarkation Camp, Étaples — War Diary 1–30 November 1918.

WA240 222 [240ba], IV Corps (British Army) War Diary, Appendices, 1–30 November 1918.

WA241 230/[241bk], 62 Infantry Division (West Riding) (British Infantry) — War Diary, 1–30 November 1918.

KIPPENBERGER MILITARY RESEARCH LIBRARY (KMRL) NATIONAL ARMY MUSEUM (NAM)

Averill, L.C.L., *First Generation New Zealander*, No. 1992.1215.

Clarke, Cyril, 'History of 15 Howitzer Battery,' NZFA, 1914–1918, RV6627.

Clarke, 41487 Private Magnus Burns, Canterbury Regiment, Diary 30 December 1917–4 January 1919, No. 2008.957.

Collis, 17879 Driver Leslie (Les) James, New Zealand Army Service Corps, Diary and Narrative, January 1916– March 1919, No. 1999.3248.

Coop, 48456 Cpl Norman, M.M. 1st N.Z.E.F., Diary and Postcards, No. 2002.266.

Green, 18926 CQMS Harold, Diaries 1902–1919, No. 1997.817.

Second Lieutenant Ivor Griffiths, Diary, NZ Machine Gun Battalion — Western Front —WW1, No. 1993.973.

Hart, Brigadier-General Herbert, Diary 22 August 1918–18 May 1919.

Hutchinson, 3/203, Second Lieutenant J. D., 5th Battery, 2nd Brigade NZFA, 4 November 1918, Diary 1915–1919, RV3641.

Looms, Driver Ernest Henry, NZFA, Diary October 1915–February 1919 — Western Front — WW1, No. 1998.222.

Miller, 21858 Rifleman Edward Percival Miller, 1st Battalion, 3rd New Zealand Rifle Brigade, letters to family and friends, 3 July 1916–12 January 1919, 1987.1645.

Nimmo, 72214 Rifleman [Captain] James Matheson, 'Somewhere in France,' Marion M. Young (ed.), No. 2003.47.

McFarlane, 44589 John J., 1 Canterbury, Letter to Mother dated 1–18 November 1918, Letters, John J. McFarlane, 1 Canterbury, No. 1986.2602.

PUBLICATIONS

Annabell, Major N., *Official History of the New Zealand Engineers During the Great War 1914–1919*; Evans, Cobb & Sharpe, Ltd, Wanganui, 1927.

Austin, Lieutenant-Colonel W.S., *The Official History of the New Zealand Rifle Brigade*, L.T. Watkins, Wellington, 1924.

Barber, Laurie and Cliff Lord, *Swift and Sure: A History of the Royal New Zealand Corps of Signals and Army Signalling in New Zealand*, New Zealand Signals Incorporated, Auckland, 1996.

Becke, Major A.F., *History of the Great War, Order of Battle of Divisions, Part 1: The Regular British Divisions*, HMSO, London, 1931.

History of the Great War, Order of Battle, Part 4: The Army Council, G.H.Q.S, Armies, and Corps 1914–1918, HMSO, London, 1945.

Beckett, Ian, Timothy Bowman and Mark Connelly, *The British Army and the First World War*, Cambridge University Press, Cambridge, 2017.

Behrend, Arthur, *As from Kemmel Hill: An Adjutant in France and Flanders, 1917 and 1918*, Greenwood Press, Westport, Connecticut, 1963.

Boff, Jonathon, *Winning and Losing on the Western Front: The British Third Army and the Defeat of Germany in 1918*, Cambridge University Press, Cambridge, 2012.

Bourke, Chris, *Good-Bye Maoriland: The Songs and Sounds of New Zealand's Great War*, Auckland University Press, Auckland, 2018.

Burton, Second Lieutenant O.E., *The Auckland Regiment: Being an Account of the Doings on Active Service of the First, Second and Third Battalions of the Auckland Regiment*, Whitcombe & Tombs, Auckland, 1922.

Byrne, Lieutenant A.E., *Official History of the Otago Regiment in the Great War 1914–1918*, J. Wilkie & Co., Dunedin, nd.

Byrne, Lieutenant J.R., *New Zealand Artillery in the Field, 1914–1918*, Whitcombe & Tombs, Auckland.

Carbery, Lieutenant-Colonel A.D., *The New Zealand Medical Service in the Great War 1914–1918*, Whitcombe & Tombs, Auckland, 1924.

Chief of General Staff, Headquarters New Zealand Military Forces, *War 1914–1918, New Zealand Expeditionary Force, Its Provision and Maintenance*, Government Printer, Wellington, 1919.

Coney, Sandra, *Gone West: Great War memorials of Waitakere and their Soldiers*, Protect Piha Heritage Society, Piha, 2017.

Cowan, James, *The Maoris in the Great War*; Maori Regimental Committee, Whitcombe & Tombs, Auckland, 1926.

Crawford, John (ed.), *The Devil's Own War: The First World War Diary of Brigadier-General Herbert Hart*, Exisle, Auckland, 2008.

Cunningham, W.H., C.A.L. Treadwell, J.S. Hanna, *The Wellington Regiment, NZEF, 1914–1919*, Ferguson & Osborn Ltd, Wellington, 1928.

Edmonds, Brigadier-General Sir James, with Lieutenant-Colonel R. Maxwell-Hyslop, *History of the Great War, Military Operations France and Belgium 1918. Volume V: 26th September–11th November, the Advance to Victory*, HMSO, London, 1947.

Ellis, Roy Finlayson, *By Wires to Victory*, 1st Signal Company War History Committee, Auckland, 1968.

Ferguson, Captain David, *The History of the Canterbury Regiment NZEF, 1914–1919*, Whitcombe & Tombs, Auckland, 1921.

Gordon, Huntly, *The Unreturning Army*, J.M. Dent, London, 1967.

Gray, John H., *From the Uttermost Ends of the Earth: The New Zealand Division on the Western Front 1916–1918: A History and Guide to its Battlefields*, Willsonscott Publishing, Christchurch, 2010.

Haigh, J. Bryant, and Alan J. Polaschek, *New Zealand and the Distinguished Service Order*, Haigh & Polaschek, Christchurch, 1993.

Harper, Glyn, *Dark Journey: Three key New Zealand battles of the Western Front*, HarperCollins, Auckland, 2007.
Johnny ENZED: The New Zealand Soldier in the First World War 1914–1918, Exisle, Auckland, 2015.

Harris, J.P., with Niall Barr, *Amiens to the Armistice: The BEF in the Hundred Days' Campaign, 8 August–11 November 1918*, Brasseys, London, 1998.

Henderson, Alan, David Green and Peter Cooke, *The Gunners: A History of New Zealand Artillery*, Raupo (Penguin), Auckland, 2008.

Hull, Isabel V., *Absolute Destruction: Military Culture and the Practices of War in Imperial Germany*, Cornell University Press, Ithaca and London, 2005.

Hutchinson, Garrie, *Pilgrimage: A Travellers Guide to New Zealanders in Two World Wars*, Penguin Books, Auckland, 2012.

Ingram, N.M., *Anzac Diary: A Nonentity in Khaki*, The Book Printer, Maryborough, Victoria, nd.
In Flanders Fields: The World War 1 Diary of Private Monty Ingram, David Ling Publishing, Auckland, 2006.

Lee, Colonel J.E., DSO, MC, Duntroon, *The Royal Military College of Australia 1911–1946*, Australian War Memorial, Canberra, 1952.

Loveridge, Steven, *Call to Arms: New Zealand Society and Commitment to the Great War*, Victoria University Press, Wellington, 2014.

McDonald, Wayne, *Honours and Awards to the New Zealand Expeditionary Force in the Great War 1914–1918*, Richard Stowers, Hamilton, revised 2nd edition, 2009.

McGibbon, Ian, *New Zealand's Western Front Campaign*, Bateman, Auckland, 2016.
New Zealand Battlefields and Memorials of the Western Front, Oxford University Press, Auckland, 2001.
The Oxford Companion to New Zealand Military History, Oxford University Press, Auckland, 2000.

McKeon, William J., *The Fruitful Years*, W.J. McKeon, Wellington, 1971.

Millen, Julia, *Salute to Service: A History of the Royal New Zealand Corps of Transport and its Predecessors 1860–1996*, Victoria University Press, Wellington, 1997.

New Zealand Expeditionary Force, *Roll of Honour*, Government Printer, Wellington, 1924.

Pedersen, Peter, with Chris Roberts, *ANZACS on the Western Front: The Australian War Memorial Battlefield Guide*, Wiley, Milton, 2012.

Philippe, Nathalie, with Christopher Pugsley, John Crawford and Matthias Strohn, *The Great Adventure Ends: New Zealand and France on the Western Front*, John Douglas Publishing, Christchurch, 2013.

Polaschek, Alan, *The Complete New Zealand Distinguished Conduct Medal*, Medals Research, Christchurch, revised edition, 1983.

Pugsley, Christopher, *A Bloody Road Home: World War Two and New Zealand's Heroic Second Division*, Penguin, Auckland, 2014.
The Anzac Experience: New Zealand, Australia and Empire in the First World War, Oratia Books, Auckland, 2016.
The Camera in the Crowd: Filming New Zealand in Peace and War, 1895–1920, Oratia Books, Auckland, 2017.
On the Fringe of Hell: New Zealanders and Military Discipline in the First World War, Hodder & Stoughton, Auckland, 1991.
Te Hokowhitu A Tu: The Maori Pioneer Battalion in the First World War, Oratia Books, Auckland, (4th edition), 2018.

Stephenson, Scott, *The Final Battle: Soldiers of the Western Front and the German Revolution of 1918*, Cambridge University Press, Cambridge, 2009.

Stewart, Colonel H., *The New Zealand Division 1916–1919: A Popular History Based on Official Records*, Whitcombe & Tombs, Auckland, 1921.

Studholme, Lieutenant-Colonel John, *New Zealand Expeditionary Force. Record of Personal Services During the War of Officers, Nurses and First-Class Warrant Officers*, Government Printer, Wellington, 1928.

Tolerton, Jane, *An Awfully Big Adventure: New Zealand World War One Veterans Tell Their Stories*, Penguin, Auckland, 2013.

Vennell, Jock, *The Forgotten General: New Zealand's World War 1 Commander Major-General Sir Andrew Russell*, Allen & Unwin, Sydney, 2011.

Watson, Alexander, *Enduring the Great War: Combat Morale and Collapse in the German and British Armies, 1914–1918*, Cambridge University Press, Cambridge, 2008.

Williams, Jeffery, *Byng of Vimy: General and Governor General*, Leo Cooper, London, 1983.

Wright, Matthew, *The New Zealand Experience at Gallipoli and the Western Front*, Oratia Books, Auckland, 2017.

CHAPTERS, PAPERS AND ARTICLES

Averill, Leslie, 'Over the fortifications,' in Nathalie Philippe et. al., *The Great Adventure Ends: New Zealand and France on the Western Front*, John Douglas Publishing, Christchurch, 2013, pp. 17–25.

Bruyère, Franck, 'The story of a ladder: The New Zealand Rifle Brigade in Le Quesnoy,' in Nathalie Philippe et. al., *The Great Adventure Ends: New Zealand and France on the Western Front*, John Douglas Publishing, Christchurch, 2013, pp. 27–41.

Crawford, John, 'A year of war for the "Dinks,"' in Nathalie Philippe et. al., *The Great Adventure Ends: New Zealand and France on the Western Front*, John Douglas Publishing, Christchurch, 2013, pp. 277–294.

Farrant, Herb, 'The Battle of the Sambre: The liberation of Le Quesnoy,' in Nathalie Philippe et. al., *The Great Adventure Ends: New Zealand and France on the Western Front*, John Douglas Publishing, Christchurch, 2013, pp. 45–52.

Horman, Louisa, 'Mystery of Fraser's Bomber,' Te Ara — the Encyclopedia of New Zealand, https://blog.tepapa.govt.nz/2015/02/26/mystery-of-frasers-bomber/, accessed 1 July 2018.

Lochhead, Ian J., 'Seager, Samuel Hurst,' *Dictionary of New Zealand Biography*, first published in 1996, updated May 2002, Te Ara — the Encyclopedia of New Zealand, https://teara.govt.nz/en/biographies/3s8/seager-samuel-hurst, accessed 1 July 2018.

Lord, Caroline, 'Painting the road to Le Quesnoy,' in Nathalie Philippe et. al., *The Great Adventure Ends: New Zealand and France on the Western Front*, John Douglas Publishing, Christchurch, 2013, pp. 357–390.

Pugsley, Christopher, 'Attacking Le Quesnoy,' in Nathalie Philippe et. al., *The Great Adventure Ends: New Zealand and France on the Western Front*, John Douglas Publishing, Christchurch, 2013, pp. 295–317.

'Haig and the Implementation of Tactical Doctrine on the Western Front', Sandhurst Occasional Papers No. 8, Central Library Royal Military Academy Sandhurst, 2011.

'New Zealand: "The Heroes Lie in France" in Hugh Cecil & Peter H. Liddle, *At the Eleventh Hour: Reflections, Hopes and Anxieties at the Closing of the Great War, 1918*, Leo Cooper, Barnsley, 1998, pp. 200–212.

'Russell, Andrew Hamilton', *Dictionary of New Zealand Biography*, first published in 1996. Te Ara — the Encyclopedia of New Zealand, https://teara.govt.nz/en/biographies/3r34/russell-andrew-hamilton, accessed 30 July 2018.

Strohn, Matthias, 'Defending Le Quesnoy,' in Nathalie Philippe et. al., *The Great Adventure Ends: New Zealand and France on the Western Front*, John Douglas Publishing, Christchurch, 2013, pp. 319–333.

NEWSPAPERS AND JOURNALS

Chronicles of the N.Z.E.F.
Evening Post
Evening Star
Grey River Argus
The New York Times
New Zealand Herald
New Zealand Listener
Te Puke Times
The Observer
The Sphere
The Sun
The Times

UNPUBLISHED MANUSCRIPTS

Blyth, Lieutenant-Colonel L.M. 'Curly,' transcript of taped interview with author, 5 June 1992.

Clayton, John Derek, 'The Battle of the Sambre 4 November 1918,' a thesis submitted to the University of Birmingham for the degree of Doctor of Philosophy, Department of History, September 2015.

Cody, 6/2385, Second Lieutenant Joseph Frederick, 1st Canterbury Company, 1 Battalion, Canterbury Regiment, 'Fred and Ita — Family History,' unpublished ms, copy given to author by Patricia Fry (daughter).

Hart, Herbert Ernest (Sir), 1882–1968. Ref: MS-Papers-2945

Kennedy, Euan, correspondence with author, April–May 2018.

Kenrick, Dr H. Selwyn, Memoirs, extract from 4 November 1918, copy in possession of Mrs Cynthia Brown (daughter).

Mortimer-Jones, Clive, letter dated 25 November 1918, *Cambridge Parish News*, Cambridge Museum.

Murphy, MC, Colonel W., former Adjutant 2 Otago, 1918, interview by author, 1979.

O'Dell, MM, Laurie, interview taped by Ngahura Stoupe, 28 June 1992, copy of transcript in author's possession.

Pugsley, Christopher, All Blacks' Visit Diary, November 2000, unpublished ms.

Soutar, Trooper George Ewan, Otago Mounted Rifles, 6th Reinforcements [later Maori Pioneer Battalion], 3 November 1918, 'A Diary Kept from 10 November 1915 until Return to NZ in April 1919,' London Papers, copy in author's possession.

Stokes, 25038 Bombardier Bert Oliver, 13th Battery, 3rd Brigade NZFA, '1914–1918 The Years of World War One,' unpublished memoirs, copy in author's possession.

Varnham, Frederick Stuart, Diaries 1915–1919, transcribed by Mrs Nancy Croad, youngest daughter, copy in author's possession.

WEBSITES

Archway, Archives New Zealand, https://archway.archives.govt.nz/Home.do

Commonwealth War Graves Commission, https://www.cwgc.org/

Cambridge/Le Quesnoy Friendship Association, http://www.cambridgelequesnoy.co.nz/

'Fortified Places, Le Quesnoy,' http://fortified-places.com/quesnoy.html, accessed 30 July 2018.

New Zealand History, New Zealand and Le Quesnoy, https://nzhistory.govt.nz/war/le-quesnoy/new-zealand-and-le-quesnoy

New Zealand War Memorial Museum, Le Quesnoy, https://nzwmm.org.nz/

New Zealand WW100, https://ww100.govt.nz/

Ngā Taonga Sound and Vision, https://ngataonga.org.nz/

Ngā Tapuwae, Discover the Western Front, https://ngatapuwae.govt.nz/discover-the-western-front

Online Cenotaph, http://www.aucklandmuseum.com/war-memorial/online-cenotaph

Papers Past, National Library of New Zealand, https://paperspast.natlib.govt.nz/

Appendix

NZEF CASUALTIES — LE QUESNOY

This list was compiled by Richard Stowers and Herb Farrant, and added to by Christopher Pugsley. Please forward any additional names and details to the author through Oratia Media. The list covers period 1–7 November 1918 and those who died after from wounds received in this period.

1. **ADDIS, John Foxcroft** 54798 Private, 1st Battalion, Wellington Infantry Regiment; Killed in action 4.11.1918 aged 21; Carpenter; Son of Jessie Addis, Ellerslie, Auckland; Cross Roads Cemetery, Fontaine-au-Bois (II.D.28)

2. **AITKEN, John** 6/3979 Private, 2nd Battalion, Canterbury Infantry Regiment; Killed in action 5.11.1918 aged 28; Labourer, Winchester; Son of Walter and Christina Aitken, Govan, Scotland; Cross Roads Cemetery, Fontaine-au-Bois (III.C.13)

3. **ALEXANDER, Frederick James** 26/45 Corporal, 3rd Battalion, 3rd New Zealand Rifle Brigade; Killed in action 4.11.1918 aged 33; Clerk NZ Railways; Husband of Mrs Louie Alexander, Sutherland Road, Lyall Bay, Wellington; Previously wounded 1916; Romeries Communal Cemetery Extension (IX.A.2)

4. **ANDERSON, Ernest** 71546 Rifleman, 4th Battalion, 3rd New Zealand Rifle Brigade; Died of wounds (received 1.11.1918) 3.11.1918 aged 21; Gardener; Son of Mrs. M. J. Alderton, 2 Spencer Road, Napier; Caudry British Cemetery (IV.G.10)

5. **ARNOTT, Robert Henry** 53995 Rifleman, 2nd Battalion, 3rd New Zealand Rifle Brigade; Killed in action 4.11.1918 aged 39; Farmer; Son of William and Marion Arnott, 45 Francis Ave, St Albans, Christchurch; Born Fernside, North Canterbury; Le Quesnoy Communal Cemetery Extension (I.A.12)

6. **AYLING, Arthur Bernard** 23/58, 2nd Lieutenant, B Company, 1st Battalion, 3rd New Zealand Rifle Brigade; Died of wounds 4.11.1918 aged 26; Clerk; Son of Stanley and Minnie Edna Ayling, District Accountant, Post Office, Thames; Single of Mt Eden Road, Auckland; Born Thames; Attested 28.5.1915 Corporal, A Company, 1st Battalion; Wounded Somme, 1916; 2nd Lieutenant 24.9.1918; Romeries Communal Cemetery Extension (VIII.A.6)

7. **AYLING, Frank** 64982 Rifleman, 2nd Battalion, 3rd New Zealand Rifle Brigade; Died of wounds (received 4.11.1918) 12.11.1918 aged 31; Plasterer; Son of the late Robert and Julinda Ayling, Christchurch; Étaples Military Cemetery (XLIX.F.30)

8. **BANKS, Henry Dunbar** 33098 Lieutenant, 2nd Battalion, Wellington Infantry Regiment; Killed in action 4.11.1918, aged 39; Schoolmaster, Upper Hutt; Brother of W.A.D. Banks, Christchurch; Wounded Passchendaele, October 1917; Le Quesnoy Communal Cemetery Extension (I.B.26)

9. **BASHFORD, Herbert** (served as Alfred MARTIN) 72075 Private, 2nd Battalion Canterbury Infantry Regiment; Died of wounds (received 5.11.1918) 8.11.1918 aged 29; Orchard Labourer, Papanui, Christchurch; Son of Mr. H.B. Bashford, 9 Rooding Street, Brighton, Victoria, Australia; Caudry British Cemetery (I.A.13)

10. **BATES, George Ronald** 24/345, 2nd Lieutenant, 2nd Battalion, 3rd New Zealand Rifle Brigade; Killed in action 4.11.1918 aged 23; Awarded Distinguished Conduct Medal in March 1917; Linotype-Operator; Son of John Holman and Annie Amelia Bates, 27 Brighton Street, Island Bay, Wellington; Also served Samoa and Egypt; Wounded Somme, 15 September 1916; Le Quesnoy Communal Cemetery Extension (I.A.22)

11. **BEATTIE, Percival Moore** 38797, 2nd Lieutenant, 3rd Battalion, 3rd New Zealand Rifle Brigade; Killed in action 4.11.1918 aged 30; Sheep farmer; Son of Alfred Luther and Mary Ann Beattie; Husband of Annie Henrietta Beattie, Herepoho, Eskdale, Napier; Cross Roads Cemetery, Fontaine-au-Bois (I.E.14). The Eskdale war memorial church on State Highway 5 was designed by noted New Zealand architect James Chapman-Taylor, and dedicated in 1920. It was built in memory of Percival Beattie. Thomas Clark donated the land and his daughter Annie, Percival's widow, donated money for the building and furnishings.

12. **BEAUREPAIRE, Louis Isidore** 74852 Rifleman, 4th Battalion, 3rd New Zealand Rifle Brigade; Killed in action 4.11.1918 aged 21; Labourer; Son of Louis Isidore and Elizabeth Jane Beaurepaire, 65 Wilson Street, Hawera; Born Brisbane, Queensland, Australia; Cross Roads Cemetery, Fontaine-au-Bois (I.G.6)

13. **BERNARD, Victor Raymond**; 21/42, 2nd Lieutenant, 4th Battalion, 3rd New Zealand Rifle Brigade; Killed in action 4.11.1918 aged 28; Civil Servant, Wellington; Son of Manuel Joseph and Ann Eliza Newcomin Bernard, Jennings Street, Te Kuiti; Cross Roads Cemetery, Fontaine-au-Bois (I.G.9)

14. **BETTRIDGE, Walter** 68104, Rifleman, 3rd Battalion, 3rd New Zealand Rifle Brigade; Killed in action 4.11.1918 aged 43; Labourer, Rata; Son of Mr and Mrs A. Bettridge, Hawera; Body not identified; Grevillers (New Zealand) Memorial

15.	**BILLESDON, John William** 72614 Private, 1st Battalion, Wellington Infantry Regiment; Killed in action 4.11.1918 aged 37; Farm labourer, Morrison's Bush, Greytown; Cross Roads Cemetery, Fontaine-au-Bois (II.D.27)

16.	**BLENNERHASSETT, Arthur Reginald** 23070 Captain and Adjutant, 1st Battalion, Wellington Infantry Regiment; Killed in action 4.11.1918 aged 28; Bank clerk, Bank of New Zealand, Taihape; Son of Annie Blennerhassett, 23 River Bank, Wanganui and the late Thomas William Blennerhassett; Born Nelson; Mentioned in Despatches; Le Quesnoy Communal Cemetery Extension (I.B.22)

17.	**BLACKBURN, James Joseph** 29728 Sergeant, 2nd Battalion Otago Regiment, 2nd New Zealand Infantry Brigade; Died of wounds (received 5.11.1918) 7.11.1918 aged 28; Awarded Military Medal for conspicuous gallantry at Salesches on 23.10.1918 and the Croix de Guerre (Belgium) for similar acts of leadership and bravery in August and September 1918; Previously wounded 4.10.1917; Labourer; Son of Mrs E. Blackburn, Dromore, Ashburton; Caudry British Cemetery, (IV.D.23)

18.	**BROOKING, Arnold Whiddon** 15677 Private, 1st Battalion, Wellington Infantry Regiment; Died of wounds (received 4.11.1918) 5.11.1918 aged 22; Previously wounded in action 23.6.1917; Printer, Waitara; Son of Mrs M.H. Cubbon, South Road, New Plymouth; Caudry British Cemetery (IV.H.31)

19.	**BROWN, Robert** 53312 Lance-Corporal, 2nd Battalion, 3rd New Zealand Rifle Brigade; Killed in action 4.11.1918 aged 32; Farmer; Youngest son of James D. and Christina Brown, Wangaloa, Kaitangata; Cross Roads Cemetery, Fontaine-au-Bois (I.G.2)

20.	**BUCK, Walter Henry** 42030 Rifleman, 1st Battalion, 3rd New Zealand Rifle Brigade; Killed in action 4.11.1918 aged 34; Labourer, Te Kuiti; Son of Mary Ann Buck, 10 Paddy's Lane, Cannock, Staffordshire, England; Romeries Communal Cemetery Extension (VIII.B.6)

21.	**BURGESS, John** 65339 Rifleman, 2nd Battalion, 3rd New Zealand Rifle Brigade; Killed in action 4.11.1918 aged 21; Student, Department of Labour; Son of Mr and Mrs Alfred Burgess, Taita, Lower Hutt, Wellington; Le Quesnoy Communal Cemetery Extension (I.A.20)

22.	**CASSIDY, Frederick William** 69681 Rifleman, 4th Battalion, 3rd New Zealand Rifle Brigade; Killed in action 4.11.1918 aged 41; Bushman; Son of Frederick and Margaret Girven Cassidy, Otago; Husband of the late Mary Cassidy; Cross Roads Cemetery, Fontaine-au-Bois (I.G.1)

23.	**CHAMBERS, Douglas Harvey** 43581 Sapper, New Zealand Divisional Signals Company, New Zealand Engineers; Died of wounds (gassed 1.11.1918) 5.11.1918 aged 22; Telegraphist, Post & Telegraph Department, Wanganui; Son of Waldo Hill Chamberlain and Bertha Chamberlain, 105 Princes Street, Hastings; St Sever Cemetery Extension, Rouen (S.III.S.13)

24.	**CLOSE, Frank** 69466 Private, 2nd Battalion, Wellington Infantry Regiment; Killed in action 4.11.1918 aged 21; Farmer, Ararata; Son of Thomas B. and Margrett C. Close, Warwick Road, Stratford; Born Nelson; Le Quesnoy Communal Cemetery Extension (I.B.11)

25.	**CORMACK, Frederick Robert** 54472 Sergeant, 1st Battalion, 3rd New Zealand Rifle Brigade; Killed in action 4.11.1918 aged 29; Awarded Military Medal (October 1918); Hotelkeeper, Commercial Hotel, Waverley; Son of David and Catherine Cormack, 7 Glasgow Street, Auckland; Born Roxburgh; Romeries Communal Cemetery Extension (IX.A.14)

26.	**CORNISH, Wilfred Arthur** 67960 Private, 1st Battalion, Auckland Infantry Regiment; Killed in action 4.11.1918 aged 37; Watersider, Union Steam Ship Company, Auckland; Son of William Henry and Annie Cornish, 6 Bowling Green Terrace, Launceston Road, Callington, Cornwall, England; Born Luckett, Callington, Cornwall; Ruesnes Communal Cemetery (I.C.3)

27.	**CRAIG, Thomas Pearson** 59098 Rifleman, Trench Mortar Battery, 3rd New Zealand Rifle Brigade; Killed in action 4.11.1918 aged 29; Iron moulder, Kaiti, Gisborne; Son of Ellen Pearson Craig, Head of Muir, Denny, Stirlingshire, Scotland; Body not identified; Grevillers (New Zealand) Memorial

28.	**CRAWFORD, Henry** 72236 Rifleman, 1st Battalion, 3rd New Zealand Rifle Brigade; Killed in action 4.11.1918 aged 22; Farm labourer; Son of James and Mary J. Crawford, Lumsden, Southland; Romeries Communal Cemetery Extension (VIII.B.3)

29.	**CROTHERS, Frederick Cleveland** 26998 Corporal, 2nd Battalion, Wellington Infantry Regiment; Died of wounds 4.11.1918 aged 20; Hotel porter; Son of William and Henrietta Crothers, 12 Dudley Street, Addington, Christchurch; Le Quesnoy Communal Cemetery Extension (I.B.10)

30.	**DANIELS, James Edward** 44259 Rifleman, 2nd Battalion, 3rd New Zealand Rifle Brigade; Killed in action 4.11.1918 aged 29; Bushman, Raurimu; Son of William and Mary Daniels, Rhyndaston, Tasmania, Australia; Le Quesnoy Communal Cemetery Extension (I.A.11)

31. **DAW, Arthur Guy** 26/757 Lance-Corporal, 4th Battalion, 3rd New Zealand Rifle Brigade; Died of wounds (received 4.11.1918) 6.11.1918 aged 24; Previously wounded 31.3.1918; Farmer, Glen Murray; Son of Arthur and Alice Daw, 3 Clifton Road, Herne Bay, Auckland; Caudry British Cemetery (IV.D.5)

32. **DOHERTY, John William** 23358 Rifleman, 3rd Battalion, 3rd New Zealand Rifle Brigade; Died of wounds (received on 4.11.1918) 7.11.1918 aged 30; Miner, Waihi; Husband of Beryl Doherty, Kenny Street, Waihi; Abbeville Community Cemetery Extension, (V.B.8)

33. **DOUGLAS, Kenneth** 47127 Rifleman, 3rd Battalion, 3rd New Zealand Rifle Brigade; Died of wounds (received on 4.11.1918) 11.11.1918 aged 26; Ploughman, Waimate; Son of Kenneth and Annie Douglas, Swordale, Evanton, Ross-shire, Scotland; St Sever Cemetery Extension, Rouen (S.III.T.12)

34. **DOUGLAS, Percy Osmond** 52970 Rifleman, 2nd Battalion, 3rd New Zealand Rifle Brigade; Died of wounds (received 4.11.1918) 10.11.1918 aged 32; Farmhand; Son of Miriam A. Douglas, 178 Waihi Road, Hawera; Caudry British Cemetery (I.B.11)

35. **DUNCAN, David** 42062 Private, New Zealand Machine Gun Corps; Died of wounds (received 4.11.1918) 6.11.1918 aged 27; Farmer; Son of Mr and Mrs G. Duncan, Bulls; Caudry British Cemetery (IV.D.14)

36. **EDMONDS, James Frederick** 12/3628 Corporal, 1st Battalion, Auckland Infantry Regiment; Killed in action 4.11.1918 aged 27; Labourer; Son of Mr and Mrs E. Edmonds, Glenfield, Auckland; Le Quesnoy Communal Cemetery Extension (I.B.5)

37. **EDWARDS, Harry Grosvenor Brundell** 50506 Gunner, 6th Battery, New Zealand Field Artillery; Died of wounds 4.11.1918 aged 27; Wool-classer; Husband of I.E. Edwards, 77 Glen Road, Kelburn, Wellington; Solesmes Communal Cemetery (B.11)

38. **ELCOCK, Sidney** J 11852 Lance-Sergeant, 1st Battalion, Wellington Infantry Regiment; Killed in action 4.11.1918 aged 33; Freezing worker, Longburn; Son of Mrs J. Elcock, 1830 Fourteenth Avenue, Grand View, Vancouver, British Columbia, Canada; Le Quesnoy Communal Cemetery Extension (I.A.29)

39. **EVANS, Francis Meredith** 26/67, 2nd Lieutenant, 4th Battalion, 3rd New Zealand Rifle Brigade; Killed in action 4.11.1918 aged 24; Shot through the head under Le Quesnoy inner wall; Clerk; Son of Edward and Sarah Evans, 127 Elizabeth Street, Wellington; Born Napier; Romeries Communal Cemetery Extension (X.A.6)

40. **EVEREST, Thomas Daniel** 48822 Rifleman, 2nd Battalion, 3rd New Zealand Rifle Brigade; Killed in action 4.11.1918 aged 23; Labourer; Son of Mr and Mrs T. Everest, Springston, Canterbury; Le Quesnoy Communal Cemetery Extension (I.A.13)

41. **FARQUHARSON, William Alexander** 49366 Private, 2nd Battalion Otago Infantry Regiment, 2nd New Zealand Infantry Brigade, Died of wounds (received 5.11.1918) 7.11.1918 aged 42; Seaman, Union Steamship Company; Son of Alexander and Isabella Farquharson, Harrington Street, Port Chalmers, Dunedin; Caudry British Cemetery (IV.D.22)

42. **FERRIS, Robert Alexander** 46984 Private, 1st Battalion, Wellington Infantry Regiment; Killed in action 4.11.1918 aged 28; Painter; Son of Mrs J. Ferris, 37 Rintoul Street, Wellington; Le Quesnoy Communal Cemetery Extension (I.B.19)

43. **FIELD, Thomas Lucas** 73576 Private, 2nd Battalion Otago Infantry Regiment; Killed in action 5.11.1918 aged 41; Orchardist, Mariri; Son of George E. and Bessie Annie Field, 219 Featherston Street, Palmerston North; Born Nelson; Cross Roads Cemetery Fontaine-au-Bois (II.A.6)

44. **FITZGERALD, John Lawrence** 55845 Private, Wellington Company, New Zealand Machine Gun Corps; Killed in action 4.11.1918 aged 29; Storeman; Son of Thomas and Julia Fitzgerald, 92 Molesworth Street, Wellington; Ruesnes Communal Cemetery (I.C.2)

45. **FLEMING, John Samson** 71106 Rifleman, 2nd Battalion, 3rd New Zealand Rifle Brigade; Killed in action 4.11.1918 aged 24; Orchardist, Mosgiel; Son of John S. and Alice Fleming, Braview Crescent, Maori Hill, Dunedin; Le Quesnoy Communal Cemetery Extension (I.A.21)

46. **FLOOD, John William** 5/244a Second Lieutenant, 2nd Battalion, Wellington Regiment, 2nd New Zealand Infantry Brigade; Died of wounds (received 4.11.1918) 8.11.1918 aged 31; Accountant, Winstone Ltd; Husband of D.K. Flood, Auckland; Caudry British Cemetery (IV.D.24)

47. **FLYNN, Michael** 27870 Private, 2nd Battalion, Otago Infantry Regiment; Killed in action 5.11.1918 aged 28; Labourer, Public Works Department; Brother of Mr P. Flynn, 4 Turnbull Street, Wellington; Cross Roads Cemetery, Fontaine-au-Bois (II.A.7)

48. **FOLLETT, Hilary Leonard Charles** 71617 Private, 1st Battalion, Auckland Infantry Regiment; Killed in action 4.11.1918 aged 23; Baker, Matamata; Son of John and Etty Follett, 15 Grey Street, Feilding; Le Quesnoy Communal Cemetery Extension (I.A.6)

49. **FRY, Raymond Thomas** 4/1780 Sapper, New Zealand Engineers; Died of wounds 4.11.1918 aged 23; Carpenter; Son of Mr and Mrs T. Fry, Maihihi, Otorohanga; Ruesnes Communal Cemetery (I.A.19)

50. **GALPIN, George Henry** 63596 Private, 1st Battalion, Canterbury Infantry Regiment; Killed in action 5.11.1918 aged 30; Driver, Excelsior Laundry, Wellington; Son of James and Carrie Galpin; Husband of Elspeth G. Galpin, 16 Blythe Street, Berhampore, Wellington; Born Guernsey, Channel Islands; La Longueville Communal Cemetery (North East Corner Grave 4)

51. **GARDNER, Frank Warren** 10586 Gunner, 2nd Battery, 2nd Brigade New Zealand Field Artillery, Killed in action 7.11.1918, aged 28; Sheep farmer; Son of Mr J.H. and Mrs. M.E. Gardner, Otoko, Gisborne; Born Hull, Yorkshire, England; Cross Roads Cemetery, Fontaine-au-Bois (IV.D.7). One of the last New Zealanders killed in action with the New Zealand Division in the First World War. Hit by artillery fire that also killed Gunner D.S. Kennedy and Driver A. Mather, who are buried alongside one another.

52. **GIBSON, Llewelyn Guthrie** 38010 Private, 2nd Battalion, Wellington Infantry Regiment; Killed in action 4.11.1918 aged 21; Draper, New Plymouth; Son of Mr and Mrs J.W. Gibson, Julia Street, Pahiatua; Le Quesnoy Communal Cemetery Extension (I.B.16)

53. **GILES, Henry** 74941 [incorrectly listed under 42917] Rifleman, 4th Battalion, 3rd New Zealand Rifle Brigade; Killed in action 4.11.1918 aged 32; Farmhand, Sanson; Son of the late William and Ellen Giles, 18 Church Street, Ashburton; Romeries Communal Cemetery Extension (IX.A.17)

54. **GRAHAM, Hugh Murray** 68576 Private, New Zealand Machine Gun Corps; Killed in action 4.11.1918 aged 20; Bank clerk, Bank of New Zealand; Son of James and Elise A. Graham, 136 Tancred Street, Ashburton; Cross Roads Cemetery, Fontaine-au-Bois (II.F.22)

55. **GRANDY, Richard** 14421 Private, 1st Battalion, Auckland Infantry Regiment; Killed in action 4.11.1918 aged 33; Seaman, Huddart Parker; Son of Mr R. Grandy, 29 High Street, E14, London; Ruesnes Communal Cemetery (I.C.1)

56. **GRAY, George Cowie** 26/448 Corporal, 4th Battalion, 3rd New Zealand Rifle Brigade; Killed in action 4.11.1918 aged 29; Labourer, Railway Department, Palmerston North; Husband of Lilian M. Gray (later Pailing), Birch, Ellesmere, Salop, England; Cross Roads Cemetery, Fontaine-au-Bois (I.F.25)

57. **GREENWOOD, Eric Percy** 54684 Private, New Zealand Machine Gun Corps; Killed in action 4.11.1918 aged 30; Farmer, Opotiki; Son of Cecil and Annie Greenwood, Murgon, Queensland, Australia; Born London, England; Cross Roads Cemetery, Fontaine-au-Bois (II.F.19). A plaque exists in Old St Paul's, Wellington, to Ellen Sarah Greenwood and her great nephews: Eric Greenwood, killed at Le Quesnoy, and 13/1034 Gascoyne Cecil Greenwood (brother of Eric) who died of wounds 2.12.1915 on Gallipoli.

58. **GUNN, William George** 23/440 Corporal, New Zealand Machine Gun Corps; Died of wounds (received 4.11.1918) 5.12.1918 aged 23; Railway cadet, Invercargill; Son of Jessie Sainsbury, Mornington, Dunedin; Awarded Military Medal for operations around Messines 7.6.1917; Bois Guillaume Communal Cemetery Extension (G.15.B). In Major J.H. Luxford's book *With the Machine Gunners in France and Palestine* (page 168): "His work had at all times been of a high order, and was often performed under heavy shell fire. He never missed a fight, and in spite of the dangerous nature of his work he had the remarkable record of reaching his Company's last day of actual fighting without a scratch."

59. **HALL, Francis** 68330 Private, 1st Battalion, Wellington Infantry Regiment; Killed in action 4.11.1918 aged 39; Flaxmill hand, Tokomaru; Brother of Mrs S. Crawford, Ballybogie, Clough, County Antrim, Ireland; Le Quesnoy Communal Cemetery Extension (I.B.21)

60. **HARDING, Francis Smith** 9/1567 Gunner, 9th Battery, New Zealand Field Artillery; Died of wounds 4.11.1918, aged 24; Shepherd; Son of Mrs Ina Harding, 16 Rawiri Street, Gisborne; Solesmes Communal Cemetery (B.12)

61. **HARDY, Colin Conrad** 2/2837 Gunner, 6th Battery, 2 Brigade, New Zealand Field Artillery; Died of wounds (received 4.11.1918) 4.11.1918 aged 23; Cooper; Son of Clara Ann Hardy, 41 Glandovey Road, Fendalton, Christchurch, and the late John Hardy; Caudry Military Cemetery (B.IV.H.1)

62. **HARTLAND, Jack Wenham** 64204 Private (Signaller), 2nd Battalion, Wellington Infantry Regiment; Killed in action 4.11.1918 aged 21; Clerk, New Zealand Railways, Ohakune; Son of John Ernest and Alice Maude Hartland, 202 Manukau Road, Parnell, Auckland; Le Quesnoy Communal Cemetery Extension (I.B.1)

63. **HAWLEY, William** 47525 Private, 1st Battalion, Otago Infantry Regiment; Died of wounds (received 5.11.1918) 6.11.1918 aged 25; Orchardist; Son of John and Catherine Hawley, Earnscleugh, Central Otago; Caudry British Cemetery (IV.F.24)

64. **HAYTER, Arthur** 54745 Lance-Corporal, 1st Battalion, 3rd New Zealand Rifle Brigade; Killed in action 4.11.1918 aged 31; Bushman; Son of Mrs J.A. Hayter, Tapuhi, Bay of Islands; Cross Roads Cemetery, Fontaine-au-Bois (II.C.19)

65. **HEFFRON, William Thomas** 70281 Private, 1st Battalion, Auckland Infantry Regiment; Died of wounds 4.11.1918 aged 34; Driver; Son of the late Michael and Ellen Heffron, Waikino, Waihi; Born Auckland; Ruesnes Communal Cemetery (III.B.2)

66. **HEMSLEY, Albert Henry** 62309 Private, 1st Battalion, Canterbury Infantry Regiment; Killed in action 5.11.1918 aged 29; Farmer, Te Puke; Son of Mrs Albert Henry Hemsley, Nottingham, England; Husband of Jean R. Hemsley, 39 Kensington Avenue, Mt Eden, Auckland; Cross Roads Cemetery Fontaine-au-Bois (III.C.10)

67. **HENDERSON, David** 66167 Private, 1st Battalion, Canterbury Infantry Regiment; Died of Wounds (received 5.11.1918) 6.11.1918 aged 31; Bootmaker; Son of Robert and Catherine Henderson; Husband of Janet Henderson, Manunui, King Country; Caudry British Cemetery (IV.D.13)

68. **HENDERSON, Edward Andrew Buick** 45693 Rifleman, 1st Battalion, 3rd New Zealand Rifle Brigade; Killed in action 4.11.1918 aged 22; Farmer; Husband of F.M. Henderson, Mikimiki, Masterton; Cross Roads Cemetery, Fontaine-au-Bois (I.F.18)

69. **HILLS, Charles Francis Robert** 47888 Rifleman, 2nd Battalion, 3rd New Zealand Rifle Brigade; Killed in action 4.11.1918 aged 22; Coach builder; Son of Charles and Rose Hills, Awapuni, Matawhero, Gisborne; Le Quesnoy Communal Cemetery Extension (I.A.18)

70. **HOGG, John Alexander** 2/2437 Corporal, 15th Howitzer Battery, New Zealand Field Artillery; Killed in action 4.11.1918 aged 31; Stationer; Son of John and Jane Hogg, 40 Cannington Road, Maori Hill, Dunedin; Cross Roads Cemetery, Fontaine-au-Bois (I.F.24).

71. **HOOD, William Roland Errol** 73502 Private, 2nd Battalion Canterbury Regiment, 2nd New Zealand Infantry Brigade; Died of wounds (received 5.11.1918) 7.11.1918 aged 21; Clerk, Lands Department; Son of John and Margaret Hood, Mt Somers, Canterbury; Caudry British Cemetery (IV.D.20)

72. **HOOPER, Charles Leonard** 26000 Sergeant, New Zealand Machine Gun Battalion; Died of wounds (received 3.11.1918) 7.11.1918 aged 32; Druggist, Masterton; Son of Leonard James and Emily F. Hooper, Wellington; Mont Huon Military Cemetery, Le Treport (IX.B.2B)

73. **HOPE, Thomas Alexander** 42666 Rifleman, 2nd Battalion, 3rd New Zealand Rifle Brigade; Killed in action 4.11.1918 aged 24; Shepherd; Son of Thomas Hope, Rees Valley Station, Glenorchy, Otago; Le Quesnoy Communal Cemetery Extension (I.A.16)

74. **HORSMAN, Arthur Frederick** 51731 Rifleman, 3rd Battalion, 3rd New Zealand Rifle Brigade; Died of wounds (received 4.11.1918) 6.11.1918 aged 45; Farmer; Son of Fred and Ann Horsman, originally of Birmingham, England, and then of Waitakere, Auckland; Awoingt British Cemetery, (III.C.29). Horsman was admitted to 45 Casualty Clearing Station, one of three in the area near the cemetery. A photo of Horsman with his brother Walter James Horsman is in the Waitakere Returned & Services Association, 39 Township Road, Waitakere.

75. **HOWELL, Noah Albert** 74051 Private, 1st Battalion, Wellington Infantry Regiment; Killed in action 4.11.1918 aged 38; Farmer; Son of Jane Howell, Taneatua, Whakatane; Le Quesnoy Communal Cemetery Extension (I.B.9)

76. **HUNTER, John Joseph** 49153 Private, 2nd Battalion, Wellington Infantry Regiment; Killed in action 4.11.1918 aged 21; Hairdresser; Son of G.I. Hunter, Lovedale Road, Hastings, and the late Emma Hunter; Born Thames; Le Quesnoy Communal Cemetery Extension (I.B.18)

77. **HURLEY, Charles George** 35023 Private, 1st Battalion, Otago Infantry Regiment; Killed in action 5.11.1918 aged 31; Farmer; Son of Mr and Mrs. James A. Hurley, Wendonside, Southland; Cross Roads Cemetery, Fontaine-au-Bois (I.C.2)

78. **HURST, Christopher John** 22803 Sergeant, 2nd Battalion, Wellington Infantry Regiment; Died of wounds (received 4.11.18) 6.11.1918 aged 23; Farmer; Son of Christopher H. and Sarah E. Hurst, Te Kiri, Taranaki; Caudry British Cemetery (IV.F.17)

79. **JENSEN, Ernest** 39823 Private, 2nd Battalion, Wellington Infantry Regiment; Killed in action 4.11.1918 aged 22; Factory hand, Ararata Dairy Company, Hawera; Son of Michael and Mary Jensen, Picton; Awarded Military Medal (September 1918); Le Quesnoy Communal Cemetery Extension (I.B.14)

80. **JOHNSON, Ernest George** 12794 Gunner, 15th Howitzer Battery, 1st Brigade, New Zealand Field Artillery; Died of wounds 4.11.1918 aged 20; Farmer; Son of John B. and Jane Johnson, Te Aroha; Romeries Communal Cemetery Extension (VIII.A.7)

81. **JOHNSON, Ewart Gladstone** 59208 Rifleman, 2nd Battalion, 3rd New Zealand Rifle Brigade; Killed in action 4.11.1918 aged 21; Biograph operator, Opera House, Gisborne; Son of W.C. and F.L. Johnson, 18 Willis Street, Palmerston North; Born Sydney, New South Wales, Australia; Le Quesnoy Communal Cemetery Extension (I.A.19)

82. **JOHNSON, Harry** 47895 Corporal, 1st Battalion, 3rd New Zealand Rifle Brigade; Killed in action 4.11.1918 aged 31; Grocer, Port Awanui; Son of Charles James and Annie Johnson, Otorohanga; Romeries Communal Cemetery Extension (VIII.B.2)

83. **JONES, Edmund Michael** 65663 Lance-Corporal, 1st Battalion, 3rd New Zealand Rifle Brigade; Killed in action 4.11.1918 aged 24; Clerk; Son of Michael and Catherine Jones, 51 Central Terrace, Kelburn, Wellington; Born New Plymouth; Romeries Communal Cemetery Extension (VIII.B.7)

84. **JONES, Harold Hazelwood** 57583 Private, 2nd Battalion, Auckland Infantry Regiment; Died of wounds 4.11.1918 aged 24; Fruiterer, Henderson; Son of James Michael and Eliza Jones, 12 Station Parade, Muswell Hill, London, England; Romeries Communal Cemetery Extension (IV.B.19)

85. **JONES, Roderick Leslie** 33381 Rifleman, 4th Battalion, 3rd New Zealand Rifle Brigade; Killed in action 4.11.1918 aged 23; Labourer, Masterton; Son of Mrs W. Jones, Upper Hutt, Wellington; Cross Roads Cemetery, Fontaine-au-Bois (I.F.26)

86. **JURY, Vernon Richard** 74874 Rifleman, 4th Battalion, 3rd New Zealand Rifle Brigade; Died of wounds (received 4.11.1918) 5.11.1918 aged 31; Railway surface man, New Zealand Railways, Eltham; Son of Richard Julian and Susanna Sarah Jury, 21 Young Street, New Plymouth; Caudry British Cemetery (IV.F.27)

87. **KEAN, Peter** 23/799 Rifleman, 4th Battalion, 3rd New Zealand Rifle Brigade; Killed in action 4.11.1918 aged 36; Farm labourer; Son of Denis and Maria Kean, Waikaka, Southland; Born Otaraia, Southland; Cross Roads Cemetery, Fontaine-au-Bois (I.F.28)

88. **KEATING, Stanley Cecil** 72406 Rifleman, 3rd Battalion, 3rd New Zealand Rifle Brigade; Died of wounds 4.11.1918 aged 21; Labourer; Son of Mr and Mrs John A. Keating, Oturehua, Central Otago; Romeries Communal Cemetery Extension (VIII.A.5)

89. **KEILER, Wilbert Watson** 63353 Private, 1st Battalion, Otago Infantry Regiment; Killed in action 4.11.1918 aged 21; Labourer; Son of William and Ann Keiler, 26 Leet Street, Invercargill; Cross Roads Cemetery, Fontaine-au-Bois (I.C.10)

90. **KELLY, Robert Dyson** 38290 Lance-Corporal, 1st Battalion, Canterbury Infanry Regiment, Killed in action 5.11.1918 aged 22; Ploughman; Son of John and Sarah Kelly, Springfield,Canterbury; Maubeuge-Centre Cemetery (C.41)

91. **KENNEDY, Donald Stewart** 2/2853 Gunner, 2nd Battery, 2nd Brigade New Zealand Field Artillery; Killed in action 7.11.1918 aged 25; Clerk and volunteer fireman; Son of Mr and Mrs. John Stewart Kennedy, Queen Street, Mosgiel, Otago; Cross Roads Cemetery, Fontaine-au-Bois (IV.D.8/9). One of the last New Zealanders killed in action with the New Zealand Division in the First World War. Hit by artillery fire that also killed Gunner F.W. Gardner and Driver A. Mather, who are buried alongside one another. Kennedy and Mather are in adjoining graves under separate headstones, but who is in which is unknown.

92. **KENNEDY, Robert Tannahill** 71811 Private, 1st Battalion, Auckland Infantry Regiment; Died of wounds 4.11.1918 aged 21; Farmhand; Son of Robert and Elizabeth Kennedy, 14 Hemi Street, Devonport, Auckland; Born Glasgow, Scotland; Ruesnes Communal Cemetery (I.A.21)

93. **KIDD, Robert David** 74914 Lance-Corporal, 1st Battalion, 3rd New Zealand Rifle Brigade; Died of wounds (received 4.11.1918) 5.11.1918 aged 21; High school teacher; Son of Benjamin Franklin and Eleanor Kidd, Omata, Taranaki; Born New South Wales; Caudry British Cemetery (IV.H.9)

94. **KING, Charles Frederick** 10458 Private, New Zealand Machine Gun Corps; Died of wounds (received 4.11.1918) 15.11.1918 aged 23; Motor driver and mechanic; Son of F. and A. J. King, Hawera, Taranaki; formerly of Bottisham, Cambridge, England; St Sever Cemetery Extension, Rouen (S.III.V.13)

95. **LARKING, Frank Campbell**; 48341 Private, 1st Light Trench Mortar Battery, 1st Battalion, Wellington Infantry Regiment; Killed in action 4.11.1918 aged 36; School teacher, Rakauroa; Son of F. and Jessie Larking, 253 Cargill Road, South Dunedin; Born Otago; Le Quesnoy Communal Cemetery Extension (I.A.26)

96. **LAUER, Thomas** 34385 Corporal, 1st Battalion, 3rd New Zealand Rifle Brigade; Killed in action 4.11.1918 aged 22; Bushman; Son of Frederick and Lucy Lauer, Pukekohe; Cross Roads Cemetery, Fontaine-au-Bois (I.F.16)

97. **LESTER, Harry** 23/190 Lance-Corporal, 4th Battalion, 3rd New Zealand Rifle Brigade; Killed in action 4.11.1918 aged 23; Wharf labourer; Husband of A. Lester, 30 Bath Street, Christchurch; Romeries Communal Cemetery Extension (IX.A.5)

98. **LESTER, William Arthur** 72109 Rifleman, 1st Battalion, 3rd New Zealand Rifle Brigade; Died of wounds (received 4.11.1918) 5.11.1918 aged 20; Clerk; Son of Mr and Mrs William Thomas Lester, 3 Winchester Street, Lyttelton; Caudry British Cemetery (IV.H.13)

99. **LUCAS, Charles** 62350 Private, 1st Battalion, Canterbury Infantry Regiment; Killed in action 5.11.1918 aged 21; Flaxmill hand, Karamea; Grandson of Mrs V. Lucas, Buller Bridge, Westport; Cross Roads Cemetery, Fontaine-au-Bois (III.C.12)

100. **LYONS, Pierce** 70305 Private, 2nd Battalion, Auckland Infantry Regiment; Killed in action 4.11.1918 aged 35; Labourer, Auckland Harbour Board; Husband of H. Lyons, 543 Gallowgate Street, Glasgow, Scotland; Body not identified; Grevillers (New Zealand) Memorial

101. **McALLISTER, George Benjamin** 15583 Private, 1st Battalion, Canterbury Regiment; Three times wounded, died of wounds received the same day 5.11.18 aged 23; Grocer's assistant; Son of Douglas and Anne McAllister, Charles Street, Kaiapoi; Cross Roads Cemetary, Fontaine-au-Bois (I.C.11)

102. **McCARTHY, James Charles** 33097 Captain (Acting Major), 1st Battalion, Auckland Infantry Regiment; Left New Zealand in command of the 23rd Reinforcements; Died of wounds (received 4.11.18) 4.11.1918 aged 35 (some sources state McCarthy was killed in action); Captain 12.3.1917; Officer in command No. 1 New Zealand Division Employment Company; Stationmaster, Mt Eden, New Zealand Railways; Son of Charles and Julia McCarthy, 169 Jervois Road, Auckland; Husband of Daisy M. McCarthy, 40 William Street, Dominion Road, Auckland (2 children); Romeries Communal Cemetery Extension (IV.B.16)

103. **McCLUNG, Gilbert Edward** 70176 Private, 2nd Battalion, Canterbury Infantry Regiment; Died of wounds 5.11.1918 aged 37; Miner, Waihi; Son of Gilbert and Agnes McClung, Katikati; Étaples Military Cemetery (XLIX.C.25)

104. **McCOMBIE, Robert Hercules Brideoake** (Brideoare) 3/3507 Private, New Zealand Medical Corps; Died of wounds (received 4.11.1918) 9.11.1918 aged 27; Clerk, Holy Orders, Granity; Son of Thomas and Louisa McCombie, Laurel Bank, Monkstown, County Dublin, Ireland; Rector of St Peter's, Granity; Caudry British Cemetery, Nord (IV. D. 31)

105. **McINTYRE, Walter** 45610 Temporary Sergeant, 1st Battalion, 3rd New Zealand Rifle Brigade; Killed in action 4.11.1918 aged 22; Farmer; Son of Charles and Louisa Martha McIntyre, Ohingaiti; Born Rangiwahia; Awarded Military Medal (September 1918); Cross Roads Cemetery, Fontaine-au-Bois (II.C.20)

106. **McGEADY, James** 4/1684 Private, 1st Battalion Canterbury Infantry Regiment; Killed in action 5.11.1918 aged 37; Carter, Blackwater, West Coast; Son of Patrick and Ann McGeady; Born Ireland; Maubeuge-Centre Cemetery (C.4)

107. **McKAY, Andrew Provan** 26/1662 Rifleman; 2nd Battalion, 3rd New Zealand Rifle Brigade; Died of wounds 4.11.1918 aged 34; Farm manager, Bankside, Canterbury; Brother of Mr C.J. McKay, 286 Madras Street, Christchurch; Villers Hill British Cemetery, Villers-Guislain (VI.B.26)

108. **McKEEFRY, Michael Joseph Augustine** 39725, Lieutenant, 2nd Battalion, Otago Infantry Regiment; Killed in action 5.11.1918 aged 25; Previously wounded April 1918; Civil servant; Son of Michael McKeefry, Police Station, Rotorua; Cross Roads Cemetery, Fontaine-au-Bois (II.A.3)

109. **McKENZIE, Kenneth** 10645 Gunner, 2nd Brigade, New Zealand Field Artillery; 12th Reinforcements; Died of wounds (received 4.11.1918) 20.11.1918 aged 32; Carpenter; Third son of Kenneth and Katherine McKenzie, Mangarimu, Feilding; Born Hawke's Bay; Caudry British Cemetery (II.C.9). One of four brothers who served in the First World War. Brother 11/1351 George McKenzie, killed in action, Somme, 29.9.1916; Brother 12/190 Frank McKenzie was awarded the Military Cross, 1917.

110. **McKENZIE, Quinton** 45641 Rifleman, 3rd Battalion, 3rd New Zealand Rifle Brigade; Killed in action 4.11.1918 aged 24; Farmer; Son of Mr and Mrs D. McKenzie, Woodlands, Masterton; Romeries Communal Cemetery Extension (IX.A.1)

111. **McKINNON, Hugh Edgar** 10/135 Major, 2nd Battalion, Wellington Infantry Regiment; Killed in action 4.11.1918 aged 28; Lieutenant, 9th Hawke's Bay Company, Wellington Infantry Battalion, 5.8.1914; Company commander in attack at the Daisy Patch, Gallipoli, 8.5.1915 (wounded); Fought in forward trench on Chunuk Bair, Gallipoli, 8.8.1915, managing to escape to the rear trench when the forward trench was overrun; Promoted Major 28.9.1918; Awarded the Military Cross (1917) and Bar (early 1918) and mentioned in Despatches (early 1918); Motor agent, Carterton; Son of John McKinnon, 34 King Street, Arch Hill, Auckland; Le Quesnoy Communal Cemetery Extension (I.B.24)

112. **MacLACHLAN, Alexander** 23/233 Corporal, 1st Battalion, 3rd New Zealand Rifle Brigade; Killed in action 4.11.1918 aged 28; Farmer, Mangatawhiri; Son of Emily Keighley (formerly MacLachlan), Alston Hall Villa, Grimsargh, Preston, England, and the late John MacLachlan; Romeries Communal Cemetery Extension (IX.A.18)

113. **MANCER, Albert Edward** 24/835 Rifleman, C Company 2nd Battalion, 3rd New Zealand Rifle Brigade, attached to Brigade Headquarters; Died of wounds (received 2.11.1918) 9.11.1918 aged 23; Builder, Kai Iwi; Son of Arthur and Margaret Mancer, 34 Reith Street, Wanganui; St Sever Cemetery Extension, Rouen (S.III.T.6)

114. **MANSON, William** 26/1044 Corporal, New Zealand Machine Gun Corps; Died of wounds (received 4.11.1918) 6.11.1918 aged 30; Draper's assistant, Waimate; Son of Mr and Mrs James Manson; Caudry British Cemetery (IV.F.4)

115. **MARWICK, John Robert** 46753 Private, 2nd Battalion, Otago Infantry Regiment; Killed in action 5.11.1918 aged 27; Ploughman, Clutha; Son of John and Mary Marwick, Serrigar, St Margaret's Hope, South Ronaldshay, Orkney, Scotland; Cross Roads Cemetery, Fontaine-au-Bois (II.A.9)

116. **MASON, Leslie Merton** 10/4138 Private, 1st Battalion, Wellington Infantry Regiment; Killed in action 4.11.1918 aged 23; Farmer; Son of H. and I. Mason, Gladstone, Wairarapa; No. 1 Light Trench Mortar Battery; Le Quesnoy Communal Cemetery Extension (I.A.27)

117. **MASON, Tom Allison John** 76061 Private, 1st Battalion, Auckland Infantry Regiment; Killed in action 4.11.1918 aged 30; Builder, Potararu; Son of the late Mrs A.H. Mason, Ponsonby, Auckland; Le Quesnoy Communal Cemetery Extension (I.B.7)

118. **MASSON, Roy Roland** 67631 Rifleman, 1st Battalion, 3rd New Zealand Rifle Brigade; Died of wounds 4.11.1918 aged 23; Hairdresser; Son of George and Bessie Masson, 29 St James Street, Auckland; Romeries Communal Cemetery Extension (VIII.A.4)

119. **MATHER, Andrew** 57685 Driver, 2nd Battery, 2nd Brigade New Zealand Field Artillery; Killed in action 7.11.1918 aged 31; Bushman, Wanganui East; Son of Horatio John Mather, Stanley, Tasmania, Australia; Cross Roads Cemetery, Fontaine-au-Bois (IV.D.8/9). One of the last New Zealanders killed in action with the New Zealand Division in the First World War. Hit by artillery fire that also killed Gunners F.W. Gardner and D.S. Kennedy, who are buried alongside one another. Kennedy and Mather lie side by side under separate headstones but who is in which grave is not known.

120. **MATHERSON, Charles** 9/1580 Private, 1st Battalion, Otago Infantry Regiment; Killed in action 5.11.1918 aged 39; Labourer, New Zealand Shipping Company, Gisborne; Husband of Camelia Matheson (now Mills), Hardy Street, Grovetown, Invercargill; Cross Roads Cemetery, Fontaine-au-Bois (I.C.1)

121. **MORRISON, James Henry** 26/315 Rifleman, 4th Battalion, 3rd New Zealand Rifle Brigade; Killed in action 4.11.1918 aged 22; Hotel employee; Son of James and Agnes Morrison, 811 Outram Road, Hastings; Also served in Egypt; Cross Roads Cemetery, Fontaine-au-Bois (I.G.11)

122. **MORROW, Francis Richard** 31134 Rifleman, 1st Battalion, 3rd New Zealand Rifle Brigade; 20th Reinforcements; Killed in action 4.11.1918 aged 32; Farmer; Youngest son of the late Robert and Annie Morrow, Tapuhi, Bay of Islands; Romeries Communal Cemetery Extension (VIII.B.5)

123. **MULVANEY, Thomas** 72038 Rifleman, 3rd Battalion, 3rd New Zealand Rifle Brigade; Killed in action 4.11.1918 aged 21; Farm labourer; Son of Mrs M. O'Donaghue, Nile Street, Timaru; Cross Roads Cemetery, Fontaine-au-Bois (III.B.11)

124. **MURPHY, Francis John** 74112 Private, 1st Battalion, Auckland Infantry Regiment; Killed in action 4.11.1918 aged 35; Labourer; Son of Ellen Murphy, 4 Royal Terrace, Kingsland, Auckland; Le Quesnoy Communal Cemetery Extension (I.B.8)

125. **MURRELL, Sydney Allan** 1/557 Captain and Adjutant, 2nd Battalion, Wellington Infantry Regiment; Killed in action 4.11.1918 aged 26; Served Samoa; Remustered 12.10.1915 (Lance-Corporal); Commissioned 2nd Lieutenant 10.8.1916; Promoted Lieutenant 26.11.1917; Bank clerk; Son of John M. and Lilian Mary Murrell, 65 Ellice Street, Wellington, later 85 Rongatai Terrace, Rongatai, Wellington; Born Hobart, Tasmania; Le Quesnoy Communal Cemetery Extension (I.B.23)

126. **MURRAY, Edward** 24/844 Lance-Corporal, Auckland Infantry Regiment, attached 1st Light Trench Mortar Battery; Previously wounded Somme 16.9.1916; Died of wounds (received 4.11.1918 by artillery fire from shell that kills Privates Larking and Riddle) 4.12.1918 aged 23; Farmer, Ohau; Son of Mr S.R. Murray, 54 Coromandel Street, Wellington; Étaples Military Cemetery (XLVII.A.19)

127. **MYLES, Sidney Austin Wilson** 59696 Private, New Zealand Machine Gun Corps; Killed in action 4.11.1918 aged 22; Farm manager; Son of William and Jessie Myles, Amberley, Canterbury; Solesmes Communal Cemetery (A.13)

128. **NEILSEN, Alfred** 39551 Private, 2nd Battalion, Wellington Infantry Regiment; Killed in action 4.11.1918 aged 41; Sawmill hand, Turangaarere; Le Quesnoy Communal Cemetery Extension (I.B.13)

129. **NORTHAM, Robert Rowan** 8/3724 Private, 2nd Battalion, Otago Infantry Regiment; Killed in action 5.11.1918 aged 38; Bushman, Auckland; Husband of H.M. Northam, Ravenswood Causeway, Head Road, Sterling, Scotland; Maubeuge-Centre Cemetery (C.1)

130. **O'BRIEN, Francis Trevor Laughlin** 62601 Rifleman (Signaller), 1st Battalion, 3rd New Zealand Rifle Brigade; Died of wounds (received 4.11.1918) 7.11.1918 aged 21; Clerk; Son of A. and N. O'Brien, Putiki Bay, Waiheke Island, Auckland; Caudry British Cemetery (IV.D.10)

131. **O'BRIEN, Lawrence John** 55114 Sapper, New Zealand Engineers; Killed in action 4.11.1918 aged 28; Electrical engineer; Son of L. and M. O'Brien, Mangaweka; Le Quesnoy Communal Cemetery Extension (I.B.4)

132. PAINTER, Percival Ernest 73445 Private, 2nd Battalion Canterbury Infantry Regiment; Killed in action 5.11.1918 aged 34; Blacksmith; Husband of Christina Painter, 419 Montreal Street, Sydenham, Christchurch; Mauberge-Centre Cemetery (C.38)

133. **PARK, Thomas Joseph** 51495 Rifleman, 3rd Battalion, 3rd New Zealand Rifle Brigade; Killed in action 4.11.1918 aged 21; Fencer, Hawera; Son of Mrs B. Wurm (formerly Park), Johnson Street, Waihi; Body not identified; Grevillers (New Zealand) Memorial

134. **PERCY, Andrew** 49168 Rifleman, 2nd Battalion, 3rd New Zealand Rifle Brigade; Killed in action 4.11.1918 aged 33; Linesman, New Zealand Government; Son of Andrew and Isabella Percy, 400 Alexander Street, Hastings; Le Quesnoy Communal Cemetery Extension (I.A.10)

135. **POOLE, Samuel Joseph** 46243 Lance-Corporal, 1st Battalion, 3rd New Zealand Rifle Brigade; Killed in action 4.11.1918 aged 34; Doctor of Law, New Zealand University; Son of William and Mary Poole, Oxford Street, Levin; Born Invercargill; Cross Roads Cemetery, Fontaine-au-Bois (I.F.15)

136. **PURDY, Alfred William** 50608 Private, 1st Battalion, Auckland Infantry Regiment; Killed in action 4.11.1918 aged 37; Butcher; Son of William Purdy, Auckland; Husband of Marie Purdy, 11 Collingwood Street, Ponsonby, Auckland; Le Quesnoy Communal Cemetery Extension (I.B.6)

137. **PUTNAM, Philip Stanley** 32378 Lance-Sergeant, 1st Battalion Canterbury Infantry Regiment; Killed in action 5.11.1918 aged 27; Plumber; Son of William John Putnam, 47 Antigua Street, Christchurch; Posthumously awarded Distinguished Conduct Medal for his action at Bapaume,2.9.1918; Maubeuge-Centre Cemetery (C.39)

138. **QUILLIAM, Cecil Wilfrid** 60294, 2nd Lieutenant, 2nd Battalion, Wellington Infantry Regiment; Killed in action 4.11.1918 aged 23; Commissioned 2nd Lieutenant 2.3.1918; Law clerk; Son of Mr J.H. Quilliam, New Plymouth; Le Quesnoy Communal Cemetery Extension (I.B.25)

139. **RAE, Thomas Handley** 12/3453, 2nd Lieutenant, B Company, 2nd Battalion, 3rd New Zealand Rifle Brigade; Formerly with the New Zealand Engineers; Killed in action 4.11.1918 aged 26; Attested 28.8.1915, A Company, Auckland Infantry; Also served in Egypt with New Zealand Engineers; Promoted 2nd Lieutenant 2.5.1918; Clerk; Son of Thomas and Anne Rae, Hikutaia, Coromandel, later Ward Street then Beresford Street, Pukekohe; Born Herekino; Le Quesnoy Communal Cemetery Extension (I.A.23)

140. **RAYNOR, John** 14864 Private, 2nd Battalion, Auckland Infantry Regiment; Died of wounds (received 5.11.1918) 7.11.1918 aged 34; Sentenced to death for desertion 3.8.1917; Commuted to 10 years' penal servitude and suspended; Previously wounded in action twice, 23.11.1917 and 1.9.1918; Bridge builder, Kawhia; Brother of Mrs A. Stark, Casterton, Victoria, Australia; Caudry British Cemetery (IV.D.26)

141. **REDMOND, Jesse Thomas** 59983 Sapper, Divisional Signals Company, NZE; Died of wounds 4.11.1918 aged 33; Postmaster, Taupo; Son of John and Annie Redmond, Palmerston North; St Sever Cemetery Extension, Rouen (S. II. P. 13)

142. **REID, John** 71134 Private, 2nd Battalion, Otago Infantry Regiment; Killed in action 5.11.1918 aged 35; Storeman; Son of John and Annie C. Reid, Glenross Street, Kaikorai Valley, Roslyn, Dunedin; Maubeuge-Centre Cemetery (C.2)

143. **RICHARDS, Dudley Charles** 69727 Rifleman, 1st Battalion, 3rd New Zealand Rifle Brigade; Killed in action 4.11.1918 aged 21; Grocer; Son of Agnes Richards, 1 Fife St, Durie Hill, Wanganui; Cross Roads Cemetery, Fontaine-au-Bois (I.F.17)

144. **RIDDLE, Ewing Stevens** 32067 Private, 1st Battalion, Wellington Infantry Regiment, attached 1st Light Trench Mortar Battery; Killed in action 4.11.1918 aged 24; Farmer; Son of Marian C. Riddle, Piopio, King Country; Le Quesnoy Communal Cemetery Extension (I.A.25)

145. **RIDLAND, Alexander James** 72271 Rifleman, 1st Battalion, 3rd New Zealand Rifle Brigade; Died of wounds (received 4.11.1918) 5.11.1918 aged 36; Blacksmith; Son of William Ridland, 13 Dublin Street, Invercargill; Caudry British Cemetery (IV.F.31)

146. **RIGBY, Edward** 38218 Private, 2nd Battalion, Wellington Infantry Regiment; Killed in action 4.11.1918 aged 43; Bushman, Waipiro Bay; Le Quesnoy Communal Cemetery Extension (I.B.17)

147. **ROSE, Ernest Leslie** 15846 Corporal, 3rd Battalion, 3rd New Zealand Rifle Brigade; Killed in action 4.11.1918 aged 24; Law clerk, Wanganui; Son of J.E.M. Rose, 89 Kainui Road, Hataitai, Wellington; Romeries Communal Cemetery Extension (IX.A.3)

148. **ROSS, Samuel** 41888 Rifleman, 2nd Battalion, 3rd New Zealand Rifle Brigade; Killed in action 4.11.1918 aged 25; Motor mechanic, Gladstone; Son of Mrs E.S.A. Ross, 141 Cox St, Ashburton; Le Quesnoy Communal Cemetery Extension (I.A.17)

149. **RUSBATCH, Hubert** 72193 Private, 2nd Battalion Otago Infantry Regiment; Killed in action 5.11.1918 aged 21; Assistant slaughter man; Son of George and Jane Rusbatch, North Road, Eveline, Oamaru; Cross Roads Cemetery, Fontaine-au-Bois (II.A.8)

150. **RUTHERFORD, William** 11/2217 Driver, Brigade Ammunition Column, 2nd (Army) Brigade, New Zealand Field Artillery; Killed in action 6.11.1918 aged 29; Farmer; Son of William and Margaret Rutherford, "Hapau",Taeuru, Masterton; Cross Roads Cemetery, Fontaine-au-Bois (I.C.12).

151. **SALISBURY, Charles Arthur** 41630 Private, 2nd Battalion, Otago Infantry Regiment; Died of wounds (received 5.11.1918) 6.11.1918 aged 34; Labourer; Brother of William Salisbury, Frankley Park, New Plymouth; Caudry British Cemetery (IV.D.16)

152. **SAVAGE, Richard Attlesey** 8/727 Second Lieutenant, 2nd Battalion Otago Infantry Regiment; Killed in action 5.11.1918 aged 24; Clerk; Son of William and Mary Savage, Petone, Wellington; Husband of Ivy Margaret Savage, Sparrow's Farm, Twinstead, Essex, England; Cross Roads Cemetery, Fontaine-au-Bois (II.A.2)

153. **SCULLY, Peter Alphonsus** 24/1189 Company Sergeant-Major (Warrant Officer 2nd Class); 2nd Battalion, 3rd New Zealand Rifle Brigade; Killed in action 4.11.1918 aged 31; Railway porter, New Zealand Railways; Son of Mr and Mrs M. Scully, 99 Venus St, Invercargill; Awarded Distinguished Conduct Medal (September 1918); Le Quesnoy Communal Cemetery Extension (I.A.9)

154. **SHARP, Alfred** 71285 Rifleman, 3rd Battalion, 3rd New Zealand Rifle Brigade; Killed in action 4.11.1918 aged 32; Coal worker, Blackball; Brother of Mrs E. Lombardy, William St, Petone, Wellington; Cross Roads Cemetery, Fontaine-au-Bois (II.F.16)

155. **SHARPIN, Robert Charles** 26/254 Rifleman, 4th Battalion, 3rd New Zealand Rifle Brigade; Killed in action 4.11.1918 aged 37; Carpenter; Son of John and Eliza Sharpin, Waipukurau; Cross Roads Cemetery, Fontaine-au-Bois (I.F.27)

156. **SHELTON, Frederick** 14494 Private, New Zealand Machine Gun Battalion; Died of wounds (received 4.11.1918) 10.11.1918 aged 34; Timber worker, Auckland; Son of Frederick and Annie Shelton, Surrey, Lincolnshire, England; Étaples Military Cemetery (XLIX.F.11)

157. **SHEPHERD, Patrick John** 41028 Rifleman, B Company, 1st Battalion, 3rd New Zealand Rifle Brigade; Killed in action 4.11.1918 aged 23, on his birthday; Postal clerk; Son of Stephen and Mary Shepherd, 101 Princes St, South Invercargill; Romeries Communal Cemetery Extension (IX.A.20)

158. **SIMMONS, Gilbert John** 70547 Rifleman, 4th Battalion, 3rd New Zealand Rifle Brigade; Died of wounds 4.11.1918; Farm hand; Son of Mr and Mrs J.S. Simmons, Market Road, Auckland; Romeries Communal Cemetery Extension (IX.B.12)

159. **SINCLAIR, Andrew James** 72427 Rifleman, 2nd Battalion, 3rd New Zealand Rifle Brigade; Killed in action 4.11.1918 aged 29; Bootmaker; Son of John and Elizabeth Sinclair, Mulberry St, Kaikorai Valley, Dunedin; Le Quesnoy Communal Cemetery Extension (I.A.7)

160. **SPEEDY, Alfred Lloyd** 46398 Rifleman, A Company 3rd Battalion, 3rd New Zealand Rifle Brigade; Died of wounds (received 2.11.1918) 15.11.1918 aged 23; Warehouseman; Son of James Henry Havelock Speedy and Marion Ellen Speedy, Chelsea, Auckland, and one of four brothers who served at the front; Étaples Military Cemetery (L.C.3)

161. **STEWART, John Archibald** 41041 Rifleman, 3rd Battalion, 3rd New Zealand Rifle Brigade; Killed in action 4.11.1918 aged 43; Labourer; Husband of the late J. Stewart, Te Kuiti; Body not identified; Grevillers (New Zealand) Memorial

162. **STOCKMAN, Leslie Campbell** 17870 Sergeant, New Zealand Machine Gun Corps; Killled in action 4.11.1918 aged 24; Farmer; Son of William and Jane Stockman, now Mrs Jane Sanderson, Hunterville; Born Wanganui; Solesmes Communal Cemetery (A.14)

163. **STOW, Edward John** 35049 Rifleman, 4th Battalion, 3rd New Zealand Rifle Brigade; Killed in action 4.11.1918 aged 36; Farm labourer; Son of Edward and Eliza Stow, Tunbridge Wells, Kent, England; Romeries Communal Cemetery Extension (X.A.7)

164. **STREET, D'Arcy** 40849 Corporal, 1st Battalion, 3rd New Zealand Rifle Brigade; Killed in action 4.11.1918 aged 25; Grocer, Sumner, Christchurch; Son of Mr and Mrs Henry Street, 142 Williamson Ave, Auckland; Romeries Communal Cemetery Extension (VIII.B.1)

165. **STUART, Godfrey Leslie** 24076 Corporal, 2nd Battalion, Auckland Infantry Regiment, attached 1 NZ Light Trench Mortar Battery; Killed in action 5.11.1918 aged 22; Awarded Distinguished Conduct Medal, Somme 1918; Engine cleaner, Mercer; Son of Godfrey and Mary Georgina Stuart, Tangowahine, Northern Wairoa; Born Aratapu; Le Quesnoy Communal Cemetery Extension (I.A.24)

166. **TAFFS, Ernest Alfred** 25/470 Rifleman, 3rd Battalion, 3rd New Zealand Rifle Brigade; Died of wounds (gassed 2.11.1918) 4.11.1918 aged 34; Wounded Somme 15.9.1916; Labourer, Dalgety & Co, Gisborne; Son of Albert B.V. and Eleanor Taffs, 4 Rameez Drive, Westcliff-on-Sea, Essex, England; St Sever Cemetery Extension Rouen (H.111.S.14)

167. **THOMPSON, John Henry** 12/2133 Lance-Corporal, 1st Battalion, Auckland Infantry Regiment; Killed in action 4.11.1918 aged 30; Engine driver; Son of Mr and Mrs W.W. Thompson, 68 West Street, Greytown; Le Quesnoy Communal Cemetery Extension (I.A.5)

168. **THOMPSON, Joseph Lyons** 44803 Lance-Corporal, 3rd Battalion, 3rd New Zealand Rifle Brigade; Killed in action 4.11.1918 aged 28; Chemist's assistant; Sharland & Company, Auckland; Son of Robert Thompson, Ballylough, Bushmills, County Antrim, Ireland; Romeries Communal Cemetery Extension (IX.A.8)

169. **THOMSON, Colin** 44535 Corporal, 1st Battalion, Wellington Infantry Regiment; Killed in action 4.11.1918 aged 22; Awarded Military Medal (August 1918); Ledger-keeper, Bank of New South Wales, Dannevirke (Bank of New South Wales, Roll of Honour, Sydney, 1921, p. 385); Son of William Malcolm and Anne Elizabeth Thomson, Norsewood; Le Quesnoy Communal Cemetery Extension (I.B.20)

170. **TODD, George Johnston** 39358 Private, 2nd Battalion Otago Infantry Regiment; Killed in action 5.11.1918 aged 23; Farmer; Foster son of Mr. J. Todd, Kaitangata, Otago; Cross Roads Cemetery, Fontaine-au-Bois (II.A.5)

171. **TWEEDY, Glenholme Francis** 36193 Sapper, Divisional Signal Company, New Zealand Engineers; Died of wounds (believed to be from shock, received 4.11.1918) 5.11.1918 aged 23; Hit within a few feet of Major L.M. Inglis' headquarters when a shell burst alongside Tweedy and Corporal Gunn (also mortally wounded) while they were mending a wire to brigade headquarters; Received a few chips of shrapnel in a shoulder blade and the back of one knee; Civil servant, Post & Telegraph Department; Son of Mr and Mrs F. Tweedy, 2 Garden Terrace, Upper Carrol St, Dunedin; Caudry British Cemetery (IV.F.32)

172. **TROTTER, Arthur Joe** 69321 Rifleman, 1st Battalion, 3rd New Zealand Rifle Brigade; Killed in action 4.11.1918 aged 23; Farmer; Son of William and Margaret Trotter, Makara, Wellington; Romeries Communal Cemetery Extension (IX.A.19)

173. **TWIDLE, Vincent Stephenson** 42231 Sergeant, 3rd Battalion, 3rd New Zealand Rifle Brigade; Killed in action 4.11.1918 aged 27; Labourer; Son of Mr and Mrs E.S. Twidle, Claudelands, Hamilton; Romeries Communal Cemetery Extension (IX.A.4)

174. **WALKER, Allen Richard** 59766 Lance-Corporal, 2nd Battalion, Otago Infantry Regiment; Killed in action 5.11.1918 aged 29; Farmer; Son of Mr R. Walker, Tututawa, Taranaki; Cross Roads Cemetery, Fontaine-au-Bois (II.A.4)

175. **WARD, Thomas Frederick** 38324 Private, 1st Battalion Canterbury Infantry Regiment; Killed in action 5.11.1918 aged 30; Sawmill hand; Son of Edmund and Ruth Ward, Otekura, Otago; Cross Roads Cemetery, Fontaine-au-Bois (III.C.11)

176. **WARREN, Joseph** 35136 Rifleman, 1st Battalion, 3rd New Zealand Rifle Brigade; Killed in action 4.11.1918 aged 23; Flaxmiller, Barrytown; Nephew of Margaret Windelburn, 39 Wilson St, Wanganui; Born Ten Mile, Greymouth; Cross Roads Cemetery, Fontaine-au-Bois (II.C.21)

177. **WAITING, Henry** 47799 Private, New Zealand Machine Gun Battalion; Died of wounds 3.11.1918 aged 31; Farm labourer, Springfield, Canterbury; Son of Mr and Mrs R. Waiting, "Oaklands", Holmwood, Dorking, Surrey; Le Quesnoy Communal Cemetery Extension (I.B.27)

178. **WATSON, Thomas** 56891 Rifleman, 2nd Battalion, 3rd New Zealand Rifle Brigade; Killed in action 4.11.1918 aged 38; Labourer, Ohura; Son of John Henry and Martha Watson, Crescent Road, Birkenhead, Auckland; Le Quesnoy Communal Cemetery Extension (I.A.15)

179. **WATSON, Walter Harold** 65006 Lance-Corporal, 2nd Battalion, 3rd New Zealand Rifle Brigade; Died of wounds (received 4.11.1918) 6.11.1918 aged 26; Nurseryman; Husband of G. Watson (later James), Cashmere, Christchurch; Caudry British Cemetery (IV.D.8)

180. **WHITE, Leo Orton** 64185 Private, 2nd Battalion, Wellington Infantry Regiment; Killed in action 4.11.1918 aged 20; Tram conductor, Wanganui Tramways; Son of William Henry and Bessie Annie White, 8 Smithfield Road, Gonville, Wanganui; Le Quesnoy Communal Cemetery Extension (I.B.15)

181. **WILLIAMS, Samuel** 11762 Private, 2nd Battalion, Otago Infantry Regiment; Killed in action 5.11.1918 aged 34; Labourer, Winstone Ltd, Auckland; Cross Roads Cemetery, Fontaine-au-Bois (II.A.10)

182. **WILLIAMSON, James** 71309 Rifleman, 2nd Battalion, 3rd New Zealand Rifle Brigade; Killed in action 4.11.1918 aged 38; Sterotyper, Government Printing Office; Son of James S. Williamson, 12 Hataitai Road, Hataitai, Wellington; Le Quesnoy Communal Cemetery Extension (I.A.14)

183. **WILLIAMSON, Matthew** 14898 Corporal, 1st Battalion, Wellington Infantry Regiment; Killed in action 4.11.1918 aged 38; Labourer; Son of Peter and Agnes Williamson, Steele Road, Kaiti, Gisborne; Le Quesnoy Communal Cemetery Extension (I.A.28)

184. **WILSON, Gladstone** 13649 Corporal, 4th Battalion, 3rd New Zealand Rifle Brigade; Killed in action 4.11.1918 aged 32; Farmer; Son of Robert and Mary Wilson, Netherby, Hatuma, Hawke's Bay; Cross Roads Cemetery, Fontaine-au-Bois (I.G.5)

185. **WILSON, William Archibald** 65644 Rifleman; 2nd Battalion, 3rd New Zealand Rifle Brigade; Died of wounds 4.11.1918 aged 29; Awarded Military Medal (October 1918); Engine driver; Son of William and Jessie Wilson, New Plymouth; Husband of Olive Annie Wilson, Mission Hill, New Plymouth; Ruesnes Communal Cemetery (I.A.20)

186. **WOOD, Alan Carruthers** 4/178a, 2nd Lieutenant, 2nd Battalion, 3rd New Zealand Rifle Brigade; Killed in action 4.11.1918 aged 28; Previously wounded July 1916; Attested United Kingdom as 2nd Lieutenant 11.6.1917; Served on Gallipoli with No. 1 Company, New Zealand Engineers; Theological student; Son of Helen Wood, 55 Harrow Road, Bexley, Sydney, New South Wales, Australia, and the late Charles Wood; Husband of J.B. Wood, 31 Eversley Road, Bexhill-on-Sea, Sussex, England; Born New South Wales, Australia; Le Quesnoy Communal Cemetery Extension (I.A.8)

187. **WOODS, Lester Stanley** 55576 Lance-Corporal, 1st Battalion, 3rd New Zealand Rifle Brigade; Killed in action 4.11.1918 aged 21; Farmhand; Son of Henry and Martha Dorcas Woods, 40 South Crescent Road, Spreydon, Christchurch; Romeries Communal Cemetery Extension (VIII.B.4)

188. **WOODWARD, Alfred John** 18736 Rifleman, 1st Battalion, 3rd New Zealand Rifle Brigade; Killed in action 4.11.1918 aged 23; Lithographic printer; Son of Charles and Annie Woodward, Motueka; Born Waianiwa, Southland; Romeries Communal Cemetery Extension (IX.A.16)

189. **WRIGHT, Everard Noel** 46420 Rifleman, 4th Battalion, 3rd New Zealand Rifle Brigade, attached to 3rd Brigade Headquarters; Died of wounds (received 2.11.1918) 9.11.1918 aged 22; Ironmonger; Son of Charles and Margaret Wright, 48 Walters Road, Kingsland, Auckland; St Sever Cemetery Extension, Rouen, (S.III. FF.21)

Index

About the Author

Christopher Pugsley is a freelance historian living at Waikanae Beach in New Zealand. He was a Senior Lecturer in the Department of War Studies, Royal Military Academy Sandhurst from 2000–2012. A former infantry Lieutenant Colonel in the New Zealand Army, he is regarded as one of New Zealand's foremost authorities on New Zealanders at war.

Christopher Pugsley in Paris. Deanna Pugsley

His publications include, *Gallipoli: The New Zealand Story* (shortlisted Watties New Zealand Book of the Year 1984) which has remained in print since first publication [a Turkish edition was released in 2015]; *On the Fringe of Hell: New Zealanders and Military Discipline in the First World War* (1991); *Anzac: The New Zealanders at Gallipoli* (1995); *Te Hokowhitu A Tu: The New Zealand Maori Pioneer Battalion in the First World War* (1995); *The Anzacs at Gallipoli* (1999); *From Emergency to Confrontation: The New Zealand Armed Forces in Malaya and Borneo 1949–1966* (shortlisted Templer Medal 2003); *The Anzac Experience: New Zealand, Australia and Empire in the First World War* (Shortlisted Templer Medal 2004, Finalist in History, Montana New Zealand Book Awards (2005); *Sandhurst: A Tradition of Leadership* (co-editor, Third Millennium, 2005); *Kiwis in Conflict: 200 Years of New Zealanders at War* (co-editor, 2008); *Fighting for Empire: New Zealand and the Great War of 1914–1918* (2014); *A Bloody Road Home: World War Two and New Zealand's Heroic Second Division* (Third place Templer Medal 2014, Finalist Ernest Scott History Prize 2015, Winner, NZ Heritage Book Award 2015). *Remembering Gallipoli: Interviews with New Zealand Gallipoli Veterans*, co-edited with Charles Ferrall (2015). His history of film in New Zealand, *The Camera in the Crowd: Filming New Zealand in Peace and War, 1895-1920* was released in 2017 with Oratia Books.

He was Historical Director for *Gallipoli: The Scale of our War* at Te Papa Tongarewa — Museum of New Zealand in Wellington, which by May 2018 has had over two million visitors to the exhibition since its opening in April 2015. He is the principal historian and narrator for the Ngā Tapuwae audio guide in the series of New Zealand heritage walks for Gallipoli and the Western Front commissioned by the New Zealand Ministry of Culture and Heritage. He has also scripted and narrated a New Zealand silent film compilation of the First World War for Ngā Taonga — Sound & Vision that has been released to schools. With the exception of Libya he has walked every New Zealand-related battlefield in Europe and the Mediterranean.

He is an Adjunct Professor in the School of Humanities, University of Canterbury, New Zealand; Senior Research Fellow in Humanities at the University of Buckingham; a Distinguished Alumni of the University of Waikato; and a Fellow of the Royal Historical Society. He was elected a Vice President of the Western Front Association in April 2013. He was appointed an Officer in the New Zealand Order of Merit in the 2015 New Year's Honours List for services as a military historian.